The FOUNDING FATHERS of ZIONISM

Benzion Netanyahu

"A brilliant, elegantly written work, highly original and personal in its portrayal of five of the most important of Zionist theorists, from Pinsker to Jabotinsky. The author is not only a renowned scholar, especially of the Inquisition in Fifteenth Century Spain, but also was himself an activist in the Revisionist Zionist movement and an aide to one the founders about whom he writes. The book helps understanding of the diverse political views in Israel today."

—Michael Curtis distinguished professor emeritus of political science at Rutgers University

The FOUNDING FATHERS of ZIONISM

Benzion Netanyahu

First printing: March 2012

Copyright © 2012 by Benzion Netanyahu. All rights reserved. No part of this book may be used or reproduced in any manner whatsoever without written permission of the publisher, except in the case of brief quotations in articles and reviews.

Balfour Books
P.O. Box 2180
Noble, OK 73068
1 877 887 0222
www.balfourtitles.com

Co-published with:

Gefen Publishing House Ltd.
6 Hatzvi St
Jerusalem, 94386
Israel
011-972-2-5380-247
www.gefenpublishing.com

ISBN: 978-1-933267-15-9

Cover and Interior by Brent Spurlock, Green Forest, AR

Printed in Israel

For my beloved son

JONATHAN

Who sacrificed his life in

defense of his people at

Entebbe on July 4, 1976

Contents

1. Foreword to the English Edition 8
2. Leo Pinsker 10
3. Theodor Herzl 66
4. Max Nordau 106
5. Israel Zangwill 144
6. Ze'ev Jabotinsky 184

Foreword to the English Edition

Modern Israel was built on the intellectual foundations laid by Zionism's founding fathers, much as the United States was built on the principles formulated by America's founding fathers.

The historical, moral and political arguments developed by Leo Pinsker, Theodore Herzl, Max Nordau, Israel Zangwill and Ze'ev Jabotinsky changed Jewish history.

They argued that the Jewish state would save the Jewish people and serve, in the words of the great English writer George Elliott, "as a beacon of freedom amidst the despotisms of the East."

These ideas have withstood the test of time. As the founding fathers predicted, without a Jewish state European Jewry was doomed. Equally, they argued that once the Jews would gather their exiles in the Promised Land and reestablish their sovereignty, they would show remarkable recuperative powers. The founding fathers of Zionism did not think antisemitic attacks would necessarily disappear once the Jews had a state of their own, but they argued presciently that a state would give them the power to defend themselves against such assaults.

The antisemitism which the founding fathers warned against, and which ultimately culminated in the Nazi horrors, has been replaced by the current onslaught of militant Islam on Israel and the West. Then, as now, the supporters of the Jewish people, and all free peoples, have much to gain from studying the insights of these prophetic men of genius. Ideas matter in the battle for freedom. They were crucial to the success of Zionism, the Jewish national movement. And they are crucial today.

In the current struggle of Israel and the West against a violent and intolerant creed, the ideals of Zionism's founders matter more than ever. They retain their pivotal importance for securing the Jewish future, and thus the future of Judeo-Christian civilization as a whole.

These five essays, three of which were originally written in Hebrew, were intermittently published over several decades—some before the Holocaust, others after the establishment of the State. Only minor editorial changes were made since. Readers will judge for themselves the merit of the analyses and the accuracy of the predictions contained in these essays, and especially the timeless relevance of the teachings of the Founding Fathers of Zionism.

B. Netanyahu

Jerusalem

Leo Pinsker
Chapter 1

A Russian physician and writer, Pinsker was born in 1821. He was the founder of Hovevei Zion (Lovers of Zion), a Jewish national movement which was the precursor of Herzl's Zionist Organization. Pinsker died in 1891.

(the following was originally published in *Road to Freedom*, Introduction, Scopus Publishing Co., New York, 1944)

I

The national movement in modern Jewry was born both in an inopportune time and an inappropriate place. All other movements of modern European nationalism arose between 1815 and 1878, between the Congress of Vienna and the Congress of Berlin. Had the Jewish national movement emerged in this interim, it would have probably benefited from the mutual support of all other movements of national liberation. In 1881, however, when Jewish nationalism finally sprang forth, the heyday of the national idea was over and a rampant Imperialism had set in. Holding in check the remaining irredenta pockets, this Imperialism coincided with another development which further enervated the movements for self determination. The colonial expansion, with its widening spheres of trade, was paralleled by an ever-growing industrialism, and the latter gave rise to the cosmopolitan socialist creed, with its anti-national bias. It was the ill fate of Jewish nationalism to be born at a time of an ascending imperialism. It was its double misfortune that it had to rise in the shadow of the anti-national world movement of Marxism.

The development of the Jewish national movement was even more hampered by the fact that it was initiated and centered in Russia. Russia exemplified both the trends of Imperialism and Marxian Socialism. No other Imperialism of the 19th century was involved in such bitter conflicts with the principles of nationalism as was that of Russia. Whereas the colonial aspirations of the western powers were directed toward extra-European territories, where nationalism was still inchoate and primitive, the established policy of the Russian empire was one of expansion westward on the continent, where the national feeling was mature and predominant. Moreover, in the path of Russia's expansion there were people of racial affinity to the Russians, and the idea of Pan-Slavism, promulgated by the Slavophiles, had struck deep roots in Russian national psychology and tinted Russian Imperialism with a national color. Herzen, the inspiring liberal publicist, and for decades the leading figure of the Russian Intelligentsia, lost his influence when he declared his support for the national revolution in Poland. It was largely on account of this aversion to all separatist national aspirations on the part of the Russians that the public national movements in Russia were brought to a standstill after the Polish insurrection of 1863.

While the Slavophiles, the right wing of the Russian Intelligentsia, gave popular backing to the ideology of Imperialist Russia, the left wing, represented by the revolutionary elements, was equally set against the nationalist viewpoint. Russian revolutionary thought, which began with the advocacy of constitutional democracy and continued with the repudiation of every form of government, finally took a sharp turn toward Marxian philosophy with its anti-national outlook. Nevertheless, it was Russian Marxism to which the subjected national elements turned their eyes. Since the Russians did not help the oppressed nations to overthrow the Czarist yoke in the name of Nationalism, these nations attempted to help the Russians overthrow that yoke in the name of Socialism. Russian Socialism gathered, like a vast river, all the streams of revolutionary energy that flowed toward it from the subjugated peoples. It was this development that made Russian Socialism more powerful and determined than any other socialist movement in Europe; but the same development also contributed to the weakening of the national fronts.

Thus, the forces that militated against Nationalism in the Europe of the eighties—Imperialism and Marxism—were more firmly arrayed against it in the Russia of that time. Even the strong national movements of the Poles and Ukrainians, which were of long standing and were rooted in their homelands, had to bow before the gales of governmental despotism and counter governmental revolutionism. The fact that the Jewish national movement was born and developed in that country and that period constitutes decisive proof that its rise was an unavoidable historic necessity, or more exactly, that there were powerful factors which overcame all the difficulties and forced Jewish nationalism to the surface in Russia in the crucial year of 1881.

*****

In order to understand these factors, one must pause to ask why modern Jewish nationalism appeared on the scene later than any other national movement in Europe. One must further query how it happened that the Jews of western and central Europe were gradually losing their national consciousness at the very time when the nations in whose midst they lived were constantly developing it. These questions are not as insoluble as they appear to be. The answer is incorporated in a long and involved historic process undergone by the Jewish people alone.

That the Jews were the only people to retain their national identity among the nations even without a country of their own, has been pointed out innumerable times. The main cause of this outstanding phenomenon, however, has not yet been properly understood. It lay in the fact that among all the nations of the ancient world, the Jews were the only one whose national consciousness was developed to its maximum degree. The loss of their country could not render them a deadly blow for the simple reason that, in certain respects, they never lost it. "A country," Mazzini rightly said, "is not a mere territory; the particular territory is only its foundation. The country is the *idea* that rises upon that foundation." The Jews had proven the veracity of this conception which applies, however, only to peoples who had reached a high state of national consciousness. They kept alive the *idea* of their country even though they lost its material foundation, and this idea served as a unifying bond almost as potent as a real territory. Nevertheless, under the harsh conditions of dispersion, that idea alone could hardly assure the existence of the Jewish nation, and in order to keep their nationalism alive, the Jews had to perpetuate most, if not all, of the elements that constitute a nation.

This seemed an arduous task whose fulfillment was in contrast to all realistic calculations. The Jews wanted to maintain their national language, but this entailed an enormous spiritual strain, since their national language invariably differed from the languages they had to speak in their adopted countries. They wanted to perpetuate their national culture, but again, this differed from the culture surrounding them. Their desire to preserve their racial bonds was likewise in opposition to the natural process of racial intermingling that affected *all* wandering nations. In like fashion, the national laws and traditions they desired to uphold were usually in contrast to those of the lands they lived in. Even the aspiration for their historic homeland was challenged by the natural inclination and the economic necessity to strike roots in their countries of residence. In brief, Jewish nationalism in the Diaspora followed the line of strongest resistance, and in order to maintain it, the Jews had to fulfill a task which seemed impossible for a nation: *they had to lead a dual existence in all spheres of life.* How could they perform this task if not by sharply separating the two aspects of their existence, by sanctifying one and secularizing the other? Indeed, only religious sanctification of the national elements seemed able to sustain them under such adverse circumstances. Thus their language, their race, their national laws and traditions, as well as the memories of their historic homeland, came to be considered sacred and were surrounded with a religious halo. While in ancient times Jewish religion was but one of the Jewish elements, and was not uniformly adopted by all the sections of the nation, all the national elements were now to become part of a common dominant religion. Thus Jewish nationalism became so entwined with Jewish religion that the two seemed identical.

This Jewish nationalism was dealt a shattering blow in the middle of the 18th century. Until that time Jewish religion, its shield, was attacked either by Christianity or by Islam, that is, by rival religions. The fact, however, that both Christianity and Islam sprang from Judaism gave the latter a powerful immunity against the claims of the former to superiority. But in the middle of the 18th century Judaism was threatened not by a rival religion, but by the enemy of all religions: free thought. There began the inexorable march of science against all imposed dogmas and accepted ideas.

It was impossible that this assault of enlightenment which was to shatter the positions of all positive faiths should not adversely affect the Jewish religion as well. The non-coercive criticism of the free thinkers achieved in a period of a few decades what the Inquisition, with its drastic measures of compulsion, could not achieve in centuries. Jewish religious laws came to be considered a superfluous burden, a mere remnant of a superstitious past; and since the *national* laws and traditions appeared inseparable from religion, they were likewise regarded as unreasonable, if not entirely meaningless. Hebrew, the language of the prayers and religious lore, was looked upon as part of the traditional rites. Its literature, which was confined to religious themes, was seen as a pernicious form of dialectic distracting the Jewish mind from modern culture. The national laws against intermarriage, long regarded as religious precepts, were treated with the same indifference. Since the aspirations for national restoration were embodied in the belief of redemption by Divine Power, they were also viewed as no more than a religious myth which, of course, should be discarded. Therefore, when the colossal structure of Jewish religion, so painfully erected for many generations, began to crumble, it threatened to bury under its debris the vital elements of Jewish nationalism that were involved in its construction.

In order to save itself, Jewish nationalism had to be released from the tottering structure of religion to which it was confined. Instead, it was restricted to it even more. The reason for this development lay in external pressure. Jewish emancipation, which paralleled the movement of enlightenment, was granted on the definite premise that the Jews belonged not to a different nationality, but to a different religion only. This had been made plain to the Jews first by the French National Assembly and later by all Parliaments of Europe. The Jews stood in front of a perplexing dilemma: to relinquish any hope for human rights, or to classify themselves as a religion. Though few among them would readily admit that they did not belong to a separate people, they had all been accustomed to seeing in religion the essence of their nationality, and the answer they gave to the Western European nations—that they belonged to a religious sect and not to a national group—was the fruit of self-deception rather than of hypocrisy. It was the result of religious hypertrophy from within and the tremendous lure of emancipation from without.

Having classified themselves as a religious sect, the Jews rendered their nationalism defenseless, because religion was retreating everywhere under the powerful attack of enlightenment. In order to check this process, conservative Jews fought enlightenment, while part of the enlightened Jews, seeking to reconcile religion with modern conceptions, advocated religious Reform. Both schools of thought agreed that Judaism was in essence a religion, and both felt the ground trembling under their feet. The movement of enlightenment continued to advance, and together with it grew the estrangement from the Jewish religion, and with this, the trend toward assimilation.

There was, however, a small fraction of enlightened Hebraists who attempted a seemingly impossible task. They undertook to nurture the vitals of Jewish nationalism as independent from religion. They began to raise the Hebrew language to modern standards. They took its literature out of the confines of religion and used it for all literary needs. They delved into the unknown realms of the Jewish past and recounted for the first time the complete history of the Jews. They spoke of Palestine not in terms of religion, but in terms of geography and history, glorifying it in song, drama and novel, and reawakening the longing for the ancient homeland. At the beginning of the seventies, after almost a century of education in this direction, the national idea was finally declared as the all-embracing force in Jewish life. Western Jews were hardly impressed by this progress of national thought. The rapid cultural assimilation of the small western communities and their emancipation, granted upon the understanding that they belonged solely to a religious sect, undermined the influence of the Hebrew nationalists. But their influence was strong in Russia.

*****

In Russia lay the center of gravity of the Jewish problem during the whole of the 19th century and down to the end of the First World War. Although in that period Russia held within its boundaries two-thirds of the Jewish people, only a few decades earlier it was practically Judenrein. The large concentration of Jews in Russia did not come as a result of immigration; and if not for the expansion of Russia itself, if not for its absorption of the greater part of Poland, which for centuries had served as the assembly place of Europe's persecuted Jews, Russia would have continued to remain Judenrein.

Russia hated the Jews long before she knew them. There were no Jews in Russia during the Middle Ages; yet the ambassador of the Moscovite Grand Duke, Basil III, at Rome, stated in 1526: "The Moscovite people dread no one more than the Jews, and do not admit them into their borders." This enmity of Russia toward the Jews was not only part of the heritage she received from Byzantium together with Christianity and its governmental system. It also had another cause which can easily be detected. The most violent outbreaks of hate against the Jews in Europe of the Middle Ages occurred wherever the clash between Christianity and Islam was most forceful and determined. Even countries which participated in the Crusades only through military expeditions have been swept by a storm of religious frenzy. In the lands where the actual conflict took place, religious zeal was even more intense. Such countries were Spain and Russia, the western and eastern gateways of Europe, through which Islam attempted to invade the continent. It was toward the end of the 15th century, at about the same time that Spain succeeded in driving the Islamic Moors out of the Iberian peninsula, that Russia succeeded in freeing herself from the yoke of the Islamic Tartars. The wars of liberation that were waged in Russia, like in Spain, in the name of religion, though they concealed a potent national feeling, made both countries the least tolerant to any non-Christian faith. For a Jew to enter Russia was as dangerous as to re-enter Spain, and it was only because there were no Jews in Russia that the fate of their brethren in Spain did not befall them.

It is important to consider all this, because the Jewish question in Russia of the 19th century bore, in many respects, the earmarks of the Middle Ages. From the point of view of Russian Czarism, the problem had but one solution: conversion or expulsion. The same alternative was offered by Russian Czars in the 16th and 17th centuries to the Jews in the annexed provinces of Poland. Refusing to give up their faith, the Jews in these provinces turned westward to their brethren in the Polish Kingdom, increasing continually the density of the Jewish population in the constantly narrowing boundaries of Poland. Towards the end of the 18th century, with the last partition of Poland, this process came to an end. There was no longer a Poland into which the Jews could be dumped. Russian Czarism restricted the Jews to the Polish territory occupied last, and prohibited their entrance into Russia proper. The Jewish problem, however, was not solved by this measure. On the contrary, it became more involved by the very fact that the Jews, who were now subjects of Russia, were compelled to live among non-Russian elements and had no access to the Russian people.

Finding it difficult to drive out the large Jewish masses from their Pale of Settlement, Russian Czarism concentrated on the alternative of conversion. As in the Middle Ages, the government conducted a systematic campaign against Jewish religion, going even to the length of confiscating and burning all Jewish religious books. A flood of persecutions descended upon the Jewish communities, aiming to turn the Pale into a veritable hell, while privileges offered lavishly to converted Jews were calculated to break the backbone of the Jewish morale. But those who agreed to embrace Christianity formed a negligible number. The failure of Czarism in this direction was in line with the traditional failure of Christendom as far as the subjection of Judaism was concerned, and the reaction which the governmental attempt evoked was similar to the traditional reaction to such attempts: it strengthened the tenacity and steadfastness of the Jews in their religio-national faith. Realizing that to achieve large-scale conversion the Jews must be made to cooperate, the government looked to Jewish assimilation in the West and believed that it had hit upon the necessary formula: religious conversion must be preceded by cultural assimilation, and cultural assimilation should be preceded by enlightenment.

Thus, the government adopted a plan of luring the Jews to conversion through enlightenment. The failure of this plan, however, was predetermined by the attitude toward religion on the part of both the Russian and Jewish movements of enlightenment. In contradistinction to the development in Western Europe, the Russian movement of enlightenment did not commence with an all-out attack upon religion. Moreover, it arose at the very time when the idea of a Christian State was again in the ascendance, even in France. A section of the Russian intelligentsia, represented by the Slavophiles, transferred this idea to Russian soil. Stressing Russia's Christian character, the Slavophiles gave modern formulation to medieval conceptions; and, since Russia had never before been given to an anti-religious mood or philosophy, the idea of the Slavophiles found fertile ground. The all-out attack against religion in Russia was made at a comparatively late date, in the middle of the 1860s, with the appearance of the Nihilists and the Social Revolutionists, of whom Bakunin was most typical. But the influence of the Slavophiles was predominant in the first half of the 19th century and was still strong towards its end. It was not without this influence that the banner of Christianity was raised on high even by the greatest of the Russian authors, including Dostoyevsky and Tolstoy.

If the Russian movement of enlightenment in general took a positive stand toward the Christian religion, the Jewish movement of enlightenment in Russia, led and molded by Hebrew writers and scholars, was imbued with deep respect toward Jewish religion. Hoping that, as in the West, Hebrew would serve as a temporary medium of modern education which would lead to Russian cultural assimilation, the government gave its blessing and support to the Hebrew movement of enlightenment. But the experiences of the West were not repeated in Russia. Here the Hebrew movement constantly increased its ranks, while the acquisition of Russian culture was limited to a small section of the Jewish population. Had Russian Czarism adopted a policy of distributing the Jews throughout Russia, a policy that would have brought the dwellers of the Pale into closer contact with the Russian people, it is possible that Hebrew would have lost ground. But the policy of the government in narrowing the Jewish zone forced the Jews into greater isolation, and as a result, the modern Hebrew movement was given the opportunity in Russia which it had nowhere else: to create the national-minded Jew.

Modern Jewish Nationalism had been in the making in Russia long before it appeared on the scene. At the end of the 1870's it was ripe for emergence, but it needed external pressure to be crystallized into a movement. This pressure was provided by the pogroms of 1881. In the same year, even before the pogroms in Russia took place, there were pogroms in Germany, and the newly launched movement of antisemitism took the entire country by storm. German Jewry was not aroused—as if the fierce hatred were not directed against it. If Russian Jewry proved less lethargic, it was first of all owing to the stirring national slogans of the Hebrew movement of enlightenment. The fact that outside attacks were needed to pave the way for the principles of the Hebrew nationalists, does not minimize the significance of their effort. As in the case of other historic peoples, Jewish national consciousness could be fully awakened only in the face of grave national danger. In 1881, war was declared on the Jewish people, and "war is a forcible teacher," according to Thucydides.

Nevertheless, it was not only the preliminary educational work of the Hebrew movement of enlightenment, plus the events of 1881, that gave rise to Jewish nationalism in Russia. No national movement appeared in times of catastrophe without a concrete plan for liquidating that catastrophe. The Jewish national movement brought with it a solution to the Jewish question: it pointed to Palestine as the best possible outlet from the labyrinth of the Diaspora. But, this solution became possible because at that very time Palestine emerged from the legendary mist in which it was enveloped and entered the realm of realistic politics and general public interest. The Russian-Turkish war of 1877-78 again aroused the Eastern Question and, as a result, Palestine was again put on the map. The Congress of Berlin gave Britain the Island of Cyprus—a stepping-stone to her long anticipated control over the Near East—and turned public attention in the same direction. And finally, the occupation of Egypt by Great Britain in 1882 placed the lands of the Pyramids and the Bible in the center of public interest. It was not, of course, the first time that the Eastern Question had attracted wide attention. This was also the case in 1831, during the occupation of Palestine by Mohammed Ali, and again in 1854 during the Crimean War. But never was it raised in so forceful a manner as at the beginning of the 1880s; and what is more important, never before was it accompanied by other factors essential to the creation of a national movement in Jewry. It was indeed a fortunate coincidence that the Eastern Question arose at the start of the Eighties when Jewish nationalism was ready to emerge, and when a wave of persecutions had strengthened the national mood and increased the readiness to undertake the national solution. No great phenomenon can ever be brought into existence by a single factor. It was the meeting of the three elements in a crucial historic moment: the emergence of national consciousness, the pressure of a national tragedy and the appearance of Palestine on the political horizon, that gave birth to the national movement in Jewry.

Whether this movement could withstand the icy climate in which it was born depended on the measure of its inner strength. The force that sustained this movement in the face of all hardships was not only engendered by historic necessity, but was also inspired by unshakable conviction of a number of towering personalities. Of these, the most outstanding was one who for a long time seemed to be lost in assimilation, but who, at the decisive moment, became the most forceful protagonist of Jewish nationalism and the first leader of the Jewish national movement. He was Leo Pinsker.

II

No better illustration could be provided for the theory that leaders of peoples are products of their generation than that offered by Leo Pinsker. There was little in which he preceded his time, although he was always among the few who took the first steps forward. He had the open-mindedness and fortitude of one who refuses to support unfounded assumptions, but is ready to proclaim and champion any principle as soon as its truth was substantiated. Pinsker's conclusion were based not on vision, but on analysis. He was more of a pioneering scientist than of a far-seeing prophet. All in all, he was one of the truest representatives of Russian Jewry in the critical transformation period of the 19th century.

The various movements and schools of thought that reshaped Jewish life in the 19th century all had their share of influence on him. But the most profound and lasting influence was that of the Hebrew movement of enlightenment, although Pinsker himself was not one of its standard bearers or even of its rank and file. The basic conception of this movement were transmitted to him from childhood by his father, one of those early Hebrew intellectuals whose ideological path ultimately led to the revival of Jewish nationalism. Moreover, Pinsker's father was outstanding among those intellectuals. He belonged to that group of excellent men of learning, who rose in the second quarter of the 19th century and who created what became known as the Science of Judaism. Due to their unrelaxing efforts in searching the ruins of

Jewish Diaspora life, the colossal building of Jewish history could finally be reconstructed. For his field of research, Pinsker's father chose the Karaites (The Jewish Reformists of the 10th century), a most controversial subject in those days. While western Jewish scholars, who fought for religious reformation, viewed the Karaites as their spiritual predecessors, traditionalist Jews regarded them as heretics and would have liked to see their memory sink into oblivion. Pinsker's attitude differed from both these groups. He did not fight for religious reformation, nor did he share the zeal and hatred of the conservatives. His interest in the Karaites derived from the fact that they were members of the Jewish people and their history was part of Jewish history. This attitude towards the Karaites, shown by Pinsker as well as by other contemporary Hebrew scholars, attested to the fact that the center of gravity was for them shifted from the Jewish religion to the Jewish people.

After more than two decades of inquiry into the subject, Pinsker summarized his findings in his *Collection of Antiquities*. This book, although full of illuminating data for scholars, does not provide easy reading for the average person. For the latter, his other book was even less attractive. It was an *Introduction to Assyrian Vocalization* and dealt with the foundation of the Hebrew grammar. But, behind these apparently dry studies was a passionate desire to revive the national language and to restore the nation's history—two of the most vital elements in modern Jewish nationalism. Indeed, Pinsker was an intense Jewish nationalist, and both the sufferings and hopes of his people were an integral part of his emotional life. In keeping with the prevalent outlook of his time, he failed to view the restoration of the Jews to their homeland as a practical project. But he well realized that the homelessness of the Jews was the source of their misery and tragic situation among the nations. His soul was tormented by the national distress; and since his pain was not relieved through a national effort, it could find expression only in his burning prayers and moving lines of poetry. Once, young Pinsker witnessed his father's tears when the latter prayed for the salvation of his people. It was a sorrow which bore deep into the child's heart and imbued him with undying determination to change the lot of his people for the better.

Pinsker's father came to Russia at the beginning of the reign of Nicholas I. Young Pinsker, who was born in 1821, was then only a few years old. His transplantation to Russian soil took place before Poland, his native country, had left an imprint on his development. His birthplace, Tomashov, a small, drab town, was quickly erased from his memory by the vivacious and gay city of Odessa, which was henceforth his home. Had Pinsker remained in Tomashov, or had his parents settled not in Odessa but in any other place in the Pale of Settlement, it is hardly imaginable that he would have become the father of the Jewish National Movement. Odessa, as we shall see, played a tremendous role in shaping his character and determining his course of action.

There were few places in Russia of the time which could offer comparatively agreeable conditions, from both the spiritual and material points of view, to Hebrew scholars like Pinsker's father. Since the conservative masses of the Pale of Settlement fought the exponents of enlightenment tooth and nail, Odessa was for the latter an island of freedom in a raging sea of hatred. But not only was internal spiritual oppression unknown in Odessa; also external tyranny toward the Jew was considerably relieved in it. Imperial Russia was interested in the development of that city as its biggest commercial outlet on the Black Sea, and the Jews, as well as other trading elements, were considered best fitted to achieve this goal. At the time Pinsker and his family came to Odessa, the entire Pale of Settlement groaned and smarted under the oppressive measures of the Russian Czar. But Odessa was hardly affected by them. Indeed, free spirits do not thrive under conditions of abject slavery, and the feeling of individual and national self-respect with which Leo Pinsker was so thoroughly imbued, could nowhere develop in Russia so fully as in the atmosphere of partial freedom which was peculiar to Odessa. It was this atmosphere which first gave impetus to his demand for the emancipation of the Jews in Russia and later to that of national independence.

Odessa soon became the center of the Jewish movement of enlightenment. Some of the friends of Pinsker's father, who gravitated to that city, established there a school for modern Jewish education which was the first of its kind in Russia. Pinsker, the elder, was one of the teachers in the school and it was there that young Leo received his elementary education. Nevertheless, he did not gain there much knowledge of Hebrew. Hebrew studies were secondary in the school's curriculum, a fact that brought much grief to his father. To the latter's friends, as to most bearers of enlightenment, the study of German came first. German was for them the language of advanced studies, high culture, and enlightenment. Russian was also taught in that school, but mainly for official and utilitarian purposes. There was little to be learned in Russian, they thought. In 1835, when the school was established, modern Russian literature was only in its early stages. And although it already produced a Pushkin and a Lermontov, the enlightened Jews of those days could hardly have been influenced by their literary greatness. Later, when Leo Pinsker entered the Russian Gymnasium of Odessa, his Hebrew studies were entirely interrupted, and although he continued to study German, which he was later able to use fluently and efficiently, the Russian language, literature and history became the center of his studies. He was among the first Jews in Russia to receive a thorough and systematic Russian education.

These were the darkest days of the Pale of Settlement. Drastic restrictions and large-scale deportations, accompanied by recruitments of Jewish children to the Russian Army, followed each other relentlessly. Young Pinsker though, experienced very little of these horrors. He lived in a community of merchants and enlightened Jews who enjoyed special privileges at the hands of the Czarist regime. Hebrew writers and fighters for enlightenment could even count on financial support from the government. Pinsker's father was among those who received governmental honors in recognition of his scholarly attainments. The government, after all, did not seem to be the enemy of the Jews. Its attitude appeared harsh only toward the fanatic and ignorant elements, while the enlightened had known only its favor. This was the climate of opinion among most of the Jews of Odessa and this, one can assume, was the state of mind of young Pinsker, who became before long a determined fighter in the movement of enlightenment.

Like all other followers of enlightenment among the Jews, young Pinsker must have been grateful to the Czarist regime for the educational possibilities it had made available to the Jews, and was doubtless especially appreciative of the fact that a number of universities were opened to Jewish students. In fact, he was among the first to take advantage of that offer. After graduating with distinction from the Gymnasium, he entered the Lycée of Richelieu in Odessa, where he studied law. It was a short time after Spiransky had completed the codification of Russian Law—an accomplishment which was widely hailed by governmental and intellectual circles— and the study of law had become a growing fad. Pinsker certainly knew that, as a Jew, he would be unable to practice law under the then existing limitations. He might have reassured himself with the hope that the restrictions would be removed before his studies would be concluded. But upon leaving the Lycée, the young man of twenty-one, well fortified with legal knowledge and ready to enter the sphere of practical life, realized clearly that the field of his vocation was tightly closed to him only because he was a Jew.

Half a century later, another young Jew who was destined to become the successor of Pinsker in leading the Jewish national movement, experienced the same frustration and disappointment. Theodor Herzl, too, graduated from a law school and was prevented by the law of his country, Austria, from realizing his ambition to become a judge. Herzl turned to the field of drama and *belles-lettres,* in which he soon achieved a position of prominence. Pinsker, if he lacked the inspiration of a poet, undoubtedly had the making of a great publicist.

But what could a Russian Jewish publicist write about at the time of Nicholas I? There was no Russo-Jewish press in existence, and if there were any attempt to create it, the governmental censorship would have immediately nullified it. From Pinsker's scant writings, one clearly sees how he hated to dodge issues and mince words. He could express his thoughts only in a straight-forward manner, in complete accord with his inner beliefs, or else he had to keep his silence. This perhaps accounts for his literary inactivity over long periods, despite his unquestionable talent for writing and originality of thought. In any case, when Pinsker was graduated from the Lycée he did not turn to literature, but to teaching. He became an instructor of the Russian language at a Modern Hebrew school in Kishinev.

Pinsker's acceptance of this position should be evaluated as a pioneering effort rather than a professional undertaking.[1] At the time he became a teacher, education was for all enlightened Jews not only a profession, but also an ideal. It was regarded as the main aspect of the Jewish problem, as well as the key to its solution. As far as Pinsker was concerned, education, particularly Russian education, became the alpha and omega of his program.

At about the time Pinsker assumed his position in Kishinev the whole of Russian Jewry, including the Jews of Odessa, were disputing the government-sponsored plan to establish a chain of modern schools in the Jewish communities. While the enlightened Jews greeted the plan with enthusiasm, the conservatives flatly rejected it. Although the opposition of the latter to the plan stemmed from their general opposition to enlightenment, it was bolstered by the fact that they clearly sensed the Czarist motives and intentions. The enlightened Jews were inclined to believe that the government's move indicated its leaning toward progress and civilization. Viewing the matter retrospectively, the fallacy of this assertion must have soon become apparent. Nicholas I, who hated every movement of free thought, who

---

1 In later years he demanded from the Society of Enlightenment, in which he took a leading part, that it assist only those Jewish students who, after finishing their studies, would devote themselves for some time to educational work in Jewish communities.

developed censorship to an extent incredible even in Russia (there were twenty-two distinct censorships), who terrified and persecuted the greatest Russian writers, under whose rule Gogol was silenced, Dostoyevsky sentenced to penal servitude, and Belinsky spared from arrest only through an early death, this Nicholas I suddenly was concerned with the enlightenment of the Jews, the most humiliated of his subjects, in order to make them more civilized and progressive? "Progress?" commented Nicholas I upon a ministerial report which included this term, "What progress? This word must be deleted from official terminology."

If it was incredible that Nicholas I favored the enlightenment of the Jews for cultural reasons, it was even less believable that this enlightenment was launched as a preliminary step to their emancipation. Those who spoke of emancipation during his reign were immediately suspected of high treason. "Man is created free, and is free even if born in chains," wrote Friedrich Schiller. But when Zhukovsky attempted to publish the translation of these words, he was forbidden to do so, even though he was the court poet and the tutor of the Crown Prince. *Uncle Tom's Cabin* was forbidden to be published in Russian translation, since it evoked too much sympathy for slaves and might arouse opposition to despotic rule. Certainly, Nicholas I did not aim at the emancipation of the Jews as the enlightened among them were inclined to believe. At what did he aim, then? This question was answered unequivocally by the majority of the Jewish masses: he aimed at the souls of the younger Jewish generation, or more exactly, at their conversion to Christianity.

Pinsker, it seemed, gave little thought to the government's intentions. Whatever those intentions might be, he believed, the beneficial influence of modern education upon the Jews of the Pale could not be doubted. The Kishinev school in which he taught was one of those planned to be established by the government and he could certainly find no fault with the fact that the school's program was based on more modern principles, or that it provided for the study of Russian. On the contrary, in Kishinev he had the opportunity to learn the conditions of life in the Pale of Settlement, its cultural backwardness and stereotyped forms, which greatly contributed to the poverty of its masses; and he became all the more convinced of the need for bringing to this foul and decayed atmosphere the new spirit of enlightenment. In any case, he himself could not stand that atmosphere for long. After one year of service in that school, he left Kishinev for Moscow where he took up the study of medicine.

*****

The University of Moscow was then the most important center of the Russian intelligentsia, the birthplace of all social and political ideas that determined Russia's historic course in the ensuing years. The two groups of the intelligentsia, the Slavophiles and the Westerners, were strongly represented there. Despite basic differences of opinion, a certain brotherly understanding existed between these circles, especially between their younger representatives. Youri Samarine, a noted Slavophile, described their relations in these glowing terms: "They met every day, lived in friendship and formed, as it were, one society, that stood in need of each other by good will, common pursuits, and mutual esteem. Under the conditions existing in those times, polemics in the press were out of the question, and, as in the epoch before the invention of printing, the place of such polemics was taken by oral disputations."

The Westerners, who upheld western science and liberalism, were more to the liking of the young Jewish student, the son of a Hebrew advocate of Enlightenment, than the Slavophiles with their Christian-national-Slavic outlook. This much one can say with certainty. But, one can also safely assume that the Slavophiles contributed in no small measure to Pinsker's ideological development. In Moscow, he became acquainted with the specific conception of the Russian national problem, as well as with that of nationalism in general, as expounded by the Slavophiles. The Slavophiles stressed religion, race and history as major forces in the molding of a nation. The Westerners, on the other hand, showed little interest in the racial and national problems of Russia, and put emphasis on individual freedom and general democratic principles. If the Slavophiles contributed to Pinsker's national outlook, the Westerners promoted in him the belief that the Jewish problem was in essence the same as that of the bulk of Russia's population.

Both conceptions manifested themselves in Pinsker's later proposal for the solution of the Jewish question. In the period under discussion, however, as well as in that which followed it, the precepts of liberalism were uppermost in his mind. The general conditions which prevailed in Russia seemed to justify the views of the Westerners. Russian Jews suffered from expulsions, restrictions and drastic conscriptions. But what about the Russians themselves? The great majority of them were virtually the chattels of the upper class. They could be sold and bought, tortured and humiliated. They were beasts of burden, slaves, "dead souls". "Who can be happy in Russia?" asked the poet Nekrasov. The fate of the Jews seemed no exception. The liberation of the Russian Jews would come with the liberation of the Russian people, just as the emancipation of the western Jews had come with the emancipation of the western peoples. This was the lesson indicated by the objective conditions. Nevertheless, even without these considerations, liberalism was then for young Pinsker, as it was for every enlightened Jew, a synonym of freedom and progress. It was an age of unshaken optimism for the final victory of the liberal idea. No reaction or oppression could shatter this faith of the enlightened Jew.

The year 1848, in which Pinsker completed his studies at the university, saw the outbreak of new liberal revolutions in Europe, and marked new triumphs for the liberal idea. In Russia, however, it signified the bolstering of reaction and the retreat of enlightenment. Nicholas I, the "policeman of Europe," who checked the revolutions of the Hungarians and the Poles, proved to be even more strict in policing Russians. In his firm determination to uproot liberalism in Russia, he soon decided to dry out its source: free thought and enlightenment. Ordered to follow the Medieval path, his Ministry of Education attempted to "base all teachings on religious truths." In the universities, the study of history and philosophy was prohibited, and in the press and literature every sign of liberalism was severely punished. Since the Russian intelligentsia was all but stifled, there was hardly any possibility for public activity on the part of the Jewish intelligentsia. Upon his return to Odessa in 1849, after a short visit to Germany, Pinsker had to devote himself exclusively to his professional work as a physician.

In this way alone could he give expression to his deep altruistic feelings and his genuine desire to help the suffering and the poor. He had already manifested these feelings in a striking manner when in 1848, on the eve of graduation, he interrupted his studies and willingly threw himself into the fight against the cholera that was sweeping Moscow. After establishing for himself an enviable medical reputation, he again showed the same altruism and the same readiness for sacrifice. When in 1854, a horrible epidemic of typhus wrought havoc among the Russian armies fighting in the Crimea, Pinsker volunteered to serve in the military hospitals, and won the esteem of the authorities for his exemplary devotion. Twice he braved death in answer to the call of his conscience. Not only was his altruism manifested in these actions, but also his deep sense of duty as well as his unflinching courage. If not for these undeniable qualities in Pinsker's character, he would not have become later champion of his people at the time of catastrophe.

The end of the Crimean War, or rather the death of Nicholas I, which occurred at the same time, sealed the first period of Pinsker's life. On the whole, it was for him a period of study, research and spiritual growth, but of total inactivity in public affairs. It was, however, this period in which the basis was laid for his future undertakings in Jewish life.

III

If the first period in Pinsker's life coincided with the reign of Nicholas I, the second paralleled the reign of Alexander II. By no means should one see in this an artificial division of biographical data. This division, which is evident in the careers of almost every man of prominence in Czarist Russia, emanates from the fact that Russian life revolved around the character and policies of its Emperors. As late as the middle of the 19th century, Marquis de Custin rightly stated that the "Empire is the ruling Emperor," and that the "Emperor is God the Lord…. In our days there is in the whole world no single man who has at his disposal such unlimited power as the Czar." This unlimited power of Czarism was challenged by the intelligentsia, that particular group in Russian society which arose at the beginning of the 19th century, and the clash between the intelligentsia and the autocracy was the essence of Russia's history until the revolution of 1917. Since the strategy employed by the Russian Emperors differed according to their temper and reasoning, every change in the Russian throne affected especially the intelligentsia, whose fate was linked with the outcome of the conflict.

Pinsker was a member of this intelligentsia. The extent of his ability to act, to speak and to write for the public largely depended on the policies adopted by the omnipotent power of the country—the Emperor. During the last years of Nicholas I, when Pinsker's political conceptions were crystallized, any public action was hardly possible. The ascendance of Alexander II to power brought with it more favorable conditions. As soon as circumstances permitted, Pinsker's public activity began.

Pinsker had to wait for such an opportunity, since in common with other bearers of liberalism in Russia, he was no revolutionary activist. This point must be born in mind. Russian liberals believed in evolution and enlightenment, and not in acts of violence. Mindful of the attempt of the Decembrists to dethrone him and conscious of the liberal revolutions in Europe, Nicholas I saw in the Russian liberals the vanguard of revolution. He dreaded Liberalism more than Socialism. But the true revolutionary type appears in Russia only with the Socialist movement. Pinsker had never accepted Socialism. His non-revolutionary stand is therefore understandable; it was in line with the general policy of the Russian liberal intelligentsia.

This policy seemed all the more justified after the coming of Alexander II to power. Although there were no revolutionary outbreaks, Russian Czarism was compelled to change its course. The force of argument and reasoning transcended any class interests or governmental ambitions. Even Nicholas I, the stubborn reactionary, had to indicate in his last days that a change in his system might not be out of place. "My successor," he said on his deathbed, "may do as he pleases, but I cannot change!" His successor, Alexander II, "did as he pleased" and inaugurated the "Epoch of the Great Reforms."

Heeding the voice of the liberal intelligentsia, he abolished a number of severe censorship rules and liberated the serfs. In the army, in the economic sphere, as in education, important steps were taken to place Russia on a par with western countries. More leniency was shown also to the Jews. The conscription of Jewish children was completely abolished. To the enlightened and the merchants more privileges were granted, while the restrictions of the Pale of Settlement were somewhat eased. The Jewish intelligentsia was fully convinced, as was the Russian liberal public, that total freedom was in the offing. Its task seemed quite clear. It had to mobilize greater support on the part of the Russian public for the demand of emancipation, and to prepare the Jews morally and culturally for an active, beneficial part in the life of the new, free and Europeanized Russia.

In order to achieve these aims the small group of Jewish intellectuals in Odessa took a daring step. They established a Russo-Jewish organ—the first periodical in Russian to deal with Jewish affairs. The publication which appeared in 1860, under a triple editorship in which Pinsker participated, was called *Razsviet* (the Dawn), indicating the firm belief of its initiators in the new era that had begun with

Alexander's rule. They were bitterly disappointed to find that the new era differed little from the old as far as the censorship limitations were concerned. Their demands for free expression were systematically suppressed, as were their attempts to point out the injustice of the special disabilities imposed upon the Jews. They could write freely only about the need for Russian education among the Jews. But this alone could hardly attract a wide reading public. In any case, some of the initiators were greatly dispirited and, after a few months of uneventful existence, the publication was discontinued.

The accepted view is that in this period Pinsker favored the assimilation of the Jews among the Russians, in the usual manner of the western assimilationists. As a matter of fact, however, his approach to the Jewish question was based on a national, rather that an assimilationist, outlook. His real point of view was expressed not in *Razsviet*, of which he was only associate editor, but in the succeeding publication of which he was founder and editor-in-chief. It is quite possible that because of the differences of opinion between him and the chief editor of *Razsviet* concerning the whole approach to the Jewish question, Pinsker undertook the editorship of the new publication.

He called this publication *Zion*. In contrast to *Razsviet*, whose declared program was to help the Jews to become Russified, the aim of *Zion* was to foster the Jewish national spirit in those who were on the road to Russification. "History had imposed two duties upon the Jews," says Pinsker in his programmatic article, "one of responding to the call of their time and native land, and one of being true Jews. Engaged in satisfying the first need, the Jews detached themselves from their past and race as well as from their whole course of life. Our task, therefore, is to revive in their hearts the meaning of the great past of the Hebrew nation as well as the purport of its present." For Pinsker, then, it was the will of history that the Jews remain true to themselves, and a "true Jew" was for him one who is attached to his past and race. By omitting any reference to the Jewish religion, Pinsker clearly indicated his national stand. According to Pinsker, the Jews are a racial and historic group and not a religious sect as preached by the assimilationists. The study of Jewish history is urged by him in the same article not in order to clarify the essence of Judaism, or more exactly, of the Jewish religion, as conceived by the western Reform scholars, but rather in order "to awaken in our hearts respect and love for our nation." His conclusions were based largely on introspection. He himself was not religious; nevertheless, he was strongly conscious of his attachment to the Jewish nationality. In fact, the problem that then troubled him most was how to protect this nationality from misguidance and disintegration.

He was of the opinion that Russian Jewry had reached the same crossroad upon which the western Jewish communities stood on the eve of Emancipation, and he was loath to see a repetition of the process of western assimilation in the ranks of Russian Jewry. By assimilation he meant not cultural conformity, but actual separation from the nation's body through intermarriage, or rather through the abandonment of its race, and lack of vital interest in its fate, that is, its past, present and future. "The great past of the Hebrew nation!"— For the son of the Hebrew scholar and historian this was a living conception.

In this approach to the Jewish question Pinsker was far ahead of his time. The emphasis he put upon race and history as the two basic elements of national life, attest to his insight into the nature of nationalism. Race and history, he thought, were among the major factors that had sustained the Jews as a national group. Race and history have remained the principal factors that still make for their separatism. Pinsker might have been influenced in this respect by Slavophile thinkers who stressed the importance of these two elements in the shaping of nationalism. But while at the center of the Slavophile ideology stood the religious factor, for Pinsker religion was only a secondary force.

There were, of course, other points of difference between the conception of Pinsker and that of the Slavophiles, the representatives of Russian national ideology, regarding the essence and meaning of nationalism. Besides stressing the religious factor, the latter paid due attention to other elements in the national scheme. "What is a nation," asks the Slavophile Kireievsky, "but a body of convictions which are more or less expressed in its manners, its customs, its language, the notions of its mind and its heart, the relations of its society—in fact, its whole life." Two decades later, when writing his *Auto-Emancipation*, Pinsker came much nearer to this understanding of nationalism. "They lack most of the attributes which are the hallmark of a nation," he writes there about the Jews. "They lack characteristic national life which is inconceivable without a common language, common customs and common land." At the beginning of the Sixties none of these elements were regarded by him as vital to Jewish national existence. What country should be considered the homeland for Russian Jewry? What should be their customs, their language? Pinsker would doubtless have answered that the land should be Russia, the customs—Russian customs, and the language—the Russian language.

Nevertheless, his advocacy of Russification should by no means be construed as an endorsement of assimilation. It was for him an expedient towards establishing closer relations with the Russian people, in whose land the Jews lived by historic decree, and it was limited to that. Hebrew played no role in his national conception, as was later true also of Herzl. He regarded Hebrew as dead for all practical purposes, and he thought that it would remain the property of a limited group of scholars for the purpose of historic and literary research. In any event, since the masses of Russian Jewry had not mastered the Hebrew language, he wanted Russian to replace the Germanic jargon which was predominant among them. He opposed German education among Russian Jewry, although, like most Russian intellectuals of the time, he regarded German as the best medium for enlightenment. He insisted on Russian education alone, because more important to him than a higher degree of enlightenment was the creation of mutual understanding between the Jews and the Russian people among whom they lived. In brief, his theory of Russification meant not assimilation, but social and political cooperation.

That this was Pinsker's conception at the time is evident from another article of his, which was published in the same periodical. *Osnova*, a Ukrainian publication, came out with an anti-Jewish attack claiming that nothing is more harmful to a nation than the residence in its midst of foreign nationalities who are indifferent to its fate. "Does not this imply," asked Pinsker, "that there must be in every land only one nation that rules over the rest and devours the rest; one nation to which all other nationalities must cleave, or else that nation will consider them harmful and will threaten them with extermination or expulsion? Do you believe that the destiny, the interests and the spirit of one nation have to dominate the entire existence of the other nationalities? Do you, too, like the Inquisition in the Middle Ages, fail to see that the multiplicity of forms is life and that death alone is uniform?" The implications of this moving argument are quite obvious. Pluralism of national bodies was, for Pinsker, in complete accord with the process of life, while assimilation meant arbitrary interference with that natural process, its distortion and termination: death.

From the above article against *Osnova,* one can also learn how Pinsker then visualized the ultimate solution of the Jewish problem in Russia. *Osnova* had reproached the Jews for their failure to adopt the Ukrainian language. Pinsker repudiated the contention that such a development had to take place. The Jews, he claimed, are obliged to study the common language of the country which is the language of *all* its peoples as well as of the State; but that language is Russian and not Ukrainian. Since the Jews form an integral part of the Russian corporate body, they have obligations toward this body alone and not toward any of its component parts. Ukrainians have no right to ask the Jews to adopt the Ukrainian language, just as the Jews have no right to ask the Ukrainians to adopt the Jewish or Hebrew tongue. In Pinsker's conception, therefore, the Jewish nationality was placed on the same level with the other nationalities of Russia. And he believed that the future democratic Russia would allow the existence and free development of its various national groups which would be united by ties of a common language, common culture, and common devotion to the State.

This was the ideal of Pinsker at the time, and this was the ideal of the best among the Russian liberals. Enlightenment was sought by them not for the sake of assimilation, but for the sake of freedom and higher forms of expression. "What is the ideal of education?" asked Pirogov, a noted Russian educator, who was Pinsker's friend. "Choose your own way and be a man! Each of us, whatever his national race, can become a real person with the aid of education. Every one can reach this goal in his own way, in keeping with his racial characteristics and his national conception of the ideal man, without failing in his duties as a citizen of his country. Moreover, it is only through education that one can bring out the fine qualities of his nation." Hoping through education to forge a Russia that would present the picture of a commonwealth of nations, living together in peace and harmony under the banner of a republic or a constitutional monarchy, Russian liberals were faced with the opposition of the oppressed nations who refused to share their views and their hopes. The latter disdained to compromise on what they considered their rightful aspirations, and, encouraged by the reforms of Alexander II, demanded nothing less than *complete* independence and *immediate* freedom. Thus, we see that at the very time that the serfs were liberated, the Polish revolutionary national movement again burst forth in open revolt.

In 1812, at the time of the Napoleonic wars, the Jews, who had come under Russian rule only a few decades before, refused to side with the Poles, the allies of Napoleon. "It is a matter of surprise," wrote Nicholas I when he was still Crown Prince, "that in 1812 the Jews displayed exemplary loyalty to us and assisted us wherever they could at the risk of their lives." In the Polish insurrection of 1831 the Jews of Poland again displayed the same loyalty to Russia, and Nicholas I officially expressed his Imperial satisfaction with the behavior of the Jews during the revolt. But the long reign of his persistent tyranny destroyed even the loyalty of the Jews. In 1863, the Jews of all the districts of the Pale of Settlement, which had belonged to Poland before its last partition, supported enthusiastically the Polish revolution. The year 1863 marked the beginning of Polish-Jewish revolutionary cooperation which was destined to play a tremendous role in the history of the Russian revolutionary movement and—through it—in the history of Europe and the world at large.

No information is available as to Pinsker's attitude toward Jewish participation in the Polish revolution. *Razsviet* had ceased publication two years before the revolt. Like most Russian periodicals at the time, its life was cut short by the harsh governmental restrictions. "Because of the prevailing censorship conditions," Pinsker wrote in later years, "my patience was exhausted after a while, and I soon resigned from the editorial board so that I would not have to be present at the demise of the periodical." Consequently, he had no desire to establish a new organ from which we might have learned about his reaction to current events. However, from the above exposition of Pinsker's views regarding the national question in Russia, one can easily adduce his negative attitude toward the active Jewish stand in the Polish rebellion. Even if he were in sympathy with the national aims of the Poles, he could not see any point in the Jewish attempt to advance these aims. The Jews had no territorial ambitions in Russia, nor could they have any. Their salvation lay, he was certain, in Russia's democratization and that meant, in the first place, the education of all its various national elements along western lines. In the year of the outbreak of the Polish revolt, there was established in St. Petersburg a Society for the Enlightenment of the Jews. Some years later there was established in Odessa an affiliated body, in which Pinsker was a leading force from the very beginning.

In 1864, on a visit to the Germanic countries, Pinsker might have gained support for his views from the leaders of the Jewish communities with whom he came in touch. Only a few years earlier, in 1862, the Jews of Germany were granted equality of rights. But what was responsible for their emancipation? The prevailing opinion was that the emancipation of the German Jews was determined at the very moment that their Germanization was initiated by Moses Mendelssohn. It was impossible, they thought, to ignore the rights of highly educated people, who had mastered the national language and took active part in all the phases and forms of the national activities. A whole century had to pass from the time that Mendelssohn had translated the Bible into German before the Emancipation of the Jews was granted. It might take decades in Russia too, Pinsker thought, but its achievement was beyond doubt if the Jews of Russia, like the Jews of Germany, became entwined in the nation's life.

Besides, the Emancipation of the western Jews was achieved—against the will of the autocratic rulers—at the wish of the peoples themselves, or rather of their liberal elements. This reasoning seemed to apply to Russia even more than to the western countries. The Czarist regime was opposed to the Jewish emancipation, but the future of Russia lay in the hands of the Russian people. If a communion of feeling were established between large sections of Jews and Russians, especially between the Jews and the Russian intelligentsia, the achievement of Jewish emancipation would follow as a matter of course. In 1869, the Society for the Advancement of Enlightenment in Odessa founded a new Russo-Jewish weekly, *Den* (The Day), whose principal aim was to cement Russo-Jewish relations. Pinsker and his associates were very optimistic about the possibilities in this direction.

In the midst of these optimistic dreams about Russian-Jewish collaboration, there came, like a thunderbolt out of a clear sky, the Odessa pogrom of 1871. This was not the first anti-Jewish outbreak in Odessa. Anti-Jewish riots were a yearly occurrence there, and in 1821, 1849, and 1859 they assumed the proportions of mass attacks. The outbreak of 1871, however, was a far more serious affair. It could not be seen as a spontaneous outburst, since it bore all the earmarks of an organized pogrom. It raged for four consecutive days without interference by the police, who looked idly on. Moreover, it was openly instigated by the Russian and Greek intelligentsia who incited the rabble against the Jews. Orshansky, the secondary editor of *Den*, stated clearly that the "intelligentsia manifested more hatred toward the Jews than the mob, and even encouraged the pogromists with words and money." In the institutions of learning, teachers justified the pogroms to the students, and in the press not a voice was raised in defense of the Jews. The demand of *Den* to punish the rioters led to its suspension by the government.

To the Russo-Jewish intellectuals in Odessa this pogrom marked a crisis whose extent can be gauged from the fact that the Society for Advancement of Enlightenment was dissolved shortly thereafter. "The pogroms against the Jews in Odessa," wrote Soloveichik (Pinsker's co-editor of *Raszviet* and *Zion*), "entirely destroyed the belief of the leaders of the Odessa Society that their work had any chance of success. They were compelled to realize that Jewish attempts to get closer to the Russians would yield no practical results as long as the mass of the Russian people was engrossed in ignorance and subjected to civil backwardness." This admission marked the first retreat of the movement of enlightenment, although it did not express the essence of the crisis. The crux of the problem lay no more in the "ignorance" and "backwardness" of the Russian masses, but in the very hopes for partnership with the intelligentsia against the reactionary forces of the government. A careful observer like Pinsker, one can assume, could not fail to see that the events of 1871 spelled doom for these hopes. The Odessa pogrom was the work of both the local intelligentsia and the common man of the street, no less than that of the authorities. On whom then could the Jews rely? What point was there in the whole campaign of enlightenment? Likewise, he must have noted the fact that pogroms broke out in Odessa more often than anywhere else in Russia, although Odessa was the home of a Jewish community to which the enlightened pointed as an example for other Jewish communities in Russia. Besides, Odessa was the gathering place of many national groups. Why, then, were the Jews singled out for outrage and persecution?

No doubt, he thought, something was basically wrong with his formula of enlightenment and his conception of the future. The whole policy of the generation was placed in grave doubt and lost its appeal for him. For seven years he withdrew from any activity in the movement of enlightenment. But time had healed the wound in his soul. In 1878, when the Society for Enlightenment was reconstituted, we again see him active in its midst. Perhaps he was influenced by the powerful movement of the Populists which, in the middle of the Seventies, stirred the country with its call to the young intelligentsia to "go to the people," to educate the ignorant peasants, to teach them the Russian language and literature, and to bring them the fruits of modern civilization. That which the Russian intelligentsia had to do for the Russian people, he might have thought, the Jewish intelligentsia had to do for the Jews. In any case, his renewed activity in the movement for enlightenment, as well as the tense political life during and after the Russo-Turkish war (1877-1878), undoubtedly helped to weaken the impression of the Odessa pogrom. He certainly became inclined to believe that the outbreak in Odessa was, after all, a mere episode, a product of temporary and local conditions. He might even have forgotten it altogether.

But the new wave of bloody terror in 1881, which swept, like a hurricane, across scores of Jewish communities, convinced him of the true character of the Odessa riots. They were not a passing occurrence, but a chronic illness. All the phenomena that accompanied the pogrom in Odessa—the connivance of the authorities, the participation of the intelligentsia, the hostility of the masses, the instigation of the press—were now repeated on a nationwide scale. In 1881, Pinsker parted once more from his friends in the Society for Enlightenment, and this time forever. He realized the ineffectiveness of their program for the solution of the Jewish question. He recognized the futility of his own endeavors and the failure of his whole life-work. It became appallingly apparent that his activity up to that moment was based on nothing but false assumptions and unfounded hopes. He was sixty years old when he discovered the grave and tragic mistake of his generation.

IV

"Once I dreamt a dream about a glorious Judaism," wrote Pinsker in one of his letters, "but when I awoke from my sleep the time—at any rate, the proper time—had passed." He thought, it seems, that his hopes for an emancipated Jewry in Russia (the "glorious Judaism" to which he referred) were responsible for the fact that for many years he failed to achieve anything in the direction of national restoration, and that when he recognized those illusions for what they were, the "proper time" for action had already passed. Had Pinsker of the Eighties, Pinsker the nationalist, arisen in Russia at the beginning of the Sixties, in all probability his fate would have been no better than that of Moses Hess, who at the same time, in Germany, came forth with the Jewish national idea. The national movement could not come into being merely by the will of a few individuals, however forceful, convincing and persistent they might be. It had to undergo a long process of growth in which the movement for enlightenment had its share, and it was the result of certain historic factors that appeared only at the beginning of the Eighties. A younger Pinsker would probably have accomplished more than the sickly sexagenarian. In the personal sense, therefore, his "proper time" might have passed. But historically, Pinsker did not come too late. He came at the right moment.

He proclaimed his belief in the national solution, however, when the national movement was already on the march. His *Auto-Emancipation*, which contains that new proclamation of faith, was published in September, 1882. Four months before its publication, Laurence Oliphant, the great Christian Zionist, had recorded his participation in a meeting of delegates from twenty-eight committees for Palestine colonization. "My correspondence from all parts of Russia," he noted, "tells me that the movement is universal."

The movement, in fact, had burst forth soon after the pogroms, which commenced on April 15, 1881, six weeks after the assassination of Alexander II. As the same Oliphant rightly stated: "The idea of a return to the East has seized upon the imagination of the masses and produced a wave of enthusiasm in favor of emigration to Palestine, the force and extent of which only those who have come in direct contact with it can appreciate." Both the imagination and enthusiasm appeared spontaneously, but they were nurtured and fired by the bearers of the Hebrew movement of enlightenment who now took a radical national stand. In the confusion and despair that followed the pogroms, and in the chaotic exodus that ensued, the Hebrew nationalists alone had offered a courageous program of action. They were quick to draw conclusions from the turn of events, and supported by the national-minded elements which their education had reared, they took the initiative in directing the Jewish masses to the path of national restoration.

One cannot determine with any certainty the exact date of Pinsker's conversion to the national idea. In any case, in March, 1882, less than one year after the outbreak of the pogroms, we find him advocating that idea in personal talks with Jewish leaders in the west. Having scant knowledge of the Hebrew language, Pinsker could not draw direct inspiration from the vigorous pronouncements of the Hebrew nationalists, chief among whom were Smolenskin and Lilienblum. Besides, his original exposition of the Jewish Question testifies to the fact that both his analysis and conclusions were products of his own mind, reached after deep and lengthy meditation. Nevertheless, the general principles of the Hebrew nationalists were common knowledge toward the end of 1881. One may, therefore, assume that the same ideological forces that contributed to the creation of the Jewish national movement had also their share of influence on him.

From the moment the national idea ripened in his mind, Pinsker became a changed man. Heretofore, he was a communal worker, cautious and restrained; from then on he became a frontline fighter, vigorous and determined. Somehow, all his previous endeavors seemed to him experiments whose conclusions he awaited with skepticism. Even in the most reassuring moments, he must have experienced that vague uncertainty, that peculiar feeling of walking on air, which always accompanies realistic observers swayed by a false doctrine. That feeling had now entirely disappeared. Instead, there came a mathematical certainty of the solution to the problem that troubled him most. Now he was in complete accord with himself, for "now," as he wrote to a comrade in arms, "we have discovered the aim of our lives in our innermost, deep conviction."

Pinsker was gripped by the national idea with the force of a prophetic mission. On his own initiative, he left Russia to traverse central and western Europe, in order to offer his plan of salvation to the leading Jewish figures of the day. On previous visits to the western countries, he had approached the representatives of western Jewry with a sense of awe. He regarded them not only as great leaders, but also as his spiritual guides, and their opinions served to spur him on in his efforts for Russification. This time, however, Pinsker came not to learn, but to teach. Certain of the validity of his reasoning and the open-mindedness of the western Jewish leaders whom he had known, he could hardly believe that he would fail to convince them.

"I visited many of them," he wrote the following year to Levanda, "I put all my soul into the argument. I made use of all the facts, trying to play upon all the strings of the human heart." But the results were disheartening. Some of them opposed him violently; some listened to his words with sympathy; but only one or two expressed agreement and encouragement. His conversation with the Chief Rabbi of Vienna, Dr. Adolf Jellinek, which was recorded by the latter in his publication *Neuzeit*, reveals the nature of the clash between the two viewpoints, that of Emancipation and that of national rehabilitation.

This meeting was probably the first encounter Pinsker had with the western Jewish spokesmen. He turned to Jellinek first, because the latter was a close friend of his father, who had spent many years in Vienna in historical research. Pinsker became acquainted with him in 1864, gained his friendship and was impressed by his striking personality. A noted author and forceful orator, Jellinek was one of the foremost western Jews, and his conversion to the national idea would enormously heighten its prestige. Pinsker knocked at his door with tense expectation.

Jellinek hardly recognized him. The past fifteen years had left their impression on Pinsker's face. But perhaps deeper than the mark of age, was the imprint of the last year, with the moral crisis it entailed for him. The outward changes in the aging man were accompanied by inner spiritual changes which were clearly visible in his countenance. This was no more the hopeful and content Pinsker of the 1860s. This was Pinsker as we know him from his last picture: a man who looked deep into the intricacies of the Jewish tragedy, who realized the enormity of the task he voluntarily undertook, but was ready to bear it with unlimited patience and endurance to the very end; a man who was capable of smiling with grief, calmly and thoughtfully, but who had lost the art of laughing. That was the new Pinsker whom Jellinek failed to recognize.

When Pinsker began to expose his views, he was even more surprised. In fact, he was shocked. The nerves of the Russian Jew, he thought, must have been shattered by the tragic events. Here was a man who had not only adopted the ridiculous notion of the "national Jew," but was also attempting to convert him, Jellinek, to this absurdity. But the shock was mutual. The Viennese leader, once so admired by Pinsker, proved to be a bitter disappointment. How short-sighted were the arguments he raised against him! "You exaggerate the importance of antisemitism," Jellinek had said. "This poisonous plant which sprouted on the banks of the Spree will wither faster than you imagine, since it has no roots in history." As if 1800 years of repeated persecutions and flaming Jew-hatred did not provide enough historic roots for antisemitism! "The large masses of Russian Jewry are concentrated in compact areas; hence the extent of the animosity toward them." As if the Jews were not forced into this concentration by that very animosity, and as if antisemitism were unknown in Germany and other countries where their numbers were much smaller. "We feel at home in Europe, and we consider ourselves Germans, French, English, Magyars, Italians, to the marrow of our bones." The Oberrabbiner of Vienna seemed to overlook the fact that the decisive factor is not how the Jews feel about the nations among whom they live, but how those nations feel about them. "The new inventions of our time, the telegraph and press, transmit the news of every atrocity to all corners of the world and facilitate the defense of the oppressed Jews in Russia." But the same inventions also transmit the antisemitic propaganda that accompanies every act of atrocity, and who can say which will be more effective. "The Jews of Russia have a guardian angel in the person of the Russian Empress, who is the daughter of the Danish King. Is it possible that the daughter of one of the most liberal princes of Europe will not tremble when Ignatiev and his associates enact cruel laws against the Jews? We should put our hopes in her." This is how one of the greatest spiritual leaders of western Jewry understood the historic events of 1881. He advocated the old Jewish folly of relying on benevolent Christian rulers, as if they could reduce the force or velocity of the antisemitic flood. No plan for changing the objective conditions; no plan for a secure future; no proposal for independence. The old Jewish habit of looking to the ruler for help and succor, trembling with fear when he is unfriendly, praying for him when he is benevolent, this was the only "advice" the spiritual leader could give a whole people over whom the threat of total destruction hung like the sword of Damocles.

This conversation was repeated many times over. But the more he spoke with these people of Vienna, Berlin, Frankfurt, Paris, and London, the more convinced he became of the indisputable nature of his assertions. He felt with all his might that he was speaking the truth, a truth confirmed by tragic experiences, by the dictates of logic, by the laws of life. To agree with his opponents meant to succumb to lies. He had hoped that his brethren in the West, who lived under conditions more favorable than those in Russia, who commanded power and prestige in various fields of activity, and were capable of large-scale planning and organization, would undertake the task of liberation. But his attempt to win over their leaders failed completely. What was left for him to do? A Jewish member of the British Parliament, Arthur Cohen, "the only one who fully understood me," as Pinsker wrote, advised him to present his case before the bar of public opinion. He urged him to put his ideas on paper. Pinsker returned to Berlin and there, in the cradle of modern assimilation, he wrote his manly call to his "brothers in race," which he entitled *Auto-Emancipation*.

*****

It was not for nought that this pamphlet opened a new era in the history of the Jewish people; it is undoubtedly one of the greatest documents that has ever been written on the Jewish question. The eloquence, clarity and simplicity of its style, together with its orderly and scientific analysis, are not the product of literary ability and analytical capacity alone. The power of documents like *Auto-Emancipation* lies in the fact that they present truths arrived at after the costly blunders and ceaseless searchings of entire generations. Its clarity of style represents clarity of thought and its forceful expression is a reflection of the force of the idea. *Auto-Emancipation* was written under the inspiring pressure of a momentous idea that *had* to find expression. When Ruelf had highly praised the style of *Auto-Emancipation* and compared it to that of Boerne, Pinsker replied: "I would have written it even with the coarse style of a peasant."

He wrote this manifesto of faith under the impression of his conversations with the leaders of assimilation, and he made them the target of the sharpest arrows at his disposal. His aim was to destroy their groundless optimism, to reveal the bare realities of their shameful condition, to expose the dangers which threatened them on every hand, but which they preferred to ignore. Western assimilationists claimed that the time of fraternity had arrived, that the Jews were being greeted with a growing feeling of comradeship. Pinsker unsparingly revealed to them what they really felt in the depth of their hearts, what innumerable manifestations and repeated events confirmed and substantiated. "No matter how much the nations are at variance with one another, however diverse their instincts and aims, they join hands in their hatred of the Jews. On this matter all are agreed." The assimilationists maintained that there was a marked difference between the attitude toward the Jews in the western countries and in Russia. They pointed to the equality of rights they enjoyed as proof that they were admitted into the family of nations. There was a difference in degree, Pinsker asserted, but not a difference in kind; the antipathy, as such, exists in all places and at all times. "In the great majority of cases, the Jew is treated as a step-child, in the most favorable cases he is regarded as an adopted child; never is he considered a legitimate child of the fatherland." He told them how they appeared in the eyes of the nations: foolish and contemptible. "You are foolish because you expect of human nature something which it has never produced—humanity. You are also contemptible, because you have no real self-estimation and no national self-respect."

In this harsh realism of Pinsker is expressed the new approach of modern Jewish nationalism not only to the Jewish question, but also to the problems of the world at large. It meant first of all the abandonment of the utopias of the 18th century, which were used as battle-cries in the great revolutions, but which were never realized in international political life. The inspiring slogans of Equality and Fraternity served at best as a basis for internal democracy, or rather for the relations between the individuals of one nation, but never as a foundation for the relations between national bodies. The Jews demanded the fulfillment of the democratic principles as individuals and citizens of the State; they refused to realize that they were also members of a separate national group to which the same principles never applied. This is what Pinsker meant when he said that *humanity* has not yet been produced by human nature. By "humanity" he did not mean, of course, kindness of soul or expressions of sympathy and understanding for one's fellow-man, which are daily manifestations; by "humanity" he meant the application of the cosmopolitan principle, the placing of the entire human race above any individual feelings or national interests. "We must recognize that before the great idea of human brotherhood will unite all the peoples of the earth, millenniums must elapse; and that meanwhile a people which is at home everywhere and nowhere, must everywhere be regarded as alien."

The nations of the world have little faith in brotherly international relations. Nevertheless, Pinsker pointed out, they normally live in relative peace. The Jews believe in cosmopolitan fraternity, while in effect they are always in a state of war. They are in such a state, even in the most democratic countries, because the forces which dominate the relations between nations are based on biological and psychological factors that are stronger than any philosophy of equality. In analyzing these factors as they operate in the relations of the nations towards the Jews, Pinsker demonstrated his deep insight into the elements of the Jewish question. Normal relations between national groups, he thought, are not based on mutual love, but on mutual respect. The Jews cannot be accorded national respect because they lack its prerequisite: national equality. "The Jewish people has no fatherland of its own, no center of gravity, no government of its own, no official representation." Since they do not control any of the forces that are at he disposal of other nations, the disrespect of the nations toward them is predetermined.

If there was no mutual respect between the nations and the Jews, there was mutual fear. The nations feared the Jews because of their failure to destroy them. The Jews feared the nations because of their attempts to destroy them. "The ghostlike apparition of a people, without unity or organization, without land or other bonds of unity, no longer alive, and yet moving about among the living—could not fail to make a strange, peculiar impression upon the imagination of the nations." This particular fear, which Pinsker called Judeophobia, strengthened the hatred of the nations for the eternal alien. The Jewish people represented in their eyes a "ghost which is not disembodied like other ghosts, but is a being of flesh and blood, and must therefore endure pain inflicted by the fearful mob who imagines itself endangered." That fear, which was elevated by Pinsker to the status of a primary factor in the spread of Jew-hatred, was already recognized by Boerne. The latter, however, failed to detect its motives. For Boerne, like for many others, it was Christianity that engendered the peculiar dread of the Jew. For Pinsker, it was the loss of Jewish statehood and the abnormal position of the Jews among the nations. "There is something unnatural about a people without a territory," he writes to Levanda, "just as there is about a man without a shadow." The rise of Christianity and the loss of Jewish statehood occurred simultaneously; hence the confusion in the minds of the observers. In fact, although religious agitation contributed no little to the aggravation of the Jewish tragedy, the real trouble, he thought, lay in the national degradation which enabled that agitation to assume its drastic form.

To these psychological factors—disrespect and fear, both of which stem from the homelessness of the Jews—Pinsker added an anthropological one: racial antagonism. Race, as we have seen, was for Pinsker one of the basic elements of nationalism, and he was among the first to see in it one of the fundamentals of the Jewish question. "The German, proud of his Teutonic origin, the Slav, the Celt, not one of them admits that the Semitic Jew is his equal by birth." It is primarily the Jewish race, and not the Jewish religion, that antisemitism fights. And as long as this race will lack the elementary conditions of power, no democratic constitution will be able to put it on equal footing with other races.

Pinsker came to the conclusion, therefore, that the "prejudice of mankind against us rests upon anthropological and social principles, innate and ineradicable." Since they are ineradicable, it is futile to combat them. "We must reconcile ourselves once and for all to the idea that the other nations, by reason of their inherent natural antagonism, will forever reject us. We must not shut our eyes to this natural force which works like every other elemental force; we must take it into account." The Jewish question was never solved in the Diaspora, he thought, because the entire existence of the Jews among the nations was contrary to the laws of human nature. Therefore, those who try to solve it under the conditions of dispersion are heading for repeated failures and catastrophes. Relying upon the democratic law and their patriotic contributions to their respective countries, the western Jews were lulled into a sense of security. "Idle delusion!"—warned Pinsker. "You may prove yourselves patriots ever so true, you will still be reminded at every opportunity of your Semitic descent. This fateful *memento mori* will not prevent you, however, from enjoying the hospitality extended, until some fine morning you are cast out of the country, until the skeptical mob reminds you that you are, after all, nothing but nomads and parasites, protected by no law."

One can properly appreciate Pinsker's vision if one recalls that fifteen more years of antisemitic agitation, accompanied by violent outbursts of hate, were required to make even such far-seeing men as Herzl and Nordau realize what Pinsker foresaw at the beginning of the 1880's. In 1882, there was no Dreyfus case in the West, no street demonstrations proclaiming "Death to the Jews." In fact, the situation seemed to be well in hand. The Reform Rabbis, in their sumptuous temples, continued to preach about the mission of Judaism, while their flocks continued to deviate from that Judaism and seek closer attachment to the various nations. Nothing could shatter the deep-rooted illusion that their equality was irrevocable, not even the riots that broke out in Germany the year before, nor the first antisemitic congress that convened in the same year at Dresden. These "new" manifestations were regarded by them as summer storms of short duration. The greatness of Pinsker lay in the fact that he sensed the meaning of these foreboding signs, and realized that only a brief time was left the Jews for their national salvation, "Shall we be satisfied with this period of respite," he repeatedly asks in his *Auto-Emancipation,* "or will we rather use this respite to draw the proper moral from the experience accumulated, in order that we may escape the new blows which are sure to come?" Emancipation, he thought, was not the greatest achievement of Jewry in the 19th century, but the greatest opportunity afforded to the Jewish people for the normalization of its life and for its national restoration. And he took the outbreak of antisemitism as a warning that the time for this opportunity was almost gone. Indeed, his sharp sense of time told him that the eleventh hour for Jewry had struck. "Let 'now or never' be our watchword!," he exclaimed. "Woe to our descendants, woe to the memory of our Jewish contemporaries, if we let this moment pass by!"

He clearly saw that the Jews of the West, as well as the East, intended to let that great moment pass by. They wasted it in repeating their old palliatives, and in giving the usual Jewish answer to every calamity: flight before the enemy, and creation of new centers of dispersion, only to find there their old foe—antisemitism—in a new disguise. Thus, they were "revolving perplexedly in a magic circle, allowing a blind fate to rule over them." They never reflected and stopped to ask themselves "whether this mad race, or rather this mad rout, will ever come to an end." Obviously, the Jews themselves were to blame for the fact that they had wandered aimlessly over the globe for many centuries. "We sailed the surging ocean of universal history without a compass," says Pinsker, "and such a compass must be invented."

Here Pinsker was in error. The "compass" had long been invented, although it was rarely put to practical use. Pointing to Palestine, it repeatedly directed strong, though mystic, Messianic movements, and finally the realistic national movement of the 1880s. Nevertheless, when Pinsker wrote his essay on the Jewish Question, he doubted the practicability of the Palestine project. Although he declared Palestine the best possible choice, he refused to grant that it was the only choice. Even should Palestine prove unavailable, he thought, the idea of Jewish territorial concentration must not be rejected. Moreover, Pinsker's "compass" implied not only a fixed country of destination for the Jewish migration movements, but also a constructive and far-reaching plan for national rehabilitation. Such a plan was sorely needed even by the nationalists of the early Eighties, whose entire program consisted of one point: immigration to Palestine. Contrary to their assertions, Pinsker pointed out that immigration should not be the beginning, but the culmination of the national effort and that it must be preceded by a world-wide organization of the national forces, by the creation of an acknowledged Jewish representation, by the acquisition of a country politically assured for Jewish national concentration, and by the mobilization of the large funds required for transplantation of masses.

This plan, which was later reborn in Herzl's mind and presented by him as Political Zionism, seemed so self-evident to Pinsker that he wondered what had prevented the Jews from adopting it long ago. He evidently pondered much on this point, since he sensed that in this curious failure of so many generations to restore their independence lay the kernel of the entire Jewish question.

It was not merely the lack of political wisdom that was responsible for that failure, he thought. While the destruction of Jewish statehood affected the political thinking of the Jews, the degeneration of the national soul which came in its wake constituted even a greater danger. If the Jews did not see their way clear during all the periods of persecution and misery to re-establish themselves as a nation, it was first of all because their urge for freedom and sovereignty had become dulled or had even disappeared. "We must prove," says Pinsker, "that the misfortunes of the Jews are due, above all, to their lack of desire for national independence; and that this desire must be awakened and maintained in time if they do not wish to be subjected forever to a disgraceful existence—in a word, we must prove that they *must become a nation*."

Thus, Pinsker transferred the center of gravity of the Jewish problem from the outer world to the Jewish people itself. The Jewish tragedy is caused not only by the attitude of the nations; it is also, and primarily, a result of the attitude of the Jews. It is a product of their stubborn adherence to the bodies of other nations in contradiction to the natural laws of nationalism, and of their refusal to change their abnormal existence. In the same manner, the solution, like the problem itself, depends first of all on the determination of the Jews to take their fate into their own hands. The whole conception of the movement of enlightenment and emancipation was based on dependence upon other nations *from* whom emancipation was expected and *by* whom emancipation had to be granted. Pinsker changed this conception radically: not Emancipation, but Auto-Emancipation. His message to the Jewish people was that its salvation rests not with others, but within itself. And although he pointed out that "the struggle of the Jews for national unity and independence will win the support of the peoples by whom we are now unwanted," he repeatedly emphasized that the dynamo of the whole movement must be found in the heart of the Jewish people. He placed as a motto at the head of *Auto-Emancipation,* the slogan of Hillel: "If I am not for myself, who will be for me?" for he realized the profound truth that his American contemporary, Charles Dudley Warner, so forcefully expressed: "There was never a nation great until it came to the knowledge that it had nowhere in the world to go for help".

*****

The influence of *Auto-Emancipation* at the time of its appearance can hardly be overestimated. Although it lacked any authoritative backing and was published anonymously as "An Appeal by a Russian Jew," it aroused a violent reaction—friendly and antagonistic—from the foremost Jewish spokesmen in the West and the East. Its attack upon the conceptions of western Jewry was promptly met by some leading western publications, but the sharpness of their counterattack provided proof that *Auto-Emancipation* had hit the mark. Although the number of the western recruits of *Autoemancipation* was at the beginning very small, they were imbued by it with an indomitable spirit that could withstand the pressure of any opposition. Emma Lazarus, who was one of these recruits and the first to proclaim modern Zionism in America, was so certain of the powerful effect of *Auto-Emancipation* that already in November, 1882, she wrote in one of her *Epistles to the*

Hebrews, that "with his fiery eloquence and his depth and fervor of conviction, this anonymous author could scarcely fail to enkindle the imagination of his Jewish readers, even if he stood alone."

But Pinsker did not stand alone. While in the West *Auto-Emancipation* heralded the beginning of the national movement, in the East it contributed to its enforcement and expansion. In the multitude of views and paucity of plans which characterized the national movement in Russia, Pinsker's *Auto-Emancipation* served as a cohesive force, from both the ideological and practical points of view. Moreover, it helped to consolidate the national movement by bringing to the fore Pinsker himself. Hardly known heretofore outside of his home town, Pinsker became, thanks to *Auto-Emancipation*, one of the most admired men in Russian Jewry. The measure of his influence may perhaps be gauged by the fact that Gordon, the preeminent Hebrew poet, who was then still skeptical of the nationalist solution, wrote a special poem about *Auto-Emancipation* and dedicated it to the author. It was because of *Auto-Emancipation* that Lilienblum, the strong-minded and conscientious Hebrew publicist, sought Pinsker's acquaintance and comradeship—a comradeship which was to play a decisive and beneficial role in the history of the national movement. Lilienblum, who from the very outset viewed Pinsker as a prospective leader, proved to him the feasibility and inevitability of the Palestine project, thus removing the only difference of opinion between Pinsker and the nationalist camp. After yielding on that point, Pinsker knew exactly where he belonged. He eagerly engaged in extensive correspondence, answering questions, refuting arguments, and stimulating to action every one who showed signs of cooperation. He became the central figure of the national movement, its heart and brain.

Nevertheless, he looked for leadership not in himself and not in Russia. "In the years I have lived in Russia," he wrote, "I have met a great many men of great personal charm and high ethical standards, but I have not met any I could picture as leaders." The lack of leadership qualities among Russian Jews, which he attributed to their oppressive environment, was not, however, his main objection to establishing the center of the movement in Russia. It was one of the western countries, he maintained, that must serve as the center of the national movement, because only the western Jews commanded the political influence and financial means necessary to carry out his plan of action. Likewise, he thought that were the leadership of the movement to be drawn from Russian Jewry, the Jewish question would appear as a specific Russian problem, while he, Pinsker, viewed it as a world problem and only as such did he visualize its solution. "Exalted and talented people," he wrote, "could turn our Jewish question into an international question, subject to the judgment of the nations, and then we would not lack influential friends as well." Besides, he realized the enormous difficulty that the national movement, political in essence, might face in a Russia that prohibited all political organizations, if the movement would lack the political authorization of other European Powers. "We must proceed legally, in order to gain the approval of the governments," he wrote in November 1883. "In Europe we shall have no difficulty in the matter. But in order to receive it also here in Russia, we shall have to try to establish a precedent in Europe." Pressed to the same conclusion by added thought and factual experience, he became in coming years even more emphatic on that point. "It is imperative that the Russian societies have a foothold outside of the country," he wrote in January 1885. "Without this foothold we lose our spiritual existence and our practical work is also endangered."

He preferred Germany to England and France as the headquarters of Jewish leadership because Germany, geographically in the heart of Europe, offered more advantages as a center for a world movement and because Germany, at the time of Bismark, commanded tremendous political influence and carried greater weight with Russia. "Only from Germany," he wrote to Ruelf, "could our national will sound its voice for the first time. From there it will also be possible to influence our Government to show greater understanding of our demands. But first of all, the mist must be removed from the eyes of the German Jews.

They ought to grasp with clear vision the gravity of the danger which awaits us as a result of our general situation."

Would they grasp this danger? He believed that the Jews of Germany—the birthplace of the newly born movement of antisemitism—were more liable than the Jews of other western countries to realize that the same perilous forces which threatened the Jews of Russia were confronting them, too. He understood that this implied a complete revolution, not only in the views of German Jewry, but also in the character of its representation. He knew that there was not one group among the Jews of Germany, as well as among those of other western countries, whose ideas were similar to those he advocated and on which he could count for support. "That biting truth whose representative I deem myself, cannot be joined with the existing programs of any of the parties in Western Europe. Such a party must be created *ex nihilo*." But from the countries of the West, and especially from Germany, he received only few signs of encouragement. Persistently he cultivated these contacts, hoping they would develop into larger circles. But all his endeavors in this direction met with failure. Embittered almost to the point of despair, Pinsker writes in January, 1884: "It is easy to make demands in the matter, but how can they be carried out? Who can give us the mythological Hercules to clean out the stables of Augeas? Who—the trumpet of the Messiah, in order to arouse these half-alive people? For this there is needed a whole legion of prophets, in order to breathe a life-giving spirit of enthusiasm into this pile of debris. Try and make Falstaff into a Hamlet!"

The "legion of prophets" arose indeed fifteen years later with the appearance of Herzl, Nordau, Zangwill and their crusading associates. It was only then that Pinsker's dream of establishing the leadership of the movement in a western country was finally realized. It was then that the first Congress could be convened and the Jewish question placed before the governments of the world and made an international issue. Pinsker knew that his diagnosis regarding the potentialities of a national Jewry in the West was correct. But he could not be satisfied with that knowledge alone. The more he met with obstacles in the West, the more he turned his attention to the movement in the East. He never had doubts regarding the ultimate triumph of the Jewish national idea in Russia. "Public opinion in Russia will be with us," he wrote shortly after *Auto-Emancipation* had been published. He realized, however, that even in Russia the movement could not rely on the "prominent Jews" and that its mainstay would be the middle-class—the source from which it sprang. Thus, already in November 1882 he writes that "I, and not I alone, decided that the basis of our organization must be laid in the middle class. It is our most wholesome, most reliable element. In it there still lives the consciousness of national dignity, and it alone is capable of a single purpose and aspiration." Having arrived at this correct appraisal of the national element in Russian Jewry, he could confidently predict the process of development. "Once we have a strong, well-knit association, impelled by one idea, our prominent Jews will participate and our western brethren will be drawn in, sooner or later."

The year following the publication of *Auto-Emancipation* passed, however, without any attempt on his part to engage in organization. Pinsker even opposed such attempts when they came from local centers. "For a long time to come," he stressed, "it shall be necessary to look for our supporters and to seek their whereabouts. As long as we are not certain in advance that we shall have a strong and influential drawing-power on those outside our camp, we ought not, with our lesser forces alone, enter the struggle for a cause upon which depends the entire future of our people." The organization should be called into being, he believed, only after the ground would be properly prepared from an ideological point of view. "Before it will be possible to do anything," he wrote in July 1883, "the national conscience must be awakened unceasingly. This is the preliminary work which faces us, or at least me, for, to my regret, I have already aged and made a late start." Carefully, but pointedly, he added however: "Perhaps some additional things will yet come at the end of my life."

These things came sooner than he expected. One month after writing the above words, he met in Odessa two outstanding Jewish intellectuals—Dr. Max Mandelstamm of Kiev and Dr. Hermann Shapira of Heidelberg—who were to become moving spirits in the Jewish national movement. These two, together with Lilienblum who constantly pressed Pinsker to assume organizational tasks, convinced him that the time had come to pass from the period of propaganda to that of organization. They formed the initial group which undertook to unite into one organizational frame all the nationalist circles and societies that were spread throughout Russia. After more than a year of activity in this direction, that goal was finally reached with the convening of the first Jewish National Conference (and the establishment of the umbrella organization of Hovevei Zion).

The place of that Conference was Kattowitz; its opening date—November 6, 1884. Both the place and the date mark milestones in Jewish history. From then on, the driving forces of Jewish nationalism were provided with a center and direction. The chosen leader was Pinsker.

V

Nothing was more distasteful to Pinsker's nature than the task which was imposed upon him in Kattowitz. "You can believe me," he wrote to Ruelf immediately after the Conference, "that it distressed me greatly when I saw that there was no one at the meeting more fit to serve as chairman than my humble self." He assumed the responsibility of leadership with a heavy heart, as an inescapable duty, but with the hope that new forces, which could replace him, would soon be drawn to the movement. He undertook this task because he realized that the first years of the movement's organizational activity were the most difficult and decisive. He wanted it to proceed from the very outset in the proper direction.

He failed, however, to achieve this aim. Were he to have his own way in the movement, he would have devoted all its organizational and financial means to the strengthening of its ranks in Russia and abroad until a Jewish Congress could be convened to place the Jewish question before the governments. But he did *not* have his own way. Greatly lacking in political understanding, the masses of the Pale could not yet perceive the implications of such a long-range plan. They gave credence only to concrete, tangible facts and were greatly impressed by them alone. This forced Pinsker to devote most of his energies to the provision of such facts, and consequently to the support of the colonizational effort in Palestine, which he considered premature and of no real consequence. Moreover, as far as this effort was concerned, Pinsker was faced with a *fait accompli*, because the Palestine colonization had begun spontaneously before the movement was officially launched. Realizing that the failure of the first Jewish settlements might adversely affect the movement as a whole, he considered those colonies a strategic position that must be held at all cost.

The cost which the young movement had to bear, however, was above its apparent powers. The financial help needed for the maintenance of the colonies drained all its resources and became its sole concern. Pinsker and his organization almost collapsed under the burden, but the position was held until help arrived from a most powerful source—Baron Edmond de Rothschild, who shouldered the expense of the various settlements and greatly lessened the financial worries of the movement.

But then arose a new problem regarding the relations between the Administration of the Baron and the settlers in the colonies. The latter hated the system of regimentation which was imposed upon them by that Administration, and their relations with it were often strained to the point of complete break. In spite of the fact that Pinsker sympathized with the settlers and understood their motives, he very often found it necessary to side with the Administration; for he realized that should

Rothschild withdraw his support, the whole colonization effort might be disrupted. There is little doubt that Pinsker's policy of keeping the balance between the Administration of the Baron and the rebellious colonists was instrumental in furthering the colonization of Palestine and even in saving it in critical moments.

The problem of maintaining balance confronted Pinsker not only on the Palestine scene, but also in the Russian organization. In Russia, there was the constant friction between the various factions, especially between the Conservatives and the Enlightened. These formerly rival groups, which were now united on one national platform, still viewed each other with continued suspicion and persistently strove for hegemony in the movement. Pinsker knew that upon the handling of this problem depended the fate of the entire organization whose component elements were not yet consolidated into one cohesive unit, and whose delicate structure might easily fall apart as a result of careless action. As one who belonged to the group of the Enlightened, Pinsker had to face attacks of the Conservatives who often failed to understand his intentions and his purely national point of view. Despite his patient and impersonal stand, this rivalry between the groups increased daily, and in the second Convention of the national movement, which took place in Drusgenik, in 1887, it came to a head. As a result, there followed a change of leadership in which the conservatives acquired the majority, without, however, impairing Pinsker's position. Hopeful that the new set-up had settled the conflict, Pinsker again left for the West to strengthen old contacts and develop new ones. He was greatly encouraged by the reception given him in some western capitals and by the support which was forthcoming to the movement as a result of his tour. Upon his return to Russia, however, he realized that the antagonism to his leadership on the part of the Conservatives had not lessened. His health entirely ruined, his patience strained to the limit, and his position in the movement viewed by him as a stumbling-block to its internal peace and unity, Pinsker insisted that his resignation be accepted. Two years later, when again forced into leadership, even the most rabid opponents of Pinsker had to acknowledge his complete disinterestedness, genuine idealism and selfless devotion to the cause of his people.

During the entire period of his leadership, Pinsker did not take any political steps to realize the final aims of the movement. He even refrained from negotiations with the Turkish Government that then ruled over Palestine, and hesitated to interfere with the agents of the Baron who were active in Constantinople, because he did not as yet see a national force in the west that could represent the Jews in a manner more influential than that provided by Rothschild as an individual. Political activity in the name of the movement was also proscribed by the very fact that officially the movement did not exist at all. During the entire 1880s, it was an underground movement, and although there was no interference by the authorities, the Third Section, the Russian Secret Police, looked upon it with constant suspicion and was ready to attack it at a moment's notice. With no political backing for the movement outside of Russia, it was the major concern of Pinsker and his associates to obtain some form of legalization for the activities of the movement in Russia itself. As long as this was not obtainable, many were afraid to join the ranks of the movement, or even to support it financially. Finally, after seven years of relentless effort, legalization was obtained with the establishment, in 1890, of the Society for the Aid of Jewish Farmers in Palestine and Syria. This was perhaps the most important achievement of the organization in Pinsker's time; from then on the movement in Russia grew and spread by leaps and bounds.

Pinsker was not satisfied with the achievements of the movement. He dreamed of a Congress, of a world Jewish representation, of placing the Jewish question on the international agenda. Instead, he saw the organization limited, in effect, to Russia, immersed in puny colonizational projects, with no political work, not even a large-scale propaganda effort. Yet, he achieved the maximum under the circumstances. Not only did he establish the national ideology, but he also gave the movement an organizational framework, united and consolidated its various groups and opposing factions into one national force, strengthened the foundations of the Palestine colonization, achieved some form of legalization for the movement in Russia, and last but not least, laid the basis for a world-wide national organization.

Pinsker died in 1891. Four years after his death, when Herzl appeared, he found nuclei of the organization in almost every country in Europe. He found them not only in Russia and the Balkans, but also in Austria and Germany, in France and Britain. The supporters won by Pinsker in various European centers rallied around them a group of followers. These were the organizational units upon which Herzl leaned and which enabled him to create his World Zionist Organization. Moreover, the immediate circle of adherents that gathered around Herzl in Vienna, his abode, was an outcome of Pinsker's educational efforts. There, in Vienna, one of Pinsker's disciples, Nathan Birnbaum, had published a periodical entitled *Self-Emancipation*. Ninety percent of those who participated in the First Zionist Congress had already been converted to the national idea before Herzl came to the fore.

It was of a leader like Herzl that Pinsker dreamed. It was to a movement like his that he aspired, and it was the line of action followed by Herzl that he considered the only one capable of leading to the realization of the Jewish hopes. Pinsker looked for leaders in the West. He tried to place the crown of leadership upon certain individuals. But leaders do not appear by invitation. They arise on their own initiative, or they are forced into leadership against their desire, by the pressure of events. It was the renewed outbursts of antisemitism in France and Austria in the middle of the 1890s that brought Herzl to Zionism. But if the tempo of his advance was much faster than that of Pinsker, his gains more significant, and his impact far wider, it was not only because of his singular dynamic qualities, but also because the initial thrust was already behind him.

That thrust was made by Pinsker, who did not expect any immediate successes, but who taught the small groups of his followers: "the first brave warriors fall." Not only is his objective historic task reflected in these words, but also his subjective attitude toward it. His governing idea was: action in line of duty, and although he died as a leader of his people, it was the fate of the unknown soldier that he was prepared to share. Shunning publicity, fame and honors, he was ready to give his best, anonymously, for what he called "the battle for the honor of our nation." His idealism was indeed of the highest type; therefore it could not fail to have an inspiring, deep and lasting effect on the whole national movement.

Theodor Herzl
Chapter 2

Born in Hungary in 1860, Herzl became an iconic figure in the drive to establish a Jewish state. He wrote The Jewish State, created the World Zionist Organization which he then led, and negotiated with world leaders for the creation of a Jewish state. Herzl died in 1904.

(the following was originally published in *Introduction to Herzl's Letters* [Hebrew], Hoza'a Medinit, Tel Aviv, 1937)

I

Perhaps the greatest riddle in the mysterious phenomenon of Herzl is the unique admiration for him, which persists even today. I say "even today" because the years that passed since his demise have been marked by historic changes that once would have taken centuries to transpire—years in which wars and revolutions have occurred, the likes of which the world has never known, when entire ways of life were destroyed and a new world was built upon their ruins. Who among Herzl's contemporaries, among the many statesmen, authors and rulers dominant in that era—who died in 1904, as he did, or even in 1914—still lives with such intensity in the consciousness of his people? Without any hesitation we could reply: not one of them.

Paul Painleve, a man of vision and a keen statesman, who was several times prime minister of France, took note of this unique adulation for Herzl when he wrote the following words: "The more Herzl's death becomes remote in time, the more the regal character of this man is revealed. Its glory and radiance will continue to increase until the day will come when the whole world will recognize him as one of the foremost specimens of the human race and one of the shapers of history. This process is currently underway."

It is no wonder that Herzl's renown and the special accord given him extended beyond the confines of his people. For it was through Herzl that the world first came to know Zionism, which is recognized by all nations to be a necessity. Moreover, Herzl met during his lifetime with many enthusiastic non-Jewish admirers, who almost always accorded him understanding and respect. What is remarkable, however, is the general adoration for him which exists today among his own people. For throughout the time he worked on behalf of his brand of Zionism, he had to fight a war with Jewish opponents, both outside and inside his movement. Truth be told, his faithful adherents among the Jewish people were a small minority. Even his rule over the Zionist Organization was maintained not because his policy was accepted, but rather because of his powerful and inspiring personality, and because, as everyone knew, the organization was his own creation.

No one thought it possible during Herzl's lifetime to gain control over an establishment which everyone regarded as Herzl's personal innovation. Still, resistance to him continually grew, igniting into a flame when provided a spark in the form of the Uganda issue, and reaching its peak when some members of his movement openly demanded that he resign its leadership. In fact, Herzl died during a particularly turbulent moment in this heated conflict—a conflict which was so fierce that Nordau saw it as the direct cause of Herzl's untimely death.

If so, the question we posed appears even more perplexing: How did this remarkable turnabout occur? How did a man who was surrounded just before his death by such fierce opposition become, so soon after passing away, an object of adulation even among his most hostile opponents? Something occurred here which is difficult to fathom. His many opponents fell silent one by one after his death. Even the most stubborn of them, Ahad Ha'am, posthumously anointed Herzl a legend and described him with the very same words of praise he used of Moses—a degree of praise beyond which a man like him could not go. Only six short years went by before Nordau could declare with certainty: Herzl has no more opponents.

Therein lies the mystery. Had his opponents accepted the opinions they had once belittled? Had Herzl's death served as a cause for reflection which transformed their views of the Jewish situation in the world?

Did those who did not want Herzl to guide them during his life suddenly become his disciples after his death? Surely, the answer to each of these questions is an emphatic no. For even after his death, his opponents continued to deny his teachings no less than they did during his life. In fact, not only did they deny them, they fought ferociously against their acceptance. Their war against Herzl's supporters dragged on for eight long years after his death, until his supporters were banished from their seats of power in the Zionist Organization; his great standard bearers, Nordau and Zangwill, were opposed to their last days with such bitterness that after their death their antagonists tried to erase their memory as if they had never lived!

What then is the source of the adulation for Herzl? Does it emanate from his charismatic personality, which even after his death continued to influence with the same magical force it did during his lifetime? Does it stem from the great inheritance which Herzl left to *all* Zionists—namely, the great institutions he created, which are also used by his opponents—*particularly* by his opponents—for their needs and plans? But if this is true, it would be appropriate for them to declare openly: "We honor Herzl's personality, Herzl the founder of institutions, Herzl the organizer. But Herzl's teaching, the idea for which he created all these institutions, the idea whose realization became his life's aim and for which he worked himself to death—that idea we reject and in it we do not recognize Herzl's greatness at all."

If they said this, then their attitude toward Herzl would be understandable. But they do not say this. Instead, they often claim that they are in fact fulfilling Herzl's testament; and even socialist Zionists do not shy from saying this, although Herzl fundamentally opposed socialism and stressed this opposition at every opportunity. For Herzl was certain that socialism does not fit human nature, and especially not that of the Jews, "who were and have remained individualists from the days of Moses up to this very day." Herzl did not see Jewish socialism as anything more than an abnormal phenomenon that was a byproduct of the abnormal existence of the Jews, and he saw as one of the great virtues of Zionism the extent to which it *removed* Jews from socialism's sphere of influence.

Accordingly, when Zionists succeeded in detaching Jewish students in Vienna from the socialist movement, he describes this fact in his journal in the spirit of a victory celebration. And he adds: "It is possible, some of them think, that we will establish socialism in the future Jewish state. *But this is not my view.* Certain matters we might organize better than we did in the old society, but in general, everything will remain the same."[1] Indeed, Herzl stressed again and again, that "it is a folly for Jews to be connected to socialism, which will soon eject the Jews from its midst,"[2] and that for the Socialists the Jews were only serving as "the Negro, whom they will cast aside after he had served his purpose"[3] (a prediction proven word for word by the cruel fate of the Jewish revolutionaries of Russia). Despite all this, the Zionist socialists declare, just as do those who have remained adherents of Hovevei Zion, whose conflict with Herzl needs no elaboration, that they are following in Herzl's footsteps.

Was Herzl's teaching one of those theories that contain internal contradictions, from which one can raise points of contention to its general principles? No, Herzl's teaching was consistent to the highest possible degree. It is a single, solid edifice, from which a lone brick cannot be removed without toppling the whole structure. Or Was Herzl's teaching one of those vague doctrines with multiple meanings, from which one can extract all kinds of interpretations and explanations? But Herzl's teaching was phrased with so great a clarity that it does not leave room for mistakes and errors. So how then can the *opponents* of Herzl's teaching say that they are actually following in his footsteps? The only answer one may give to this question is seemingly paradoxical: To the very extent that they are following in Herzl's footsteps, to that extent they are not following in his footsteps at all.

---

1 *Diaries*, III, "Mizpe", 1929, p. 103.
2 ibid, p. 102
3 Theodore Herzl, *Zionism*, State edition, 1937, p. 47

I'll try to make myself clear.

Zionism has become an integral part of the Jewish world view throughout the world. Today, in the 1930s, it is virtually clear to Jews everywhere, even to those outside the sphere of Zionism, that the only concrete solution to the Jewish question is the concentration of the Jews in their own land. All other theories regarding the possibility of a normal existence for Jews in alien lands are bankrupt. So this idea, which for a long time was regarded by many as an absurd daydream, which Herzl "waved like a banner on high" and proclaimed before the world, has now become a generally accepted idea. In this regard, they are all following in Herzl's footsteps.

But however much we value Herzl's activities in publicizing this idea, we should not assume even for a single moment that this idea, in the form in which it is so generally accepted, was in any way unique to Herzl. For this was an idea shared by many Jews, from Hovevei Zion to Pinsker to Hess to the Rabbis Kalisher and Alkalai. This was basically also the idea of Shabbetai Zevi, of Shlomo Molho and probably also of Don Yosef Nasi. It was the idea of all Jews who carried in their soul the dream of the messianic revival of their people and saw in it an end to their suffering and torments. This "idea," that the ultimate solution to the woes and abnormal situation of Israel among the nations could only be a Jewish state, "this idea"—Herzl himself says—"is age-old, as old as the nation itself." In the general consensus which exists today regarding this idea, or more correctly, to the assumption that this idea is not utopian, not merely a daydream or a romantic aspiration, one may not see something unique to Herzl, but rather a concept that was widespread among the Jews for many generations and of which Herzl was but one of its standard bearers, no less than Hovevei Zion who preceded him, and no more than those who followed after him.

And indeed, if all of Herzl's teachings could be limited to this idea alone, if it were to include only the proofs of the necessity and requirement of a Jewish state, then the excessive and special admiration which is awarded him would be a great injustice even to his modern predecessors, like Pinsker and Hess. For while not acting as prominently as Herzl did in *publicizing* this idea, they did precede him in *the idea itself* and, because "the idea is father to the act," they would deserve no less adulation. Certainly, Ahad Ha'am would then be just in regarding the diminution of Pinsker's stature relative to Herzl's as a grave injustice. Yet, the stranger the following statement may seem, the more its truth must be reiterated: Herzl's uniqueness and greatness were not found in the idea of "the Jewish state". Herzl, to be sure, strengthened the foundations of this idea by his uniquely shrewd analysis and by bringing new arguments and proofs that the solution for the Jewish question could be found only in this idea. Still, it is clear that this idea was not the source of the *unique spiritual stature* of Herzl, a stature which the nation felt, possibly unconsciously, and by virtue of which accorded Herzl the sort of veneration which only two or three individuals were granted throughout the Jewish nation's four-thousand year history.

Herzl's special stature is inherent in the teaching which was his alone, a teaching which was not known to Hess and Hovevei Zion, neither to Shabbetai Zevi and Shlomo Molho, nor was it known to any of those millions of Jews longing for redemption. Since they did not know it, since only he knew it, only his idea produced results, or to be precise, results followed only the activity he undertook which emanated from this thought. Let us briefly outline the main features of this idea.

Herzl's unique greatness was not in teaching that the only solution to the Jewish question was a Jewish state, but rather in teaching *how to put this idea into practice*, and in explaining *the only way* in which it was possible to put it into practice. Herzl himself knew well that herein lay his entire innovation: "Because all the leaders who sought to lead you know where Zion is." So why have you not been able to come to Zion? "Because it is not possible to arrive at the goal in a straight line." Since one needs to choose a concrete path, and every such path involves obstacles and delays, and since all the previously chosen paths were quickly blocked, "this is a very complicated question."

"The problem is that of the path," Herzl said, clearly defining the crux of the matter.[4] Therefore we can say that Herzl's teaching which, as we have noted, was his alone, was *the teaching of the way to make Zionism a reality.*

II

The course of national revival which Herzl charted, and in which his entire greatness lies, was clearly not accepted in either his own time or after his death. During these years, Herzl's idea stood in sharp contrast to the method advocated by those who shared, for the most part, his analysis of the state of world Jewry, but never understood the mode of operation he espoused or the means by which he sought to realize their shared ambitions. The simple and modest approach of Herzl's opponents did not require undue mental effort. They sought to proceed toward their objective in a straight line. They wanted to follow the simple laws of arithmetic, believing this was the only practical way to achieve their desired goal. They knew that one million Jews are comprised of one million individuals, that one million acres are comprised of one million single-acre plots, and they assumed that to achieve their objective, they needed only to bring to Palestine one Jew after another and to purchase acre after acre. They never imagined that in traveling this direct path, they were bound to run into brick walls. They never paid due attention to the fact that they would encounter a government in Palestine whose opposition to the Zionist plan—an opposition they clearly felt from time to time—might take a form that would eliminate any possibility of their continued activity.

Nor did they pay much attention to the fact that there was a body of native residents in the country who formed the majority of the population and who, together with the government, could put a stop to both their immigration and settlement virtually whenever they pleased. They thought that they could avoid, or at least minimize these

---
[4] *Zionism*, p. 262-263

disturbances, by refraining from speaking openly about them, or more clearly: they wanted to proceed quietly and stealthily toward their goal. This was the vaccine with which they sought to inoculate the Zionist undertaking from the harm which threatened it. This approach led a large part of those belonging to Hovevei Zion (the organization promoting renewed Jewish settlement in Palestine) to oppose even the call to the First Zionist Congress, fearing that such a gathering might provoke the Turkish government to thwart the aspirations of the Jews regarding the Land of Israel.

And when, despite Hovevei Zion's efforts, the First Zionist Congress did take place and the Zionist Organization was established, they tried to use all their power to steer it down the same old path, which was the only path they were capable of comprehending, and which they believed could enable them to reach their objective.

Then, Herzl arose and boldly declared: No more gradual immigration! No more infiltration! For he considered the notion that the Jews could become the majority in the country through the gradual arrival of settlers, to be childish and absurd. "They, the 'Practical Zionists', thought the smarter approach was to bring, little by little, without it being noticed, hundreds of thousands of individual Jews to the Land of Israel, and afterward, once they were already there, to demand rights on their behalf." "But," asked Herzl, "in the name of God! Without it being noticed? How do they imagine that this thing will occur? Indeed, we must assume that they do not think of it at all." Since they did not foresee the problem only a few years from the time of this writing, there is no doubt they did not foresee it 40 years ago, at the time of Herzl. For even *after* the Balfour Declaration, when they opposed publicly declaring Zionist aspirations, at the time of Nordau and Zangwill and later at the Congress of 1931, the naive view that it would be possible to effect a large settlement project without the world taking notice, and without it being noticed even by the residents of the land in which the settlement was taking place, never wore off. Clearly, the wisdom of this view was no different than the wisdom of the ostrich that believes that no one can see it if it buries its head in the ground.

We see that the Jews have succeeded in bringing to the Land of Israel hundreds of thousands of people. But not only have the native residents noticed the evolution of this event, not only has the government in authority noticed it, but so, too, have all the states of the Mediterranean and, indeed, the entire world. For how was it possible to imagine that such a movement would not be noticed? Mass immigration to another country is noticed, first and foremost, in those countries from which the migrants leave in droves. For their departure leaves vacant positions in the economy and thereby causes an internal migration to those vacated posts. Such a thing cannot go unnoticed. Second, they remove property from those countries and this necessarily causes the local governments to adopt an adverse stance toward the migration. But this is not all. The migrants do not go to the new country and hide like thieves. Rather, they become active participants in its life. They scour the land. They buy real estate. They trade. They build factories. They bring with them new ways of life and new ideas. Soon, every person in the land feels their presence and starts to wonder about the future of the new arrivals in the country and their ambitions.

This is particularly true regarding the settlement of the Jews, a people the entire world knows and observes intensely and whose every migratory movement quickly stirs public opinion. How much more is this true of a movement of Jews to settle in the land of their forefathers? That is why Herzl declared loudly and unequivocally: "Anyone who thinks that the Jews can come to the land of their fathers by stealth is deluding himself and others. In no land does the arrival of Jews so hasten to announce itself as in their historic birthplace, by the very fact that it is their historic birthplace."

Since there is no possibility of a gradual infiltration which will go unnoticed, this infiltration will result in two possible outcomes, which Herzl formulated with the certainty and clarity of law: "Either the Jewish migrants will run into trouble immediately—and then the migration will cease soon thereafter—or they will manage to prosper, and their prosperity will result in a local flowering of antisemitism."

The "realist" statesmen will now counter: "Yes, Herzl did have those fantastic plans of an agreement with the Turkish government, of a charter and the like, but he ignored the reality of 'the Arab question,' and did not foresee the obstacles the Jewish settlement would encounter from this quarter." Clearly, whoever advances this argument, which in effect says that Herzl was a short-sighted statesman who failed to see something so obvious, does not follow the entire train of Herzl's thought. Could this man, who on the basis of a single visit in Egypt, and a single glance at the young Egyptians who attended a lecture of Sir William Willcocks, *foresaw all of Egypt's immediate future*, overlook something so obvious for the country on whose future and acquisition all his thoughts were centered?

To be sure, he did not refer to this issue as the "Arab question." Rather, to him it was not an Arab question, but rather another side of the Jewish question; or, to be even more precise, the question of the Jewish settlement in the Land of Israel. For in his analysis, he considered the Arab residents of Palestine to be no different than the residents of any other land. He judged their opposition to Jewish immigration— an opposition he clearly foresaw—as no different from the inevitable opposition of the residents of any country to foreign immigration, whether Jewish or otherwise. Surely, had Herzl not taken the Arabs into account or the obstacles they were liable to erect, in addition to the negative attitude of the government, he would not have opposed infiltration. In fact, his opposition to gradual immigration was based to a very large extent on his recognition of the problem posed by the resident population. He feared the "moment, which is inevitable, when the local population senses danger to its position, awakens a general alarm, and forces the government to stop any further influx of Jews."

"And what will become of the local population of the country?"— Herzl asks in his article on Leroy-Beaulieu—"According to our view, they will be better off, since work, transportation links and culture will be poured into this impoverished and depleted land." Herzl knew for certain that "the entry of the Jews means a tremendous increase in resources, which no one had expected, to a poor and desolate country." But he knew also that upgrading the country thus would not change the attitude of its resident population toward the Jewish settlement. They would only use it to their own advantage, just as many European nations had used Jewish immigration into their lands to their own advantage. He knew that under the conditions of settlement which his Zionist opponents championed, the new resources would only hurt the Jews. For such resources, which came from the pipeline of Jewish migration, would themselves be used to seal that pipeline. Therefore, he stood and warned—tirelessly repeated this warning—"It is not in our interest to come there before the right moment." We shall later see what Herzl meant by this particular expression.

Thus, having calculated his plan to the most minute detail, he foresaw the resistance that was liable to come from the existing residents of the land. In contrast, his opponents, who had difficulty in discerning such facts, failed to. Indeed, when Herzl spoke of these things, when repeating his concerns time and again, they did not even comprehend what he meant. So when did most of those who today emphasize the problem posed by the Arabs discover its existence? When the problem had already become a blatant fact; that is, only when the "moment which is inevitable" which Herzl referred to arrived.

The problem was noted with considerable clarity by a man with a statesman's sensibility, Eliezer Ben Yehuda, whose remarks on this issue Herzl jotted down: "The people (meaning the population of the Land of Israel) is like a wild animal, which can either be sicked on or diverted at every object. If the authorities give the slightest hint, the Muslims will fall upon the Jews and atrocities perpetuated on the Armenians will be repeated on us."[5] For Herzl, these remarks held nothing new in them. He only wrote beside them, simply and coolly: "Why, this is my argument, which I have long felt against infiltration!"

---

5   *Diaries*, III, p. 243

This was then the argument—an argument that today is obvious and understood, but which was neither obvious nor understood forty years ago. Herzl showed the settlement advocates of Hovevei Zion how their "straight line" would be blocked. He also explained his thinking by way of a parable of someone trying to build a house of stone. "They are dragging stone after stone to the building site and assume that as a result a house will be erected. Never!"—Herzl claimed without any reservation—"The house will never be built in that way!" For there are countervailing forces whose resistance is as certain as the laws of gravity. "It's folly to construct a building without a plan and folly for us to construct a house without being assured the land on which it is built. For without that, the owner of the land will come one day and raze the building or evict us from the house which we constructed for ourselves."[6]

The owner of the land—is not this the entire problem of Jewish existence in foreign countries? Is it not the whole problem of antisemitism? But it's as if the Jews had not experienced eighteen hundred years of attempts at settlement; they always repeated the same actions, which always ended in disastrous results. For what have Jews done until now in every country? What has the whole saga of their wanderings and exiles been if not an attempt at building and putting down roots without having a land-owner's license?

They now sought to renew in the Land of Israel this same bitter attempt, which had never succeeded elsewhere, and were thus burying with their own hands the hope for the rescue of their people. To this, Herzl declared: Stop! Do you not see that you are repeating the same miserable attempt? No, they had not seen this. But did they really have a choice? And here Herzl showed that there was a choice. With genius simplicity, he derived his conclusions from the universally known fact that every attempt by the Jews at infiltration had ended in failure because they had never possessed the right of national settlement. Therefore, it was necessary to reverse the order: it was necessary *first*

---

6   *Zionism*, p. 177

to secure the right to national settlement, only after which the attempt at immigration will not end in failure. Therefore, before the moment comes when this right is secured, Herzl opposed any infiltration.

What was the nature of this right-of-settlement to which Herzl aspired? In truth, the words "right of settlement" do not accurately describe Herzl's aspiration. He knew that there were two dominant factors in Palestine: the government that was ruling the country and the population residing in it. The right of settlement could be obtained only from the government. But since Jewish settlement was aimed necessarily at reaching primacy in the land, and since the granting of such a right would always be against the will of the extant residents, then in order for that right not to be appealed afterward by those residents in the name of their actual or perceived rights—or, to be precise, in order that there be no room for them to make such an appeal or for the local government to do so—it is necessary that the right of Jewish settlement be defined *a priori* as a right of sovereignty, one that has the power to annul all other rights. Herzl wanted to obtain just such a right, which he saw as a necessary condition for any meaningful settlement. The focus of his political activity therefore centered on obtaining this right. "Without an assured right of sovereignty"—he declared—"all this migration is a waste of effort."[7]

Moreover, it is dangerous. For he knew that if this attempt at the Jews' salvation should fail due to recklessness or ill-conceived actions, the plan for their salvation would be postponed for an inconceivably long time, possibly forever, for this was perhaps the last attempt which this downcast and desperate people would make to redeem itself. Therefore, he was careful not to risk this attempt with false promises and delusions that had no foundation in reality.

In contrast to his caution, let us consider what were the words of those who told the people that little by little, with the expansion of the Jewish settlement, the promise of national revival would be fulfilled. Those who saw no necessity in laying the political groundwork, who

---

7   *Zionism*, p. 21

mocked Herzl's diplomatic activity and accused *him* of making false promises to the people—what were all their words if not one big false promise? Indeed, this was the biggest of lies—a lie which had not a single leg to stand on.

The bitter experience of Jewish settlement has by now shown the Jews what would have been the outcome of any settlement during the period of British rule here, had it not been based on their double right to settle the land, expressed in the Balfour Declaration and the League of Nations' Mandate. For were it not for the Balfour Declaration and the Mandate, the Jews would not have managed to overcome the harsh and deliberate British obstacles to their settlement even to the extent they did, and there is no need to prove that they would have never reached the sum of six hundred thousand people in the country as they have today. Had this immigration not been preceded *by a legal right of settlement*, then any government would have seen those immigrants as merely alien intruders, and would have been obliged to accede to the will of the residents of the country. The Jews would have had no grounds for recourse—neither to the authorized government in the land, nor to any government whatsoever. In short, without the Balfour Declaration and the Mandate, which expressed legal and well-founded claims and which were upheld by international powers, the aspirations of the Jews in the Land of Israel would have soon come to an end; the Jews who had settled there would have become a hated minority and fearful of its future—like Jewish minorities throughout the world.

But Herzl was not content with a right of sovereignty alone. He knew that even if some government were to give the Jews sovereignty in Palestine, it was likely to renege on its commitments due to the residents' opposition, or its own changes of attitude, or for some other reason. Therefore, he considered it essential that this right of sovereignty be secured through political guarantees—that is, upheld legally by the great powers. Clearly, political guarantees in the case of a weak state like Turkey would have tied its hands and forced it to uphold what it had agreed to. Following the same line of thinking, the stronger the state to make the commitments, the stronger should be the political guarantees. Today, we can appreciate what Zionism's chances for survival would have been without the existing guarantees, i.e., had the British Mandate not been approved by fifty-two countries of the League of Nations, including those nations who supported Zionism because of their own internal "Jewish Question," and had not the United States, too, been a guarantor of its fulfillment. Clearly, it was in the power of these guarantees to thwart any of the attempts that have been made to weaken Zionism, had they been exercised properly. But that is a matter which we will leave out of this discussion.

But even political guarantees were not sufficient for Herzl. It was clear to him that even if there were a right of sovereignty secured by such guarantees, it would be impossible to prevent, under certain conditions, outbreaks of violence on the part of the residents of the land—thus possibly delaying the entire process of settlement, if not ending it altogether. For the right of sovereignty to be assured, not just by written agreements but actually to have practical force, it would be necessary for that right to be accompanied by an armed force of the settlers themselves, a force which could be relied on at all times and which would be capable of nipping in the bud any attempted disturbance or outbreak.

Therefore, from the outset of his Zionist activity, Herzl declared, *as a condition that was not subject to compromise* and which was self-explanatory, that Jewish military power would preserve and defend the rights of the settlers. "Clearly, we will also have an army," he said at every opportunity. Yet, this matter was not clear to Hovevei Zion, just as his opposition to immigration without political guarantees was unclear to them. So it is no surprise that it was over these two principles that Herzl and Hovevei Zion waged war from their first encounter. This encounter took place in July, 1896, when Herzl came to London for the first time and attended a meeting of Hovevei Zion. In contrast to their system of settlement, which lacked political guarantors, he set forth his founding principles:

1. "I want only a settlement which we can defend with our own Jewish army";
2. "I must oppose an infiltration" that is not founded upon a right of sovereignty.

"Then the storm broke out," he writes. And this storm, which began in 1896, is still raging about these same two issues today.

Herzl repeated his two leading principles with increasing forcefulness, without allowing any pressure or influence to sway him from his view of their primary importance. We shall cite only one further example of his views on this matter from his first speech in Vienna: "The large scale settlement which we aspire to is not possible except as a settlement which (a) is secured by its own defense force, and (b) possesses autonomy. Otherwise, we shall create new Armenians in one place or another."[8]

These two conditions were to him absolute requirements for the success of the settlement project. Therefore, he was intransigent in insisting on them in his various negotiations, whether over the Land of Israel, the Sinai Peninsula or Uganda. For he was certain that it was essential that any settlement proposal satisfy these two conditions. By itself, the right of sovereignty (or the right of autonomy) was not enough. This right, aside from needing to be recognized by international law and assured by the guarantees of several nations, had to be defended by the Jews themselves—that is, by their own military power. Without it, any right of sovereignty would be fictitious. And without it, "we shall produce new Armenians in one place or another."

III

We have spoken about the right of sovereignty or autonomy, but what concrete rights did Herzl mean by these two concepts, which he used interchangeably? It is clear that Herzl meant a whole set of rights

---

8   *Zionism*, p. 56

and not just one alone. Did he mean religious and cultural autonomy, of the kind which the autonomists in the diaspora spoke about? Did he also mean economic autonomy? Did he mean that the Jews will enjoy special rights of settlement, such as substantial inducements to immigrate and own land? Yes, Herzl's right of sovereignty or autonomy included all these things, but it also included much more.

When Herzl speaks of sovereignty, he means *state* sovereignty, and when he speaks of autonomy, he means an autonomy which constitutes the *ruling authority*. He understood that the existence of all the other rights, of culture, religion, economy and settlement, depends on this authority. In other words, he understood that even if the most desirable rights were granted to the settlers, those rights would not be secure if the settlers themselves were not the ruling authority. Therefore, we arrive at an obvious and certain conclusion: Herzl saw as a *necessary condition* for the success of the settlement project the attainment of an *autonomous ruling authority*—an autonomy which would be assured by political guarantees and accompanied by the military force of the settling people.

Herzl stated his sole objective clearly and candidly to the first Turkish statesman he met on his initial trip to Constantinople: "We want Palestine as an absolutely independent state." And when that same statesman (Ziad Paha) told him that this demand did not leave room for negotiation, and that perhaps it would be only possible to receive an autonomous state which paid taxes to Turkey, Herzl replied: "This political construct is a form of self-deception, because such states always yearn quickly to achieve complete independence."[9]

But after his first visit to Constantinople, and after speaking to several of the ministers, he soon discovered that it would be impossible to conduct negotiations with the Turkish government except on the basis of such self-deception. Therefore, he gave up on the demand of absolute independence, in the hope of obtaining the type of ruling authority which would necessarily lead to independence; or

---
9   *Diaries*, II, p. 41-42.

more precisely, to create the kind of a political entity that would be dependent on another body by only weak ties, which could soon be broken and which in any event would not have the power to disturb, even partially, the efforts of Jewish immigration and settlement. A statesman as clear-sighted as the Arch Duke of Baden knew well what he had in mind. "You want to found a state?"—he asked Herzl on one occasion—"That seems to me the only way to obtain a secure legal standing. It's possible to find a means by which to leave the supreme authority in the hands of the Sultan, for instance like the former rule of princes by the Dunau. What will come of it afterward, say, one generation on, you never know." Herzl adds: "He smiled."[10]

He smiled, for he knew very well what became of the "rule of princes by the Dunau." He knew what that "supreme authority" of the Sultan's meant, which was all Herzl would agree to as a condition of settlement. "I've spoken with the Turks," Herzl wrote to Colonel Goldsmith. "They refuse to give us Palestine as an independent state at any price, but as a vassal state of Turkey (perhaps like Egypt) we could get it. You, sir, will join the Turkish army as a general, and as such would command the army of Palestine under the supreme authority of the Sultan, and when the day comes on which the Turkish empire breaks up, *an independent Land of Israel* will fall into our hands or in the hands of our sons."[11]

Herzl therefore interpreted the right of sovereignty as very simply the right of independent state authority or, at the very least, the right of ruling authority which would necessarily lead to independence. The autonomy of which Herzl spoke was not a hollow and empty concept of a right floating in the air, but rather meant transferring, in exchange for a pre-agreed tax, the power of the country's internal rule to a Jewish ruling authority. For the sake of securing the settlement, he was obliged to obtain, as he formulated clearly, "the right of legal ownership of Palestine," and he knew that such a right could not be exercised in practice if not accompanied by state authority. For never

---

10 *Diaries*, III, p.92-93.
11 ibid, II, p. 199-200.

had there occurred a settlement of any people who aspired to proper standing in the land it sought to settle in, without the settling people first having ruling authority.

Such was the case regarding the settlements of the French and English in Canada, the English in North America, the Spanish in South America, the Dutch and English in South Africa, and such was the case with the settlements of all the world's colonial powers from the age of Carthage until modern times. Since it was clear to Herzl that he would not be able to extract from Turkey the completely independent rule which was most desirable to him, then he could not budge an inch from that minimum of ruling authority which was necessary for the settlement to succeed. Such a minimum was for him the type of settlement which was assured and accepted throughout the 19th century. This was settlement according to a charter, whose full scope contained a kind of "state within a state." Herzl's charter included everything: the right to rule and to tax payments, military defense, customs regulations, border regulations, the structure of the legal system, and regulations concerning the ownership of land—in short, a whole system of political conditions which he saw as necessary for a successful settlement.

Therefore, when he believed that he was close to reaching an agreement with Turkey, he instructed the lawyer Bodenheimer to draft a charter. According to what? "According to the regulations of the charter corporation of Rhodes, according to the regulations of the German corporation in East Africa and of the corporation of New Guinea"[12]—that is, according to the laws of settlement of the greatest colonial powers. Such was the charter he demanded from the British for their proposals concerning Jewish settlement in the Sinai Peninsula, El-Arish and Cyprus, as was the charter he intended to obtain from them for Uganda.

*****

---

12   T. Herzl, *Letters*, State edition, 1937, p. 166-167.

Unlike Hovevei Zion, Herzl knew that the process of settlement was not only that of propagandizing in newspapers or collecting donations, but one of the most complex processes which was liable to take place among the settling people and the people within the country being settled. For any complete national settlement is, in effect, an extended internal revolution which takes place in the country being settled. It is essentially a *process of national birth*, after which the country becomes a new national entity which will determine its way of life and future destiny. Herzl knew that in order for this peaceful revolution to end properly, in order for this difficult national birth to bring forth a healthy political body destined to grow and develop and not result in a premature birth which would create something that would wither and quickly die, it was essential that all the limbs and institutions of the political body be directed toward that goal. He knew that with regard to the delicate and complex process of settlement, one law not properly formed or one political institution not functioning as it should, was enough to disrupt and even prevent the entire process.

And herein is the most striking difference between Pinsker's *Auto-Emancipation* and Herzl's *The Jewish State*. Pinsker also talked of a Jewish state, but the state he envisioned was something general and amorphous. In contrast, Herzl's "Jewish State" was a machine of many screws, cogs and wheels. What was the source of this difference? Its source was Herzl being a great statesman, and hence his insistence on the importance of the details of the political arrangements he sought to bring forth. He understood that a state was a complex mechanism, whose every part had to operate in mutual accord, and that any flaw in one of its wheels was liable to prevent it from fulfilling its function— or at least from fulfilling it properly. He understood that this mutual accord was even more decisive in a settlement project, and he therefore worked indefatigably—even after he wrote *The Jewish State*—on plans for how to suit this machine to its function in the best way.

The great revolution which Herzl brought to the Jewish question and to its solution was, therefore, this: A settlement does not achieve its objective unless it is first provided with a legal right to achieve this objective, or in other words, unless the settlement is preceded by a right of settlement. This right of settlement would have no concrete value unless it was secured by external political guarantees and by an internal military force. In short, a state cannot be established on the basis of gradual infiltration. On the contrary, in order for gradual infiltration or any other infiltration to be possible, it is first necessary to establish the state.

*****

This approach was, of course, incomprehensible to the myopic and politically uneducated among the Jews. Was not this, the Hovevei Zion asked, a pipe dream, a fantasy unfounded in reality? Instead of proceeding in the clear and obvious way of adding Jew to Jew, acre to acre, Herzl, they were certain, was steeped in baseless fantasies which would never be realized. If this weren't bad enough, they also saw Herzl as preventing them, the experienced and realistic men of action, from taking their good and proper path. Of course, given the conditions of Jewish existence at the time, Herzl was seeking to achieve something that was almost beyond belief. For he aspired to create what Archimedes had aspired to obtain—a vast lever that would have the power to transform at once the condition of the Jewish people.

Herzl was not moved by the criticism of Hovevei Zion. With a firm hand, he led the Zionist movement in a direction which practically no one but him truly wanted, toward a goal which only a few understood. He knew that in order to obtain the kind of political structure which he saw as the first condition of settlement activity, he was *obliged* to follow Archimedes and find firm leverage for his idea outside the Jewish world, whose fate he sought to change. He began to operate over a huge sphere and to put out feelers in each and every place where he had hopes of finding a point of leverage. He knew exactly what he wanted to attain. He wanted to create a new political fact, and he knew that such a fact, once created, would immediately be part of the workings of a vast, almost infinite, world of existing political facts and would immediately exist on certain terms with each and all of them. For this reality to be shaped, for the necessary space to be cleared for it in the world of other political realities, it was clear to him that it was necessary first to obtain for it the general agreement of the great powers.

Thus he sought to obtain the main governments' recognition for the Jewish state even before that state had been founded in practice. Moreover, he knew that his "dream state," as Nordau called it—which so many considered a utopia that was not worth discussing with any seriousness, or worse, which was undesirable—would never leave the realms of imagination if complete and general agreement to it was not obtained. This was, seemingly, an impossibly difficult task which any other statesman would not have made a fool of himself by attempting to fulfill. But Herzl was one of those rare individuals for whom the greatest and most difficult challenges summon all their internal resources to achieve their objective, perhaps for whom only the greatest of tasks can move them to such action.

With unprecedented consistency, incomparable stubbornness, and unrivaled confidence in his ultimate success, with innovations that only his mind could have imagined, persuasive arguments that only he could have uncovered, and with the influence which only his personality was capable of projecting, Herzl acquired, step by step, the consent of all the major powers to his idea of a Jewish state: Germany, Austria, Russia, Italy, England, and indirectly, France as well. Surely, had this consent not been obtained, had Herzl not introduced into all the world's ruling circles the recognition that "a Jewish state is a world necessity," and that it was the only possible and desirable solution to both the Jewish question and the question of Palestine, there would have been no grounds whatsoever for any hope of fulfilling the national aspirations of the Jews.

Herzl foresaw the practical results which were to come from his activity. For in contrast to the accusations of Hovevei Zion, Herzl was a realist statesman, and all of his activities and his words were aimed, first and foremost, toward practical ends—perhaps not the inconsequential practical ends to which the eyes of Hovevei Zion were set, but those great practical ends on which his sight was directed. It was actually the "practical" Hovevei Zion who were impractical and living in a fantasy world. That was why for Ahad Ha'am and his supporters, the settlement of the Land of Israel was a matter of centuries. Herzl knew that no one man can make realistic plans for hundreds of years for the simple reason that no man can calculate the possibilities over such a long period. Yet for Hovevei Zion, the question of time did not exist at all. They acted as if they lived in a vacuum—as if the entire world would stand still and wait for them to complete their endeavor. But Herzl knew that every time the sun rises or sets, something changes in the world. He knew that one can make plans over at most a few decades. For that too, one would need a great statesmen.

Herzl knew something else, which Hovevei Zion (apart from Pinsker) had not even considered. He knew that even if it were possible to conceive of rescue operations whose implementation required hundreds of years, world Jewry did not have those hundreds of years at its disposal. He listened carefully to what was happening in his times and heard the thunder rumbling from of a gathering storm of Jew-hatred, coming closer and closer. It was clear to him that *the Middle Ages would be revisited upon the Jews in all the states of Europe*, and he repeated this observation time and again. He saw that "the stone is rolling down the mountain slope," and he knew where it would stop, "at the bottom, the absolute bottom!" "Will it be devastation by the forces of revolution?" (as happened later to the Jews of Russia) "Will it be confiscation by the forces of reaction?" (as happened later to the Jews of Germany) "Will they expel us? Will they murder us? *I anticipate all of these things and more."*[13]

He saw that the glowing embers of the fires of the old Jew-hatred, which had previously engulfed all the states of Europe, were going

---

13   *Diaries*, I, p. 129

to flare up again, and that this fire would spread with the same global sweep it had in the past. "I am not a speculator of catastrophe," he wrote in 1903 to the Hungarian Jew Erne Mezei, "but catastrophe will come upon the Jews of Hungary too, in brutal fashion, and the later it comes the more severe it will be; the stronger they become, the more savage it will be. There is no escaping it. Meanwhile, we [Zionists], who are now being mocked, have risen and are building a homeland for those very people who today do not want to know a thing about us."[14]

For at the distant edge of those decades which he envisioned so clearly, the specter of the *catastrophe* appeared before him like a dark shroud which blocks all lines of sight and buries all plans and calculations. It was clear to him that what awaited the Jewish people behind that shroud was extinction. For this people could be compared in his eyes to a man whose enemies had tried to drown him by holding his head under the water. Yet because that man had uncommon endurance and could hold his breath a very long time, they had tired of holding him down and let go of him for a little while. But only for a little while. And now that man, instead of using the precious time afforded him to escape his enemies, to leave the place which they control, was blithely breathing the air he was given, not suspecting the intentions of those seeking to kill him.

Indeed, Herzl saw the Jewish people sinking once more—and this time, perhaps permanently—into the terrible servitude and endless harassment which had marked their darkest periods, and he understood that there was a necessity to use *swiftly* the brief period in which the emancipation had granted the Jews a measure of liberty. He understood that in order to preempt the catastrophe, there was a necessity for a *swift* rescue. Therefore, he did not daydream about plans which may require centuries, but took hold with all his might of the political reality of *his own era*, a reality in which he saw the emerging contours of the next generation.

---

14   *Letters*, p. 266

He knew that the Land of Israel was in the hands of Turkey. Upon analyzing Turkey's political situation, he felt certain that it was headed for disintegration. But he feared the division of Turkey, because he knew that such a division could deliver Palestine into non-Jewish hands, and that it was impossible to know how the new owners would view his aspirations and whether Palestine would not be considered by them too precious to hand it over to the Jews. For he also made an assessment of the future of Palestine, and realized the value which it would acquire both politically and economically, even though few of his contemporaries paid any attention to this. It was clear to him that this value would soon be discovered by everyone. "How long do you think"—he asked Lord Rothschild—"how much longer will no one notice all the advantages which it is possible to gain there? Yet then it will be we Jews—we who are always so wise and so cheated—who will miss the right moment."[15]

This moment—the division of Turkey, which was drawing close, when the value of Palestine would rise—was constantly on his mind. Even in December 1896, he writes: "The demise of Turkey—and today it can no longer be doubted—is for us the critical moment."[16] If that were true, then not only because of the hardship facing the Jews, but also for general political reasons, it was desirable for him to obtain the Land of Israel before this division occurred. He was absolutely certain that this was possible if only he had at his disposal the sums which he required. Those of today who claim political astuteness and say that this was impossible, think that there are those of us who believe that their political understanding of Turkey was greater than Herzl's.

Yet Herzl conducted personal negotiations for eight consecutive years with all the Turkish ministers. He had agents posted at Constantinople at the Yildis Kiosk. He checked which way the winds were blowing, knew all the potential pitfalls, and nevertheless was sure, particularly after his meeting with the Sultan, that it was definitely possible to obtain Turkey's consent if he only had the financial resources which

---

15 *Diaries,* V, p. 198
16 *Letters,* p. 26

he demanded in vain from the Jewish people. We have reason to accept Herzl's prognosis much more than those of the prognosticators whose judgments are based on vague opinionating.

But Herzl also took into account the possibility that due to the refusal of the government or due to a lack of resources, he would not obtain the Land of Israel from Turkey, and therefore all his political activity was aimed simultaneously toward two possibilities: to obtain it either before the division of Turkey or during the division itself. Therefore, when he saw that the process of preparing the governments and world opinion was making progress, he noted with certainty: "If I don't obtain Palestine now, I'll obtain it at the point of the division of Turkey." Why was he so certain? Because, as he put it, he waited for the division of Turkey "with a stop watch in hand," because it was clear to him that the moment of decision over the fate of the Palestine was fast approaching, and because he knew what role he, as leader of his people, must play. He did not count the number of cows and goats in the holdings of the Jewish farmers, as Hovevei Zion would do, but rather prepared the consent of the major powers.

When that same great moment which Herzl foresaw arrived during the World War [WWI] (and he did in fact say that "the division of Turkey means a world war"[17]), the agreement of the League of Nations to Zionism was ready before that body was even established. For it is important to note, that at the very time when the western allied statesmen were debating the plan of the Balfour Declaration, the same plan was before the German government—the same Germany which knew Zionism well from the days of Herzl's personal negotiations with Kaiser Wilhelm II and his ministers. And if England and France prepared this declaration,[18] it was because they knew Zionism and its aims also through Herzl's political activity. Let us bear in mind the unique adulation which Clemenceau felt for Herzl. In England, Herzl conducted, both he himself and via his assistants Zangwill and Greenberg, considerable and prolonged political activity, which

---

17 *Zionism*, p. 65
18 See Max Nordau, *Zionist Writings*, IV, Zionist Library, p.194-195.

involved all the senior members of the government and policymakers of England. Lloyd George too was brought into the sphere of Zionism by them. The role played by this man, who was at the time both a solicitor and member of parliament, in Herzl's political activity was nothing less than this: *He had drafted Herzl's Uganda charter.* And who was at the head of that same government which made Herzl the offer of Uganda?

That Prime Minister was none other than Arthur James Balfour, who by virtue of his office was well versed in that Uganda offer and in the Zionist movement with which England sought to be connected. And it was Balfour who also took part in the debate over the Uganda proposal, which was held in parliament on June 20, 1904 and in which the members of the government defended the offer against the attacks of several members of parliament. Indeed, it is difficult to find any among the great statesmen who later aided in the obtainment of the Balfour Declaration and the Mandate who were not directly won over either by Herzl and his assistants or indirectly by their political activity.

The matter is, therefore, clear. Had Herzl not prepared the consent of the major powers, had he not inculcated into the consciousness of the greatest statesmen that Zionism was *the only possible solution* to the two big and grave questions—i.e., the Jewish question and the question of Palestine—had he not made Zionism a known and accepted political factor, Palestine would have passed in time of war from hand to hand, as it had many times in its long history, and with it would have passed authority over the small Jewish settlement which survived within it after the war, and nothing would have changed concerning the fate of either the land or the Jewish people.

IV

If we had before us a map of all the stations Herzl passed on the road of his political activity, we would see that the same map also indicates the positions he reached in the course of his political thinking. What is more, parallelism of time and place is apparent not only in his specific achievements, but also in the simultaneity of the great efforts required to attain his goals. Thus, before mobilizing international public opinion for the cause of Zionism and obtaining the agreements of the great powers, Herzl searched for a fixed point to place the lever he intended to use for attaining those goals which would enable him to change the destiny of Israel. Both tasks were equally essential, and the second was harder to attain, indeed harder than the one facing Archimedes. For the latter only sought a suitable leverage point outside the existing Earth.

Herzl, on the other hand, knew that even if he built a lever, even if he located the appropriate point to place it, the planet (if we go along with Archimedes metaphor), which the lever had to take hold of, did not exist as a solid body. For until his time, it was not clearly known whether a Jewish nation, as such, truly existed. What he found in practice was not a people that could be moved and which could be considered a coherent body with a will of its own, but rather human dust, soil scattered over the ends of the earth. So Herzl began scooping up this soil, breathing life into it and turning it into a solid and cohesive body. He created the Zionist Organization, which was to become the largest administrative organization ever to function in the people's long existence in the Diaspora. And this organization was to become the solid framework which would unite within it all the fragmented powers of the people into a single robust entity.

Would that not be enough? Would the realization of activities so monumental and wide ranging be enough to ensure, when the opportunity arises, the acquisition of the right of sovereignty which was longed for? Perhaps more than all the great things he did, here we discover all of Herzl's farsightedness and his deep insight into the nature of things. He knew that this was insufficient. For the analogy of the lever, like all analogies, does not fit reality in all its detail. Yes, he knew that both the readiness of the great powers and an organized Jewish people were necessary conditions for acquiring the desired political position, which he saw as the key to national settlement and the solution of the Jewish question. But he also knew that a national redemption emanates, first and foremost, from the depths of a national will for such redemption, that all liberations start with self-liberation. It was Herzl who said at the first Congress: "Only the people itself can deliver itself. If it does not deliver itself—it cannot be delivered at all."

He knew that he had found a point of leverage for the Jewish liberation (the agreements of the great powers), that he had created a body which could be taken hold at this point (the Zionist Organization), but the essence was still missing: *He still could not see the moving force of the lever.* It was absolutely clear to Herzl that this force, in the degree which was needed to obtain results, would not come from the outside, but must come from the people itself. With the acute sense he possessed, he felt immediately that the people did not yet possess this moving force, or did so to only the smallest extent. And how did Herzl define that moving force? With a single word: will.

Herzl's "will" meant far more than the word which is commonly used, yet which often means little. Rather, like any concrete will, his "will" was comprised of several essential elements. *"The feeling of nationhood—from where shall we take it?"* Pinsker asked in deep despair. For the feeling of nationhood, the fondness for the nation's possessions, its yearning for liberation—this was, of course, the first necessary condition for achieving such liberation. But Herzl knew that on this point in particular, there was no cause for despair. He knew that the feeling of nationhood existed among the people, and certainly in a large part of it, and that this feeling would gradually spread to almost all quarters. Herzl saw the main flaw not in the absence of a feeling of nationhood, but in the presence of a feeling of inferiority which the Jewish nation had sunk into during the centuries of Exile—or, in other words, in the people's low esteem for their own capabilities and their ubiquitous conviction that the harassed, scattered and fragmented people of Israel were weak, powerless and helpless. It was clear that a people sunk in this spiritual state of inferiority, endlessly depressed by the conviction that it was pathetic and feeble, would never discover within itself the power and drive to realize what is certainly the most difficult national achievement—its own liberation.

The people's belief in their own abilities was a condition for the emergence of their will to liberation, just as the individual's belief in his own abilities is a condition for a determined will appearing in him. So Herzl began pulling this self-abnegation out by its roots, by the means which he saw as appropriate, from his deep understanding of human nature. At every opportunity that came his way, he declared loudly that the people of Israel are great and mighty, that titanic forces are pent up within them. There is, he argued, something very strong in their character, for this was the only people that had passed through so many zones of Hell in their long history of four thousand years.[19] He pointed out that "the Jewish race is more diligent than most of the peoples of the earth, and that this is indeed the reason for the great hatred toward it."[20] He declared that this race, if the world did not grant it what was necessary for its normal existence, could serve as a terrible dynamite which could destroy the entire world, and he pointed out the danger of revolution hovering over Russia through the abilities of those same Jews, while everyone was foolishly disdaining their abilities.

For even though they were mired in catastrophe, the Jews were still very strong, and therefore it was within their power to execute their own rescue operation. "Were those who founded states which are now powerful any stronger, smarter, or richer than we Jews today? Poor shepherds and hunters formed public bodies which later became states. Even in our day, the Greeks, Romanians, Serbs and Bulgarians have risen up. And this is beyond us?"[21] "No man," he replied elsewhere, "will seriously dare prove to us that we are not capable of doing *the same thing* that were done by the Balkan peoples."[22] "But what is our

---

19   *Zionism*, p. 58
20   *Diaries*, V, p. 235
21   ibid, ibid.
22   *Zionism*, p. 152

tragedy? We lack the belief in ourselves."[23] And he says: "That very day that we believe in ourselves, our moral distress will end."

To undo this moral distress, which shackled the ability of the people to raise its self-esteem, was certainly a difficult task to accomplish in the conditions of poverty, servitude and harassment in which the Jews were mired in Eastern Europe, and in the condition of conscious negation of self-identity by the Jews in Western Europe. Still, Herzl knew that without accomplishing this task, nothing would change. But how would this desired self-awareness be manifested, the skeptics asked. What use were all of Herzl's words? Would the people's belief that they were strong change the actual balance of power? Herzl knew better than his skeptics what were, in fact, a nation's actual assets. He knew that not on the basis of physical power, nor on the basis of building houses or buying up tracts of land, would a nation gain what it yearned for. A nation gains what it yearns for only on the basis of an undetectable and unquantifiable transformation in its spiritual life, character and outlook. At the very moment a downtrodden nation wholeheartedly believes in its own power and greatness, at that moment it is assured of acquiring power and greatness in practice. Of course, it is necessary for that belief to be general and overwhelming, and it is necessary for it to be based on the existence of real strengths, although such strength might be concealed within the nation and not easily discernable to all.

But a nation which does not believe in its ability to achieve great things, will never achieve them. The most awesome national power is the belief in those abilities, and only this power can pave the road to both liberation and a magnificent future. Herzl knew this secret of human nature. He knew that at the very moment when, to use the prophet Zephaniah's aphorism, "The weakling will say: I am strong!" at that moment he becomes strong in practice. If a nation says out of conviction, I am strong and forceful, then it becomes strong and

---

23 *Diaries*, V, p. 235

forceful. This is the law of greatness, and this is the law of liberation; there is no other.

The people's belief in their own powers is, therefore, the initial and primary requirement for any act of self help, any vast undertaking or great demand. The world will appreciate the power of the Jews only if they recognize their own self-worth and believe in their importance. This belief is a first condition, but it is not the only condition. For a nation to receive the right of sovereignty, for it to be a ruling authority, it is not sufficient for others to agree to grant it these rights. It must itself be ready to receive them. And to do so, it must be ready to demand them. Still, the great claims—and the claims of a state are the greatest of claims—are not based upon self-confidence alone. Here, there is something which extends beyond the realms of belief, and Herzl knew what it was: it is the daring, the spiritual courage, and the strength to grapple with fate—to take it into your own hands and bend it according to the national interest.

And this thing, which Herzl called the "courage to rule," was lacking in the Jewish people. Herzl saw it as an essential need. He regarded it so highly that he saw in it "the entire historic purpose of Jewish emancipation, which should have restored to us this quality."[24] Therefore Herzl came and declared: "Dare! Smaller nations than us have dared to claim their portion on the earth as their political property; and because they dared, because they had the courage to rule—they also got it."[25]

Therefore, Herzl's "will" was comprised of several essential elements. It was a will which had to be based on the nation's deep belief in its ability to found a state, and on its daring to claim it without relent and to take it with its own hands. He also knew that only such a will—a will which was the product of neither sentimental longing nor feeble urges that commit one to nothing—won't let anything stand in its way and will chart a course to its objective. The formation of such a

24   *Zionism*, p.33
25   ibid, p. 34

will was the aim of all his national education, just as it was the aim of his aspirations. For Herzl was set on obtaining *political rule*, and for a nation to get that power, it has to be *capable* of ruling. Obviously, ruling entails discipline and organization, and there is no doubt that in this regard his creation of the Zionist Organization was also an attempt to accustom the nation to a framework of rule before it obtained actual political power. In this sense, perhaps *especially* in this sense, Herzl saw the Zionist Organization as "the Jewish State in the making." But governance of a state, with all the duties and roles it entailed, and which always included foreign elements and is always clashing with them, is not merely a matter of discipline and organization. Such a rule entails, first and foremost, belief in the power of your strengths and your uniqueness. Such a rule entails *daring* and also, as Nietzche put it, "the will to power." That is why I would sum up Herzl's entire understanding of the internal conditions for the liberation of his people in three words: believe, dare and desire, and that is why he stated even at the start of his activity: "We are close to Jerusalem to the extent that we *desire* Jerusalem. It is a question of the will that beats within us. Our role is to awaken that will, to rouse it, and if possible—to spur it on."[26] Therefore he repeated and emphasized this point near the end of his life and even raised it to the level of a first principle: "If you will it, it is no dream…"

V

These were the main principles of Herzl's teachings. As we have noted, he saw their full implementation as the unshakable foundations of the national edifice he wished to build for his people. Therefore, all his activities and statements were primarily directed at their fulfillment. But the all-too- sophisticated and wise will still ask: What were all these activities and statements anyway? What did all his diplomacy, all his discussions with statesmen consist of? What did all his remarks

---

26   *Letters*, p. 76

about changing the character of the people comprise? Was not this merely talk? For there was nothing here that was realistic, tangible and concrete.

Quite true. And we can even expand on the above—since even the Zionist Organization, which Herzl created, was not a "concrete" thing. Organization and discipline are not tangible and concrete, but the sort of things which are based on spiritual strength. Indeed, all of Herzl's activity was floating in mid-air. However, it was not by accident, but rather by design that Herzl gave his work this character. For from *the very beginning*, he insisted that the national activity he pursued is based on what can be neither quantified nor measured, and his opinion on this matter was the source of disagreement with the first Jewish millionaire he met on his way. Why? Because he knew that money and material power could not serve as the *foundation* for the political entity to which he aspired. He knew that only by the power of the spiritual and symbolic, only by that power which human beings have no control over, but rather which controls them, would it be possible to propel forward this monumental mission whose name was: creating a nation and founding a state. He knew that "monumental issues do not require a solid foundation," that "only an apple needs to be laid on a table in order not to fall, but the earth floats in space."[27]

The practical activities would certainly need to come later, in one fell swoop and in vast quantities, like the natural and rich harvest of all his "non-practical" activities, and they would have to be great and monumental, and suited to their purpose. He was as certain that they would come, as he was that two times two equals four. All his political activities were ordered in his mind like a series of mathematical formulas, which he saw as directed toward the goal.

But was this mathematics? No. It was something infinitely deeper and more complex. For a political reality has no fixed elements, but rather such that change and switch constantly. To be filled with the kind of certainty that Herzl possessed, one had to have the sort of deep and

---

27 *Diaries*, II, p. 24

penetrating insight, the sort of vision with which one could uncover the hidden forces that were capable of founding a state and with which one could clearly understand the significance of the moment that was fast approaching. It was clear to him that the moment of opportunity would come. He could not know for sure whether it would take five years or ten or twenty, but he knew it would come. He also understood that in order for that precious moment of opportunity not to pass in vain—the nation had to be prepared, and all its resources ready to seize and take control of it. Therefore, all of Herzl's political, organizational and educational activity was directed toward that moment.

This was Herzl's plan, a plan which was based on both his laws of liberation and his foresight. Did history confirm his plan? Did he move to anticipate events correctly? To these questions, we can respond unequivocally: A prophet has not yet arisen among his people whose words have come to fruition in so brief a period as have the words of Herzl. The great moment came, as he prophesied, bound together with the storm of a world war, and bearing in its wings an exterminating attack on world Jewry, which began with the massacre of the Jews of Ukraine (during the Russian Civil War) and continues to spread to the present day. Herzl's political activity resulted in the fact that the Jews, whom he had united in a political organization, were recognized as a political entity, and that their aspirations, which Herzl had publicized and proven their significance for the world, became part of the international political system. Indeed, due to the war, those aspirations had become so important that *the major powers turned to the Zionists*. This fact, which was clearly proven by Nordau[28], was also verified by Dr. Weizmann's secretary during the period of the Balfour Declaration and by other testimonies and documents which cannot be refuted. At that moment, Herzl's idea should have been realized.

Here we arrive at the thing which Herzl tried to accomplish, but in which he did not succeed. Herzl failed to change the character of the people. This change, which, as we have said, Herzl viewed as

---

28 See Max Nordau, *Zionist Writings*, IV, p. 194

a necessity, was not found in the spirit of its leaders; or to be more precise, in the spirit of those who conducted the negotiations in the name of the Jewish people and afterwards conducted its affairs. When there was a need to display the *courage to rule* of which Herzl spoke, when there was a need to dare and to *demand from the world a Jewish state and the power to rule over that state*, this demand was not heard from the mouths of his successors. Ahad Ha'am no doubt warned Weizmann not to make such a demand. Weizmann himself later admitted that he never made it—an admission that later resulted in Zangwill's tempestuous attacks on Weizmann's conduct. And why did the Jewish representatives not make that demand? Because they lacked the daring, because the feeling of weakness, borne of the existence in the diaspora, had become deeply rooted in their souls, and because they did not have confidence in the abilities of their people to govern a state of their own. Thus, when Nordau later demanded the rapid transfer of half a million Jews to the Land of Israel (which might have partly corrected that fatal error), they rejected this demand, too, without making the slightest effort to execute Nordau's plan. For since they were lacking daring and faith in the abilities of their people, they were not able to summon in that decisive hour the tremendous effort and the monumental will which was necessary to perform such an endeavor. And who knows if not for that reason, and perhaps only for that reason, the great moment passed without delivering what was lodged in its wings.

But the moment did not pass *entirely* in vain. For the scope of activities Herzl performed could not possibly yield no results. Those results were expressed in the right of sovereignty which was granted to the Jews over the Land of Israel in the form and to the extent outlined in the Balfour Declaration and the League of Nations' Mandate. But this right of sovereignty was not defined in a framework of concrete political rights, nor was it developed into a policy directed toward securing the establishment of a Jewish State, because, as stated above, Herzl did not succeed to inculcate within the Jewish people the character which is essential to a political movement. In fact, all of Herzl's teachings remain alien to this day to the great majority of the Jews. The Jewish leadership today is comprised of those who fought Herzl during his lifetime, who never truly studied his teaching and never understood it.

In a certain sense, one could say that the Balfour Declaration fell into their laps out of the sky, or to paraphrase Herzl's remarks about Bismark: "They shook the tree which Herzl planted," and the fruit fell in the form of the Balfour Declaration and the Mandate. But they continued being the same "Hovevei Zion," and continued to think that they would achieve their goal by the same simple laws of addition, by adding in Palestine Jew upon Jew, by purchasing acre after acre— the same old approach which Herzl sought to expunge from their minds. They did not understand that there is no settlement without a supportive ruling authority or, at the very least, without supreme authority in the *management* of the country being settled. Therefore, not only did they fail to demand an absolute ruling authority, but they relinquished and even misinterpreted the rights which had been included in the Mandate and the Balfour Declaration. They did not duly fight for their realization. Nor did they endeavor to maintain the existence of the Jewish military force which was founded during the war, but instead treated its dismantlement virtually with indifference, and some of them even reached the incredible conclusion that the presence of such a force may be harmful as it might aggravate the Arabs.

We are suffering from this feeble spirit to this day, paying dearly for every deviation from Herzl's path. If today we agree to exclude additional parts of Palestine from Jewish settlement and remain with a corner of the land which may suffice for only an million or a million and a half Jews, then again this occurs because the course of Zionism is not guided by Herzl's teachings. For all of Zionism was worthless in his eyes, if he could not see within it a solution to the entire Jewish question. Herzl explicitly stressed this repeatedly: "We need a territory that will be sufficient to the needs of the people." Moreover, he saw clearly, as we have noted, that great waves of antisemitism were going to wash over the Jews in all the countries of the world, and that *most* of world Jewry would need an *island* to save themselves. Herzl always negotiated for obtaining a vast territory, and when in his dying days he conducted negotiations to obtain the district of Acco, it was because he saw in it what he saw in the El-Arish or Sinai settlement proposals: a springboard with which to gain ruling authority over the entire land of Israel *at the time of the break-up of Turkey*, which he was sure would come.

Need we point out the vast difference between the sovereignty which Herzl sought for the district of Acco, and the sovereignty allegedly offered the Jews in 1938 under the Peel Commission proposal? For Herzl's proposal did not entail giving up any sovereign right whatsoever, since he did not as yet have such rights in hand, and in any case did not entail abandoning sovereignty over most of the country, as had been guaranteed in the Balfour Declaration and the Mandate. In contrast, the acceptance of the Peel Commission partition plan, even if the territory allotted to the Jewish state is expanded from what is currently proposed, does entail such an abandonment. It is surely no secret that sovereign rights may easily be lost through political or military error, but are not easily regained. Moreover, is it not obvious that a nation which *willingly* conceded its land has signed with its own hand its recognition that this land was not its own and was rightly uprooted from it forever? Indeed, the self-deprecation within us works wonders. To this day, the proud and mighty spirit of Herzl has been no match for it.

John Locke wrote somewhere: "When God creates the prophet, he does not kill the man in him." Obviously, for all his being a prophet, Herzl, like any man, was liable to be wrong about this or that detail. His entire edifice was based on a single foundation: his faith in his people and in their capacity for redemption. Did he not know this people? Was he, as Nordau said, delusional regarding its qualities and capacities? True, from the beginning he attributed to it hopes which were soon proven false. But afterward, he saw everything clearly. "As

Moses aged, he always saw before him Korah, the golden calf and the faces of slaves. He was wearied by all of these sights, but nevertheless had to pull the people ever onward." Onward indeed. For had Herzl ceased believing in his people, in reforming its character, in imbuing it with political understanding, he would have been left with nothing. So, while surrounded by ridicule and opposition, he was obliged, almost entirely alone, to pave for his nation its road to redemption. He also placed them on that road, and thrust them down it. And while that exertion cost him his life, he died in the belief that his people would continue in his path.

Was he mistaken in his belief? Was this the one part of Herzl's well-thought out plan that was not thought through? The history of the coming decades will answer that question. But if we do not wish for Herzl's great undertaking to be lost in an abyss, if we do not wish for his efforts to have been in vain, if our admiration for Herzl is sincere, we will abide by his teachings, arm ourselves with his directives and take upon ourselves the spirit he attributed to us. For otherwise, a day will come which will be the darkest of days, a day of fury and terror, when our people will sink once more into the depths of slavery, when we will be robbed and despised by all the world, harassed and laid low even in the land of our forefathers. And on the tombstone of Herzl shall then be engraved a few words, which the stranger, unaware of Herzl's teachings, will not understand. But these will be the words which he himself asked to engrave on his tombstone, during a moment of grave doubt as to the outcome of his work: "His view of the Jews was too optimistic."

Max Nordau
Chapter 3

Born in Hungary in 1849, Nordau was a philosopher-critic, physician, and Zionist leader. A co-founder of the First Zionist Congress together with Herzl, he died in 1923.

(the following was originally published in *Max Nordau to His People*, "Introduction," Scopus Publishing Co., New York, 1941)

I. Background

From 1849, the year of Nordau's birth, till 1939, the year of the outbreak of the Second World War, ninety years, about the maximum span of a man's life, elapsed. The pivotal axis which runs through this period is undoubtedly the National Idea. The years 1849 and 1939 are its two poles, representing almost opposite stages in the transformation of modern Nationalism.

The year 1849 still heard the battle-cries of the popular insurrections which had started in March 1848. They were, as a serious thinker said, "the last thunders of the great storm, called the French Revolution"; but they also heralded a new era dominated by ideas not even conceived in 1789. The principles of the French Revolution, embodied in the slogan of "Liberty, Equality, Fraternity", were still valid in the middle of the nineteenth century, but their import was enlarged, and the addition proved to be the main factor of the coming age. Liberty, Equality and Fraternity were now proclaimed not only for the *individuals* of the *state*, as in 1789, but also for the *nationalities* of the *fatherlands*. In the streets of Paris, Berlin, Vienna, Budapest and Warsaw, blood was shed not only for the "rights of men", but also for the "rights of nations". The most important of the latter was, as then believed, the right of the people to be freed of oppression, internal or external. The essence of Nationalism was, therefore, the same as that of Liberalism.

Since all nations were considered potentially *free*, or, better, devoid of any right to subdue any people or race, they were all considered *equal.* As the feeling of equality was an immediate result of the idea of liberty, so was the feeling of fraternity a result of both of them. The fraternity of nations was considered the most dangerous weapon of the revolutionary uprisings since the beginning of the national movements. The Italian Carbonari fought for the freedom of Spain in 1823. When the defeated Polish revolutionaries passed through Germany in 1831, they were welcomed with enthusiasm by the sympathetic mobs. Frenchmen and Poles fought for the liberation of Italy, and the Italian and Polish refugees in France participated in the bloody events of 1830 and 1848. The organization *Young Europe*, established by Mazzini, was in fact the "First International" of Nationalism, being, by the way, strongly opposed in spirit and aims to the First International of Socialism, established later by Karl Marx.

Superficial historians have tried to explain the most important phenomena of modern European history without giving serious consideration to the Jews. Mentioning only those outstanding Jews whom they could not possibly ignore, they never explained the real sources of their historical work: the particular character of Jewish thought and the particular influence of the Jewish situation. The Jews played a leading part in the two "international" organizations mentioned above. What the Jews contributed to the rise of Socialism is well known. What they did for the growth of Nationalism is hardly known. Socialism was supported in the middle of the 19th century by only a few Jews—mostly the creators or the leaders of the movement. Liberal Nationalism, on the other hand, was the prevailing idea among the Jewish masses in Europe.

Eduard von Hartmann came very near the truth when he said that the Jews were the dominating element in European Liberal parties, although he was wrong in his analysis of the causes of this undeniable fact. Jewish influence was the eternal flame which kept the national revolutionary movements from being extinguished whenever the raging waves of reaction swept over them. How many Jews were there in Italy around 1840? Not more than thirty thousand. Nevertheless,

Nordau could state authoritatively that "from every page of the history of the Risorgimento, Jewish names shine forth among the martyrs as well as among the heroes." Jews fought for the Poles against the Russians, they fought for the Hungarians against the Austrians, they fought for the Austrians when the latter tried to liberate themselves from the heavy yoke of reaction imposed by Metternich. It was a Jew, Adolf Fischhoff, who led the rioting masses in Vienna in 1848 and was the true inspirer of the liberal revolution in Austria at the time.

Siding always with the oppressed nations and supporting the idea of national liberation, the Jews exposed themselves courageously to the revenge of the oppressors. The prisons of Europe were filled with Jews, and Jewish faces were not an infrequent sight on the scaffolds. At the time of Nordau's birth, the Jews of his native Hungary had to pay with tremendous penalties for the services they rendered to the national movement in their country. The fate of the Polish Jews was no different.

But the most distinguished support of the national idea and the greatest ardor for self-sacrifice in its name were exhibited by the Jews of Germany. It was again a Jew, Johann Jacobi, who created the National Democratic Party in Germany, and who, when participating in a delegation to Friedrich Wilhelm IV, had the courage to cry out in font of the ruler: "Woe unto the King who does not hearken to the truth!" Although their number in the Berlin population did not exceed three percent, nine percent of those killed in the streets of Berlin, when the rioting masses encountered Friedrich Wilhelm's soldiers, were Jews. The Jews of Germany were among the first to lend an ear to the words of Fichte, the trumpet of German Nationalism. Without the names of Heine, Boerne, Samson, Lasker and Bamberger, it is impossible to understand not only the revolutionary movements in Germany in 1830 and 1848, but also the drive toward German unification.

The position of the Jews in this respect was, however, paradoxical. While fighting for the sovereignty of the national idea in Europe, they disowned and cast aside their own nationality. This paradox climaxed a fatal development of intrinsic factors in Jewish history. The National Assembly of France in 1789 agreed to grant the Jews equality of rights provided they renounced their own nationality. As a result Jews for the first time in their history repudiated their identity as a nation. During the following period of reaction, which robbed them of their newly-won rights, Jews tried to regain their lost emancipation by paying an additional price: they assisted other nationalities to nationhood. Devoid of any *Jewish* national idea, and not seeking any separate national future inside or outside of Europe, they were to a certain extent correct from the standpoint of their time. Had they not assisted with such bravery and devotion the European national movements, the equality of rights they sought would have never been achieved. It was an unavoidable compensation for their help, awarded them by the victorious national movements.

No sooner had their emancipation been granted than the pendulum swung back again. Anti-Jewish attacks were resumed with increased intensity. German Jews received their equality of rights in 1869. In the same year, Smolenskin, the forerunner of the national movement in Jewry, who lived in Vienna, felt and recorded the incendiary hatred for the Jews, manifested in renewed antisemitic propaganda. To the ancient historic causes of Jew-baiting, new ones were added.

Nationalism which had approached its goal by preaching equality and fraternity among nations, quickly deviated, in most European countries, from its path, and sank into a swamp of extreme national egotism. The idea of a national mission, postulating that every nation has a special task in world history, served at first to raise the depressed national spirit and to justify the trend toward national independence. But when the liberated nations became intoxicated by the excessive power of freedom, the mission-idea quickly degenerated into a mere feeling of superiority. The notion of equality thus forsaken, there was, of course, no place for fraternity.

The national states—created, as we have stressed, by the mutual assistance of all national movements in Europe—began to erect barriers of hatred, destined to deepen separation and competition. The war of 1914-1918 was a direct result of this development, but not its last phase. The last phase transformed the idea of superiority into the doctrine, openly preached, that "superior" nations had the *right to subjugate* "inferior" ones. Its culmination was the war of 1939.

There was also another development of the national idea which quickly became apparent. This one affected the internal state of the nation, without changing for the better its external relationships. Mazzini's slogan: "Don't speak of your rights, speak of your duties," was intended to intensify the will to self-sacrifice for the national cause, but gradually developed into a deterioration of individual rights as against the duties claimed by the national state. Instead of liberalism and democracy within the state, Mazzini would see later in his own Italy oppression and tyranny. To visualize the impression which this state of things would have made on the prophet of European Nationalism, one has only to recall his saying on another occasion: "I would prefer to see the Austrians returning to Italy rather than see the Italians slaves to their own brethren".

The Jews, who were always a distinct entity among the nations, were, of course, the first to be exposed to the attacks of mutilated nationalism. Separated by no frontiers, and living *within* the nations, they were the first victims of the idea of *racial superiority* which quickly effected their degradation. Undefended by any political power and lacking even a protective sympathy of the masses (who were virtually their enemies), they were the first prey to the new brutal system of internal tyranny. But the main factor which undermined their emancipation was, of course, the ever-existing hatred toward them, occasioned by their minority status in all countries.

Many Jews sensed, if they did not understand, the special complexity of the Jewish situation even before the transformation of the national idea took place. Some of them put their hopes in the future *disappearance of nationalism* and in the triumph of international socialism. Their hopes, however, were visionary. Socialism, whenever confronted with nationalism, surrendered, and the socialist movement, wherever it came to power, had to work along national lines. Disappointed in the possibilities of cosmopolitan socialism and understanding that the victorious national movements would never accept the Jews, one of the first leaders of Socialism, Moses Hess, came as early as 1862 to the conclusion that the Jew had only one road to salvation: to re-embrace his nation and establish his own state. Only few paid serious attention to his warning. History had to teach its lesson through fire and blood. Western as well as eastern European Jews had to try many byways before coming to the right highway. The three essential stages of this process—adherence to foreign nationalism, antagonism to every nationalism, turning to self-nationalism—respectively followed each other during the nineteenth century. Nowhere else was this so clearly evidenced as in the Jewry of the Germanic countries. The first stage may be symbolized here by the names of Heine and Boerne; the second—by Marx and Lassalle, the third—by Herzl and Nordau.

II. Character

"The character of a man is his fate", said Heraclitos. Is this true? Those who think that our character is determined by the occurrences of life, by environment and education, by all that is evidently so accidental, will surely believe that "the fate of a man determines his character." These two statements, although contradictory, are each valid in respect to different characters. A feeble, soft, pliable character is quickly changed by external influences and, like wax, is capable of any transformation when it collides with firmer substances. On the other hand, a strong, solid, rigid character stubbornly paves its own way through all obstacles, yielding to nothing but its own will, and, like steel, becomes harder and tenser with the strokes of the hammer— the strokes of life. Such, indeed, was the character of Max Nordau. It exemplified the statement of Heraclitos. It did determine his fate.

The adversities of life hammered on his being from the very beginning. He was born into a very poor family who could give him nothing but inestimable hereditary qualities and deep sympathy. His mother, an unusually clever and courageous woman, of a Russian Jewish family, bequeathed him the unshakable optimism of her strong nature. His father was a teacher, respected as a Hebrew grammarian and scholar. Although he numbered among his pupils children of well-known personalities (like Adolf Fischhoff of Vienna, the tribune of the Austrian revolution, mentioned above), he was so poor at the time of Nordau's birth that he was obliged to leave his confined wife in order to earn a few pennies. "He left beside her bed," as told by a family chronicle, "a piece of bread and a jug of water;" but once, when he came back depressed after his search, he was comforted when he found his newly born son lying beside his mother in promising peacefulness. This was his fifth child, and he could not see any difficulty in his sharing with another mouth the piece of bread which he, the father, could afford from time to time.

The pedagogue himself, when hungry, found consolation in writing Hebrew poems, dramas, or essays on Judaism. Some of these essays were published, but his poetry, in which he gave vent to his emotions and longing for beauty, never saw the light. Nobody took notice of his poetical works, or paid serious attention to his other writings. This, however, disturbed him little and did not shake his faith in his literary talent. He carefully folded his manuscripts and put them one after another into the drawer of his shabby table. He was sure that a day would come when he would find a reader, both worthy and appreciative.

The careworn dreamer was right. He eventually found a worthy reader who sincerely admired him throughout his life. When his little Simon,[1] twelve years old, accidentally found those manuscripts in the drawer, he read them with such great enthusiasm that he used to consider his father "the greatest writer who ever lived." Although Max

---

1 Nordau's first name before he changed it into Max

Nordau in later years modified his evaluation of his father's writings, he never ceased to consider him "a genius whose greatness was not acknowledged." Be that as it may, the writings of the pedagogue had a fruitful influence on the boy. After reading them, the twelve-year-old came to a decision which remained with him through life. He determined to be a writer.

This decision gave him more strength and self-confidence than even his talents, which quickly distinguished him from all his schoolmates. It counteracted all the hardships that confronted him. For was it not one of life's greatest ordeals that he had to go to school wearing a coat twice his size, bought as a bargain from an old clothes vendor; or a pair of shoes which were not mates and, moreover, were both right or left footed; or a hat which kept falling down his face? Were not the peals of laughter which those clothes provoked among his school mates the blows that made the deepest impression on him? Did they not hurt and greatly depress him? Hurt? Yes, of course. Depress? Not at all. Whenever he heard laughter behind him he would turn on his tormentors and fight against odds. This being his usual answer, his soul was never affected by humiliation, and his aggressive qualities continued to grow in the teeth of opposition. His sense of right and wrong became more acute, his will more resolute, his pluck more ready. From those days he acquired the invaluable courage to fight, if necessary, as one against many.

When he decided to be a writer, he took his task seriously. Before that, the stories or songs he wrote were a personal delight, or a means of distinguishing himself among his classmates. He still did not understand that all these expressions of his soul were but the first bubbling forth of a spring before it grows into a flowing stream. After that decision he began to look at his writings from a different angle. He compared them with literary works he read, and wondered whether his own works were worthy of publication.

They seemed to him, of course, quite perfect. One day, at the age of fourteen, he found himself bold enough to send one of his sketches to a newspaper.

He was not disappointed—his work was published. From that time on his name was often found in the local press of his home-town. He had, of course, to fight from time to time against discouragement engendered by severe editors. But if one compared his swift literary ascent to the trials of many other well-known writers (Emil Zola or Jack London, for example), he seemed very lucky. This luck was not a mere accident. It emanated from a talent which repeatedly revealed itself. It was a talent which did not require a connoisseur to recommend it. Nordau's style was too brilliant, his parables too striking, his ideas too original and too clear, to remain unnoticed. The fate of his father's writings, closed forever in a drawer, could never be shared by his manuscripts.

Two years later, when the sixteen year old Gymnasium pupil was a much-admired critic and reviewer, his writings provided him not only with spiritual, but also with material comfort. From then on, his pen supported his family, enabled him to continue his studies, to be graduated from various universities, and finally, to become independent. It was, indeed, in his profession as a writer that his character was most severely tested and proven. Although knowing that his whole future and even his immediate existence depended on his writings, he never yielded to, or even flattered, any public fashion or ideas of which he did not inwardly approve. Knowing cruel poverty with all its miseries, he never sold his pen for private benefit. If freedom of individuals, of nationalities and of humanity was the leading motive of his writings up to his dying day, it was first of all a result of the fact that his soul was never affected by any sign of moral servility. Although everything he could possess depended on public taste, he never catered to it. He obstinately retained his independence.

Nevertheless, his path led him upward quickly. It was, after all, the age of "liberalism in revolt", and bold, free spirits were acceptable. When eighteen, he was already a steady contributor of the *Pester Lloyd*, the largest paper in Hungary at the time. This was indeed a pinnacle which only few youngsters of his age would have dared to hope for. But in that year he entered the university, and another magic world was opened to him. It was the world of natural science and medicine, which never ceased to fascinate him. So strong was the lure of science, that several times in his life he sought to forsake literature altogether and dedicate himself exclusively to medicine. But each time, the power of literature held him back. As he could part neither with science nor with literature, his mind combined both of them in one vigorous attempt to inspire poetry with the aims of science, and science with the beauty of poetry.

Perhaps Goethe was the first modern writer who made this attempt and succeeded. After him, only few escaped failure in this arduous and complex task. Nordau was one of the few. His scientific books have the charm of attractive novels, his novels the clear-mindedness and analytical penetration of science. Moreover, in the unification of science and poetry he later saw one of the conditions of human happiness, an idea which appeared as the main theme of some of his books.

In 1863, he was sent by the *Pester Lloyd* to Vienna as its special correspondent for the World Exposition, which took place at that time. It was his first journey into the "great unknown world." His journalistic success as foreign correspondent carried him from Vienna to Berlin, Copenhagen, Stockholm, Paris, London and Madrid, and thence to the other side of Europe—Moscow. When the lad of twenty-two, who had just been graduated from the university, was sent for the first time to Vienna, the world appeared to him much more pleasant and far less corrupt than it actually was. Until then, he had lived in the realm of books and imagination rather than with people and earth-bound reality. The years of wandering, however, destroyed many of his illusions, bred dissatisfaction and deepened his critical faculty. Twice he left Budapest for those long cross-continental journeys, the result of which were two brilliant books, *From the Kremlin to the Alhambra* and *Truths from the Land of Milliards*.

These books gave him great publicity. But what was publicity to him? He returned to Budapest determined to stay there and satisfy himself with humble medical work. Did he feel that he had said all he had to say, or was he in possession of a great idea he felt powerless to express? There were, indeed, moments of hesitation, of disbelief in himself, of self-examination, characteristic of young sincere talents not yet sure of their own particular truth. The atmosphere of the great capitals of Europe, filled with conflicting ideas, with the miseries of the present and projects for the future, attracted him intensely. He knew that his place was there, and yet he stayed in Budapest. An extraordinary man, Herman Vamberi, an oriental scholar and an international diplomat who later played an important part in Herzl's diplomatic activities, was attracted by the astonishing abilities of the young man, as well as by his strong personality. Certain that Nordau was destined to greatness, he saved him from those moments of uncertainty, and furnished him with the final impetus for decisive action. In 1879, Nordau, encouraged by his friend, left Budapest forever.

He went to Paris.

III. Attack

In the year 1881, the entire German press announced the appearance of Nordau's new book *Paris in the Days of the Third Republic*. It was a sensational document, revealing appalling traits and events of corrupt Parisian life. The Germans were delighted, the French furious. The book struck a moral blow stronger than any they had received since the humiliating Battle of Sedan. This was not, however, Nordau's object. He was thoroughly misunderstood both by triumphant Germans and beaten French.

Paris was for him only an example. It was his first attempt to attack modern civilization—that contemporary world which seemed to him "an immense hospital ward,

the air filled with groans and lamentations, and every form of suffering twisting and turning on the beds." In *Paris in the Days of the Third Republic,* he only described the manifestations of the disease, emphasized with increased fervency its destructive results, and sought to lay bare its cause. He was sure that it was "the same in all countries, although its symptoms were characterized by various local names in different places, such as Nihilism, Fenianism, Socialism, Antisemitism." He came to the conclusion that all those movements, expressing deep dissatisfaction with the existing order of things, stemmed from the same root—"the perpetual conflict between the existing conditions of the world and our secret convictions." Having reached this conclusion, he next wrote *The Conventional Lies of Our Civilization.*

Hume, one of the most daring of thinkers, came after a systematic entertainment of doubts, to the conclusion that "truths which are pernicious to society will yield to errors which are salutary and advantageous." This idea could never be accepted by Nordau. There are no truths, thought he, which are pernicious to society; there are no errors which may be advantageous. The greatest mischief of society lies in the fact that truths, which seem to be pernicious, yield to errors, which seem to be beneficial. Our conscience will never approve of it, and the more we reveal the true nature of things, the more resolved will we be to destroy the social order based on conventional lies. As long as the foundations of society are rotten, nobody should wonder when deep cracks, in the form of rebellious movements, appear one after another and endanger its whole structure.

He was surprised to see that although science had made giant strides forward since the time of the eighteenth century philosophers, the institutions of society remained almost unaltered, and the revolutions of 1789, 1830, 1848 introduced but little change, despite the many sacrifices and immense bloodshed. Convinced, nevertheless, that the social edifice was undermined, he felt that one more big push would send the whole structure crashing to the ground.

The Conventional Lies of Our Civilization was to be the dynamo of that big push. One hundred and ten years after Rousseau, and thirty years after Marx had declared the doctrines of his First International, a single man again made the heroic effort to attack the whole system of society. Truly, the book was a trumpet of revolution. Edition after edition was disposed of. During the first twenty-five years after its appearance, 59 editions were sold out, and until the beginning of the Second World War—71. It was quickly translated into English, French, Italian, Swedish, Danish, Dutch, Spanish, Greek, Czech, Turkish, Hungarian, Russian, Japanese, and Chinese. The trumpet resounded all over the globe. The impression was tremendous. Several governments took steps against it. In Russia, the book was banned. In Austria, it was forbidden and publicly burned. The Pope denounced it most fervently.

It was a cruel book, too cruel indeed for the satiated Philistines of Western Europe in the 1880s. It mercilessly exposed all conventional lies in religion, monarchy, marriage, economics and the press, all the decayed parts of the social body, into which disease had penetrated. "Literature and art, philosophy and positive knowledge, politics and economy, all are affected by its taint." Its taint was Skepticism.

Carlyle called the skepticism of the earlier 18th century the "black plague". Nordau called the skepticism of his time the "malady of the generation." The skepticism of his time seemed to him much more dangerous than that of the 18th century. The earlier one was directed toward certain institutions and common beliefs of the past, whilst the later one was directed toward the possibilities of the future. Hence, the optimism which accompanied the skeptics of the 18th century and the pessimism which, like a black shadow, followed the skeptics of the end of the 19th century.

It was a destructive pessimism, which widened and deepened man's skeptical attitude toward everything. The skepticism of the 18th century had two fixed borders which kept it within bounds. These limits were science and morality. No limits existed for the skeptics of the 1880s. They not only attacked all fields of human creative power, but singled out science and morality as their chief targets. Nordau, who likewise attacked the institutions of society, defended with the most splendid vigor morality and science—the conscience and wisdom of civilization.

Mene, Tekel, Upharsin was the warning with which he started his *Conventional Lies*. He knew where skepticism accompanied by pessimism might lead. Either society would destroy them, or they would destroy society. These twin evils cannot long remain passive. They contain effervescent qualities which corrode the vitals of humanity. Contact with morals and science renders them even more destructive. In this cancerous soil there shoots up a malignant Sophistry that turns Skepticism into a *conviction* that right is wrong and wrong is right.

The sophists appeared, indeed. Their influence spread quickly with ever-increasing force. But every sophistic epoch has its corresponding Socrates. The Socratic type endeavors to reestablish the values whose certainty was shattered by skepticism and sophism. The Socrates of the 17th century was Descartes, the founder of modern philosophy, who endeavored to reconstruct the world which the skepticism of his time had destroyed. The answer to the skeptic philosophy of the 18th century was Kantianism. The Socratic type of the late 19th century skepticism was not a philosopher who was satisfied with "pure contemplation", but a far-sighted thinker who paved the way for his ideas in storm and gale. He was Max Nordau.

The author of *The Conventional Lies*, who continued to fight against the perverted phenomena of the age in a series of books, the most important of which were *Paradoxes* and *The Malady of the Century*, began to realize the difficulty of his fight. He had taken it upon himself to check the tide of the ocean. Was it possible? Whether possible or not, he deemed it his duty. Fearlessly, he prepared himself for the greatest combat of his life. Instead of attacking institutions, opinions, and general phenomena, he decided now to bear down upon living individuals, the idols of the age, the Sophists. He knew that it was a most dangerous task, that their multitudinous adherents and admirers would turn against him with the ferocity of wild beasts. Nevertheless, he concentrated on it for a long time, intending to attack them suddenly with all the crushing power of a giant. So appeared his *Degeneration*.

IV. Warning

Bernard Shaw describes the extraordinary result of Nordau's blow. He wrote that for several years "Nordau was master of the field, and the newspaper champions of Modern Literature and Art were on their knees before him, weeping and protesting their innocence." Moreover, even the majority of the worshipers of the idols were entirely overwhelmed, and, as Shaw further tells us, "counsel on the other side mostly threw up their briefs in consternation, and began to protest that they entirely agreed with Dr. Nordau, and that though they had perhaps dallied a little with Rossetti, Wagner, Ibsen, Tolstoy, Nietzsche and the rest of the degenerates before their true character had been exposed, yet they had never really approved of them." But "counsel on the other side" were really too hasty in their surrender. Several years later they repented. What had happened was clear. The tremendous knowledge, skill and eloquence, the incontradictable logic of the author subdued them momentarily. They did not and could not understand the book altogether. They considered it the work of a great critic, a formidable and dangerous adversary with all the resources of science at his command. They considered it the work of a physician or psychologist, a disciple of Charcot and Krafft-Ebing and Lombroso, his diagnosis difficult to trifle with. They certainly did not see the Socratic champion who foresaw a great catastrophe arising from the teachings of the Sophists. How could they, indeed? The prophecy was for coming generations. Today, we begin to understand it.

This, too, was a cruel book, cruel chiefly for those who were publicly analyzed, and therefore, much more annoying and disturbing than any of Nordau's other books. It was a fierce, ruthless attack which by the most drastic means sought to annihilate the influence exercised by the leading personages of the age. The attack was made because Nordau was certain of his unerring judgment, or, better, of his vision; because he was sure of the great danger to humanity the ideas of Nietzsche and Wagner and Tolstoy and all the rest. He could not be merciful. Too much was at stake.

Some critics assumed that Nordau was wrong when he used the operating knife of the surgeon in an attempt to analyze the mental constitution of geniuses. No doubt he was wrong. The secrets of the soul, especially of a soul endowed with powerful talents, cannot be easily revealed; surely not by means of its artistic expressions alone, nor through the general biography of the artist. But, although the method may be criticized, much of the content and the major aims, were, and remain, above criticism.

The hallmark of the 1890s, during which *Degeneration* appeared, was the "revaluation of all values." It was, however, a subterranean process; implicit in the age, but unnoticed by it. Nordau alone saw "one epoch of history unmistakably in its decline, and another announcing its approach." He heard "a sound of rending in every tradition," and he knew what it meant. It meant "a practical emancipation from traditional discipline, theoretically still in force. To the voluptuary it meant unbridled lewdness, the unchaining of the beast in man. To the withered heart of the egoist it meant disdain of all consideration for his fellow men, the trampling under foot of all barriers which enclosed brutal greed. To the condemner of the world it meant the shameless ascendancy of base impulses and motives. To the believer it meant the repudiation of dogma, the negation of a super-sensuous world. To the sensitive nature, yearning for esthetic thrills, it meant the vanishing of ideals in art." It meant that day was fading and night drawing near.

No one felt as he did the inner desires of the great multitudes of humanity surrounded by the falling darkness. He heard their questions: "What shall be considered good tomorrow—what shall be beautiful? What shall we believe in? What shall inspire us?" He understood their perplexity as well as its results: "Where a fool or a knave suddenly began to prophesy... there gathered a great concourse, crowding around him to seek in what he had wrought, as in oracles of the Pythia, some meaning to be divined and interpreted." Against these new Pythian oracles, against the new false prophets, who intensified the general menacing trend instead of checking it, he aimed all his arrows with the wrath of a prophet of truth. He was certain that unless their influence was shattered, "the morrow would not link itself with today"; there would come "the end of an established order which for thousands of years has satisfied logic, fettered depravity and in every art matured something of beauty." Were their influence not destroyed, the future would not bring the hoped-for brightness of day, but the "*dusk of the nations, in which all suns and all stars gradually wane, and mankind with all its institutions and creations perishes in the midst of a dying world.*"

His opponents could laugh at all this. They could say, as Bernard Shaw did, that "this theory of his is, at bottom, nothing but the familiar delusion...that the world is going to the dogs." Delusion? Of course. In 1895 neither Bernard Shaw, nor Georg Brandes, nor other famous critics who had to defend all those attacked by Nordau, could imagine that the world was going to the dogs. Even in 1912, when Shaw reprinted his anti-Nordau essay, he did not see it. Two years later, the human volcano erupted, and the fire started, then smoldered, until it again broke out with even greater vehemence. All that was hidden in the depths of the human soul was revealed at last. Is there any serious thinker who will say today that Nazism, or Communism as exemplified in Russia for a long period after coming to power, were basically ordinary political phenomena and not a result of a fundamental change of moral values, too? Is there any serious historian who will not properly define them as they were: "Revolutions of Nihilism"? But what were the origins of those Nihilistic revolutions which covered a great part of the civilized world with a black cloud of tyranny? Their origins were theories, new theories concerning morals and society, developed and maintained by thought and art in those days when Nordau sounded the warning in his *Degeneration*.

We cannot dwell upon this at length. Let us take, for example, two of the theories most sharply combated by Nordau: Tolstoism and Nietzscheism. They were complete opposites, absolutely different in sprit and origin, but both equally destructive of the accepted moral system. For Nietzsche the accepted system was the "morality of slaves", or the "Christian morality"; while for Tolstoy it was the reverse of Christianity. Both were sophists in the eyes of Nordau, and equally dangerous. Tolstoy's main ethical law: "Do not resist evil, and suffer wrong!" was understood by Nordau as the best refutation of Tolstoy's own doctrine that "the individual lives in order to do his fellow creatures good." Was not resistance to evil precisely the greatest good that one could do one's fellow man? In opposing this theory, the most vehement indignation effervesces in Nordau's words. "Do not resist evil" meant for him exactly what was embodied in it: delivering up society to everlasting tyranny. "Individuals with anti-social impulses would soon be in the majority if the healthy members did not subdue them and make it difficult for them to thrive." Moreover, "were they once to become the stronger," Nordau foretold, "society, and soon mankind itself, would of necessity be destined to destruction."

Those who know the history of how the Communists came to power realize that the soil of revolution was fertilized less by the theories of Marxism, which called certain groups to action, than by the passivity and mental depravity of the majority of the Russian intelligentsia. The latter were, to a great extent, affected by the moral teachings of Tolstoy as well as influenced by other parts of his theory which correspond to pure Communism. It is no accident that Tolstoy was the writer most publicized by communist Russian rulers. "Do not resist evil" was an excellent mental food with which to nourish the masses and make despotism safe. Not the artistic creations of the great Russian novelist were denounced by Nordau, as the critics thought, but those "thoughts the fruit of which was the system at once Materialistic, Pantheistic, Christian, Ascetic, Rousseauistic and Communistic of Leo Tolstoy."

Tolstoy's dictum not to resist evil was, however, less repulsive to Nordau than Nietzsche's exhortation to do evil consciously. While Tolstoy's theory left room for criminal inclinations, Nietzsche sanctified crime as the highest human value. "No injury, violence, exploitation, annihilation," said Nietzsche, "can in itself be a wrong, inasmuch as life operates in its fundamental functions." The fundamental functions of life are even opposed to virtues such as diligence, obedience, chastity, piety, justice. These are, according to Nietzsche, "for the most part pernicious to their possessors." Furthermore, "praise of virtues is praise of something... which deprives a man of his noblest egoism and of the power of the highest self protection." That Nietzsche's "noblest egoism" was nothing but mere bestial lust, and that his "self protection" meant nothing but barbaric forays against the less protected, was proved by Nordau undeniably.

He did not read Nietzsche through rose-colored spectacles. He paid no attention to some of his falsifying commentators. He read what Nietzsche himself preached: "There is no good and no evil. It is a superstition and an hereditary prejudice to cling to these artificial notions." He read: "I rejoice in great sins as my great consolation," and "wickedness is man's best strength." Seeing, therefore, that Nietzsche had "become the means of raising a mental pestilence," he found it necessary to refute his theory from the anthropological, historical, philological and biological points of view. He left no stone unturned, for he realized the great danger for humanity involved in Nietzsche's doctrines, culminating in his ideal of "a herd of blond beasts of prey, a race of conquerors and masters, with military organization."[2] In those days, who thought the realization of this "ideal" possible? Who realized its moral influence, its practical value? Neither the admirers nor the opponents of Nietzsche took his teachings seriously. The former thought they were fine words, the latter—empty. Nordau alone realized the significance of Nietzsche's words. He saw them for what they were: destroying flames eating at the pillars of civilization.

Today, we see the whole building in flames. We can see the "exultant monsters," so praised by Nietzsche, returning in the flesh from the "horrible train of murder, incendiarism, rapine, torture," which he had idealized. We see their leaders, too, carrying out in practice Nietzsche's formula: "He who comes on the scene violent in deed and demeanor… what has he to do with contracts?"

What we saw later, since the 1920s, Nordau emphatically predicted. Those whom he called degenerates spoke of "their future" as an era of progress and "true liberty." Nordau, however, was certain that if the Future was destined to be theirs, it would bury all the hopes of humanity, "They are not the future," he shouted with indignation, "but an immeasurably remote past. They are not progress, but the most appalling reaction. They are not liberty, but the most disgraceful slavery. They are not youth and the dawn, but the most exhausted senility, the starless winter night, the grave and corruption."

This is what Nordau foreboded and fought. This was the content of his assault on society in order to save society, which lasted for about fifteen years and culminated in his great warning named *"Degeneration"*. Should Mr. Shaw reread the book today (during the Second World War), he would surely understand its repeated denunciations of the theories of the Ego and the "enslavement of the people by a few stronger and more violent personalities."

---

2   Quoted from Nietzsche's *Genealogie der Moral* in *Degeneration*, p. 421, New York, 1895.

V. Nationalism

"Do you not see," asked Diderot in one of his letters, "that the anticipated judgment of posterity is the sole encouragement, the sole support, the sole consolation… of men in a thousand unhappy circumstances?" The consolation of Nordau in *his* agonies, occasioned by his bitter, uncompromising fight against the greatest authorities in the thought and art of his time, was surely not the judgment of posterity, but his own judgment—his firm conviction that he was fulfilling his duty to champion the truth. He acted not for the sake of the *judgment* of posterity, but for the sake of the *salvation* of posterity. The theories spurned by him in *Degeneration* were in his eyes like black clouds hovering in the distance, and he would probably not have considered them so dangerous, had he not felt the presence of a strong wind which might carry them across the skies until the whole civilized world would be covered with darkness.

That strong wind was the *Idea of Nationalism.*

That Nationalism is a legitimate manifestation of human nature was always admitted by Nordau. Though he criticized most of the institutions and theories of his time, he never said a word against the basic validity of the national idea. Among all the "conventional lies" he found in humanity, one idea was for him an unshakable truth. It was Nationalism. Those who tried to prove that Nationalism was an invention of modern politics, conceived by Napoleon III, for example, in order to create internal dissension in foreign countries, were for Nordau "incurable imbeciles". "National consciousness," he says in his *Paradoxes*, published in 1883, "is a phenomenon that occurs necessarily and as a matter of course when the development of the individual, as also of the race, has reached a certain point." To retard this phenomenon, or to prevent it, was for him "to change the heat of the sun in midsummer." Nothing was in his eyes so deeply rooted in human nature as the idea of Nationalism; nothing so elevated. The state is the end of human nature, said Aristotle. Not the state, but the national state, corrected the promulgators of nationalism in the 19th century. Max Nordau could surely be counted among them.

If those who considered nationalism, or rather the national state, a recent innovation, seemed "imbeciles" to him, so also did those who considered the national state a passing phase. The latter believed that humanity would arrive at a condition in which small independent communities would replace the great national states. "I would prefer to believe," says Nordau, "that the organic evolution of human beings will bring them some day to a point where…the molecular motion of the brain will be imparted directly to other brains by a kind of radiation or continuous transmission. I ascribe about the same degree of probability to this imaginary onward evolution from the national state into the independent community."

In the early Eighties, when Nordau wrote the above words, revolutionary nationalism was still disturbing the peace of Europe. There still were the Irish, the Czechs, the Poles and other races that fought for self-determination. But was not Greece independent? Was not Italy liberated? Had not Germany gained its unification? The main problems of European nationalism seemed to have been solved. Read the speeches of Gladstone, the mouthpiece of Liberalism, or the writings of Kautsky, the mouthpiece of Socialism; you will see that most of the troubles caused by nationalism are considered a matter of the past. Nordau was perhaps the only one of his time who clearly understood the drama of nationalism and could foretell its denouement. The great troubles of nationalism, thought he, were not *behind*, but *before* mankind's planned advances; they are not in the past, but in the future. Modern nationalism, as he understood it, was "the fifth act of the historical tragedy, which began to play at the time of the great migration of nations." Before that fifth and final act, there was a long intermission, but it could not continue for ever. Now, at last, "the curtain has risen," said Nordau, "and the catastrophe is approaching."

It was, he felt, "impossible for Europe to escape much longer a mighty and violent rending asunder of the different nationalities."

The inevitable result would be a terrific conflict, but the problem of nationality, the thought, had to and would be solved at any price. Unequivocally, he announced the fate of Europe: "Distress and bloodshed, many crimes and deeds of violence; peoples will rage against each other, and whole races will be pitilessly crushed out of existence; tragedies of exalted heroism will be played along with tragedies of human baseness; cowardly multitudes will allow themselves to be emasculated without resistance; armies of brave men will fall with glory in the combat." Only after paying this price will the objective be reached. And Nordau warns: "*It is not probable that the twentieth century will end without having witnessed the conclusion of this great historical drama.*"

The twentieth century, as we know, was entirely immersed in this drama. We are still in the midst of it, and the struggle for the rights of nations which, some believed, had ended by the last war (World War I), is now in its new, and probably not its last, round. But here we come to the main point. One should understand that the roots of World War II lay far beyond the limits of the national problem. They derived their vitality much more from the ideas Nordau fought in *Degeneration* than from the sources of Nationalism, expounded in *Paradoxes*. If the national idea, natural and healthy in itself, has been transformed into abnormal, this was due to its merging, in the late 19th century, with ideas of the Ego, the Superman, Racial Superiority, and the like. In 1883, when Nordau wrote his *Paradoxes*, he forecast the dangers of *natural* nationalism. Ten years later, when writing *Degeneration*, he could see the perils of *unnatural* nationalism. The future dangers of normal nationalism, thwarted in its aim of self-determination, could be summed up in one word: war. The dangers of abnormal nationalism meant for him not only war, but the complete overturn of society, the return to the age of barbarism, to wild deserts long forsaken by the civilized human race.

He would never say, like Sir Walter Bagehot, that "the conflict of nations is at first a main force in the improvement of nations." War, whether it resulted in victory or defeat, was always for Nordau one of the greatest misfortunes of humanity. Nevertheless, he was not a pacifist. He thought there *was*, after all, one kind of war that was justified, whatever its result might be. This was the war for national freedom and existence, for normal conditions of national development. He would surely not say, to cite Walter Bagehot again, that "martial merit is a token of real merit" and "the nation that wins is the nation that ought to win." He knew that the results of war are in very rare cases in harmony with justice and righteousness, and that history afforded many examples of nations who had "won" although they ought not. His only advice to weak and suppressed nations, for whom he fought throughout his life, was: Be strong! Martial merit is *not* a token of real merit, but in a world of violence and merciless struggle for power, one must be able to fight like a wolf, if one does not wish to be devoured like a sheep.

Nationalism, as we see, was for him the only true element in modern European civilization, the one thing worth fighting for, as well as the determining factor in the future of humanity. But what is Nationalism? Of course, he could not avoid thinking of its nature. He could find many answers to this question, which every serious thinker since the French Revolution, and even before it, had endeavored to answer. He could think, like Locke, that nationalism is determined by citizenship in a state, or like de Boneville, that it is a kind of modern religion, or like Rousseau, that it is the sentiment of a society with a common past and common aims, or like Buckle, that it is determined by country and climate. None of these answers were accepted by him. Nationalism, he thought, is determined by something else: "Language is what determines the nationality…This alone is what decides a man's relationship to a people." Was he influenced by Fichte, who also thought so, or by the "fight for languages" put up by the oppressed nations in Austria? Was he convinced by the many reasons with which he tried to prove this supposition? In any case, it was a statement which in the coming years he himself had to refute.

It was the statement of a Jew who considered himself a German, because the German language was at that time the language of his soul. Even ten years later, when he, the linguist par excellence, could speak a half dozen tongues with equal facility, he still wrote: "We Germans." The man, who was called by many of his opponents a "Cosmopolitan Jew," for whom German was neither his mother-tongue, nor his first cultural language (Hebrew was that); who in all his books spoke not to the German nation, but to the whole world; who felt the deepest feelings of antagonism toward all ideologies of pure Germanism, which he called Teutomania—this man still said: "We Germans." It was a cataract on his far-sighted eyes, caused by assimilation, which enveloped in darkness a most important part of his field of vision. A man like him could not suffer it long. It had to be removed. The growth of antisemitism proved to be the painful operation which removed that cataract forever.

VI. Antisemitism

The transformation of pure nationalism into exaggerated nationalism—already evident in the early eighties—manifested itself, as we have said, first of all in the attitude of the European nations toward the Jews. Antisemitism broke out like a plague and swept over one country after another. Almost at the same time there were pogroms in Russia, the Rohling trial in Austria, terrific anti-Jewish propaganda in Germany and France, and a blood-libel in Hungary. From the outrage of Tisza Eszlar in 1882 until the Dreyfus affair in 1895, the time of Nordau's assault on European civilization, antisemitism had grown rapidly and continually. Had Nordau ignored antisemitism, had he treated this problem with the usual cowardice of assimilated Jews, he would not have been that courageous fighter he always was. In truth, he could neither ignore nor avoid fighting antisemitism. He spoke of it with anger at the beginning of his *Conventional Lies* where he sharply attacked the persecution of the Jews in Russia and the antisemitic movement in Germany. It was for him, as we have seen, one of the symptoms of the general disease of the age. By indicating the causes of the universal malady, and especially by fighting against them, he thought he was fighting antisemitism, too. He was still of this opinion ten years later, when the pus created by the unhealed wound of antisemitism had penetrated deeply into the body of several European nations, especially Germany. In writing *Degeneration,* he had to devote a great part of the book to the antisemitic problem. The fierce assault he launched against Wagner was to a great extent the result of the latter's antisemitic inclinations and theories. Nordau came to the conclusion that antisemitism had originated in Germany, and was a result of the special German nature and conditions. He considered it a manifestation of German hysteria and "the most dangerous form of persecution-mania, in which the person, believing himself persecuted, becomes a savage persecutor capable of all crimes".[3] Whether this definition of antisemitism was right or wrong, relating it to one place, to Germany, was a mistake which he quickly had to acknowledge. Two years after those words were said, he could feel the same public "hysteria", or "persecution-mania", or, more simply, "antisemitism", expressed in the most brutal form in Paris at the time of the Dreyfus trial.

Being a Jew, he was, of course, personally affronted with Jewish hatred. This made an everlasting impression upon him. One of his encounters with antisemitism was related by his wife, Anna Nordau. In 1893 he went together with Stephany, a Christian friend, to Borkum, a seaside summer resort. When he sat down to have his lunch at the hotel, he found a letter near his plate. Without suspecting anything he opened it and read: "Jews are not wanted here." After lunch he showed the letter to Stephany, who was very much upset by it. On the following day he found another letter. This time he did not open it, but went to his room. From then on he found open and closed letters wherever he went. He acted as if he did not notice them, because he did not want to hurt his friend. But he could not stand it much longer.

---

3   *Degeneration,* p. 209.

Thicker letters were sent to him in prose and in verse. A real attack was launched against him. After ten days he decided to leave the place.

"This incident," Mrs. Nordau tells us, "was a great shock to him. He felt abhorrence toward all that surrounded him. He immediately went to Antwerp. Alone he roamed about the museums, writing to no one, speaking to no one for several days, keeping himself apart from the whole world."

These antisemitic encounters touched the most sensitive point of his soul: the feeling of honor. He could not be indifferent toward them. His mind was consumed by them. They taught him more than information on Jewish suffering received from any other source. And he had previously received a great deal of such information! In 1881, when visiting Berlin, he made the acquaintance of Dr. G. Lowenthal, who told him about the Russian pogroms which had taken place in that year, and also revealed to him the necessity of Jewish mass emigration from Eastern Europe. Those conversations with Dr. Lowenthal may have been the inspiration of the lines against antisemitism in *Conventional Lies*. Dr. Lowenthal became one of Nordau's closest friends, but with the years each went his own way—Nordau toward the solution of world problems, Lowenthal toward the solution of the problem of his own people.

Lowenthal was the man who, more than anyone else, was responsible for Baron de Hirsch's plans for easing Jewish distress in Russia by concentrated immigration to countries overseas. He headed Baron de Hirsch's delegation to Central and South America, seeking to obtain governmental permission for a great agricultural settlement of Jews. He finally succeeded in getting such a permit from the government of the Argentine, and Jewish settlement started there. He was the living spirit of that undertaking, and on every journey he made to the Argentine, he flooded Nordau with letters, relating his accomplishments and trying to win him over to his plans. There is no doubt that this man who resembled Herzl outwardly as well as in his great love for his people, gradually instilled in Nordau the will to participate in a common Jewish effort. Nordau admired him, wrote a poignant poem in his memory, but did not join him in any active way.

Dr. Lowenthal died in 1894. In the same year, on the fifth of October, Dreyfus was arrested. As a correspondent of the *Vossische Zeitung*, Nordau had to be present at all the hearings and witness the tragic scene of January 4, 1895, when Dreyfus was stripped of his colors. He was moved to his depths. When he came home he cried out: "This man is innocent! I have striking proof of it!" He began to realize what antisemitism meant.

Several months later, in July 1895, the Jewish correspondent of another German paper who had also witnessed the Dreyfus trial and been similarly shocked, came to Nordau with a proposition containing both a confession and a demand. It was Theodor Herzl, whom Nordau had known sine 1892. Herzl came to his friend with his plan for a Jewish State. Their conversations lasted three consecutive days. Herzl had to prove that what seemed like a fantastic dream was the only practical plan dictated by a long process of history; by past, present and future. Moreover, he had to receive an acknowledgment from Nordau, the well-known psychiatrist, that he was not insane, as he was claimed to be. When the conversations came to an end, Nordau stretched out his hands to his friend and said: "You may be mad, but if you are, I am as mad as you." He was the first man whom Herzl converted to Zionism.

VII. Zionism

"Zionism has given my life its aim and content," said Nordau. After fifteen years of continual attack on the institutions and ideas of the civilized world, after waving his sharp sword of criticism on all sides, he became at last aware of the fact that it was impossible to change the course of European development. Did not his sword hit a windmill? Did not his fight resemble that of Don Quixote? Did not the barbarous outbreak of antisemitism prove that Europe was incurable? Was he to make himself ridiculous by again sounding the warnings which he had repeated indefatigably for fifteen years? Indeed, what purpose could his life have now? Had he not seen the way to a great effort of salvation? At the most critical moment of his life, Zionism gave it a new aim and content.

But Zionism gave him something else. It gave him a higher viewpoint from which many things, formerly misty and vague, were now absolutely clear; he now realized, upon introspection, how false was his conception of himself. To his astonishment he discovered that he, who had denounced the whole world as sinking into lies, was himself sinking into the greatest of all lies: the lie of assimilation.

Now, knowing himself better, he likewise knew better what nationality meant. He was not a German, and never could be one, because nationality is not determined by language only, but by factors which are much more decisive; namely, origin and history. These factors determine the fate of every individual belonging to a nation, as they give him an inheritance which constitute the core of his individuality. In his drama *A Question of Honor*[4] he gave artistic expression to this new insight. Herzl, in his criticism of the play, summarized its thesis in these words: "A man can leave a political party, but not the nation to which he belongs." Only by intermarriage can a person uproot himself from a nation, and then only in so far as his descendants are concerned. His individuality, which is an extract and an example of the qualities of his nation, may then be lost in future generations, dominated by qualities of other nations. Quitting a nation is, therefore, even from a biological point of view, an act of suicide. It shows that the individual does not value his own special qualities. This is no doubt contrary to the first law of life, and is proof of a deep feeling of inferiority.

As with nationalism, so with antisemitism—he now understood it. He had deceived himself in defining it as a "German hysteria". If it was a hysteria, it was not only German, but a world hysteria. Wherever there were Jews, there was antisemitism. All the Jews of the world

---

4 The title of the English version of "Doktor Kohn."

were under its pressure. He had deceived himself also in regarding it as a recent phenomenon. It had followed the Jews like a shadow in all their wanderings, since they had become a people without a country. The recent development of the national idea in Europe and the new trends of thought had surely added fire to the old hatred. But here he discovered the most interesting thing of all: antisemitism in its renewed form was not merely a result of the general malady, but also a major cause of it. He could, therefore, best serve not only his nation, but also civilization as a whole by devoting himself to the annihilation of antisemitism.

The way was now clear. The object of antisemitism, the Jew, should be removed from the affected areas; the source—the abnormal situation of a nation without a country—should be closed up. The Jews should be taken out of Europe to a country of their own. This was their only salvation and it should be carried out *without delay*. Having returned to his people, he realized that the future development of European nationalism, which he had clearly foreseen, was threatening them with the gravest dangers. To remove the Jews as quickly as possible from the volcanic area now became the sacred task of his life. If they were not taken out, they would, he thought, be crushed among the tremendous struggling powers.

With this conception he came to the first Zionist Congress in Basle in 1897, and delivered the speech which even Ahad-Ha'am, the most critical man in Zionism, called "an oration of a prophet."

It was the first of his many speeches, which helped so effectively to make Zionism the greatest mass movement in modern Jewry. He spoke in Basel, in Vienna, in Berlin, in the Hague, in Paris and in London, everywhere with the same unparalleled logic, the same prophetic vision and enthusiasm, and with the same radiant talent and magnetic power. To the mental qualities with which his orations were permeated, his personality and appearance contributed not a little. His prematurely white hair which adorned a leonine head lent him the dignity of age, which was in full harmony with the ripe wisdom of his sayings. His hazel eyes, usually bright with a visionary fervor, could be, when aroused by resentment and anger, as forceful as two clenched fists. His voice, capable of all oratorical variations, often resounded like the blows of a hammer on rock. He was not tall, but when he raised his arms in moments of exaltation, it seemed as if he rose to soaring heights and elevated his audience with him.

He became the greatest apostle of Zionism, battling for it in many fields, always first in the most perilous fronts, always leading the attack on the strongholds of its opponents. But the more he fought for Zionism, the more he understood how serious was the Jewish illness. It was not only assimilation which had to be attacked. It was the whole conception of the Jewish position which had to be destroyed. He could now observe a new list of conventional lies, deeply rooted in the body of the Jewish people. There were the Reformers, who believed in the Jewish mission, appointing themselves teachers of humanity. There were the Orthodox who believed in redemption by Messianic miracle, content with total passivity and condemning every national effort toward self-emancipation. There were the Socialists who believed in solving the Jewish problem by social revolution. There were the Liberals, who closed their eyes and did not see that the day of liberalism was rapidly sinking. There were all these and many more. Indeed, all parties in Jewry had their respective conventional lies, all of which were based on the assumption that the continuation of Jewish life in dispersion is possible and even beneficial.

In 1897, the year during which the first Zionist Congress convened to take the first step toward the salvation of Jewry, antisemitism received its greatest push toward *its* objective—the annihilation of the Jews. The year that witnessed the Basle Congress, witnessed also the appearance of a book entitled *The Foundations of the Nineteenth Century*, by H. S. Chamberlain. This work endeavored to give a scientific basis to the idea of the inferiority of the Jewish race, as well as to that of the menace, which it supposedly constituted to humanity. H. S. Chamberlain was Wagner's best pupil. Thanks to his efforts, the anti-Jewish racial theory was systematically spread among the German masses until it became the law of the new Germany.

The new trend of antisemitism gave Nordau the best proof of his own and Herzl's doctrines that European Jewry was steadily approaching the horror of obliteration, and that except for Zionism, there was no salvation for Jewry. "Zionism must succeed," said Nordau, "for otherwise we shall die." But the efforts of Herzl to get a political basis for Zionism in Palestine could not succeed during the reign of the Turkish Sultans. Although convinced of the necessity for quick salvation, Herzl never compromised with the idea. He was never ready to support large scale immigration of Jews to Palestine without first obtaining the political security which he thought essential to its success. He was sure that the most important part of the work had been done. The solution of the Jewish problem, i.e., Zionism, had become a political factor known to all the powers of the world. Certain that the Turkish Empire would collapse in the coming war, he died with hopes that his people would regain their land at the first political opportunity. Nordau's attitude to the practical moves of Zionism was in complete harmony with Herzl's. It was, he felt, better to wait for the right opportunity, than to act hastily and fail. Those Zionists, who did not foresee the coming world events, did not have his patience. They insisted on immediate action. Nordau, like Herzl, had patience in abundance. He believed that the tide of Zionism must be taken at its flood, or all would be lost.

The revolution of the Young Turks in 1908, though it raised the hopes of many Zionists, made no impression upon him. He placed his hopes only on the collapse of Turkey during a World War of whose coming he was certain. Time and again after Herzl's death, he pronounced before Zionist gatherings his advice, summarized in his favorite phrase: "Be patient".

Just as the rapid expansion of the Zionist movement would have been impossible without Nordau's agitation, so many of Herzl's diplomatic activities and the achievements of the movement after Herzl's time were affected only through Nordau's assistance. Often when launching some new political enterprise, Herzl could feel the powerful influence of Nordau's name. He realized it even during his conversation with Plehve, the head of the Russian Ministry of the Interior, who could not conceal his respect for "the great philosopher Nordau." But in no instance was Nordau's influence of greater utility to Herzl than in his dealings with Herman Vamberi, the traveler and writer of international fame, who was, as has been mentioned, Nordau's friend of many years standing. This friendship had grown with the years and with Nordau's literary success. Herzl's audience with the Sultan Abdul-Hamid, a diplomatic coup which he used as a spring-board for later negotiations in London, would have been impossible without the intervention of Vamberi. Though nothing revealed Herzl's sagacity in handling people more than his dealings with Vamberi, it is clear that the personal friendship between the latter and Nordau first prompted Vamberi to serve the Zionist cause.

But Nordau's direct diplomatic activities were no less important. His conversations with Clemenceau started in their early years, when the latter was still forging ahead with his literary career, and Nordau, as a critic, encouraged him. This friendship was strengthened at the time of the Dreyfus affair, when Nordau was active in that small circle of zealots for justice led by Clemenceau, and when the Zionist movement was born. Nordau had several conversations with Clemenceau on Zionism, and there is no doubt that Nordau had a great share in inspiring Clemenceau with sincere admiration for Herzl and with sympathy for Zionist aspirations. These sympathies never died and were most manifest at the time of the Peace Conference, although Clemenceau's personal attitude toward Nordau changed for the worse as a result of slanderous accusations.

Unquestionably, more than any other man, with the exception of Herzl, Nordau was responsible for the fact that Zionism was accepted with such readiness by all diplomatic circles after the first World War. Only a collection of his numerous letters could reveal what Nordau did for the infusion of Zionism in the minds of leading personalities in politics and literature in almost every civilized country from the Argentine to Greece. His outspoken support of Jewish liberation was often considered an inseparable part of his audacious fight for liberty in general. In Greece, for example, he was revered as a national hero, because of his unceasing efforts on behalf of the Greek nation and the views he expressed regarding the Macedonian problem. Streets were named after him in Athens, Salonika and other cities. The Greek Government decorated him with the "Cross of the Holy Saviors." The Faculty of Law in Athens appointed him an honorary member. Greek enthusiasts came to Paris to see him almost in the manner of pilgrims. Venizelos, the Greek politician and revolutionary fighter, was one of his closest friends to his last day. Greek support for Zionist strivings followed naturally.

The outbreak of the war in 1914 brought havoc on Palestinian Jewry. Most of the Zionist settlers were Russian subjects and, consequently, were regarded as enemies throughout the Turkish Empire, Palestine included. When Italy, then still neutral, took over the Russian interests in the Holy Land, Nordau wrote to Luigi Luzzatti, the former Italian Prime Minister, and asked him to pay special attention to the Russian Jews in Palestine, who were facing persecution. Luzzatti replied that the necessary orders had been sent to the Italian ambassador in Constantinople. This step undoubtedly helped American diplomatic intervention to avert the complete ruin of Palestinian Jewry.

On the eve of the war, in 1913 and 1914, Nordau conversed with Pichon, then foreign Minister of France, and enlightened him on Zionist aspirations. Pichon was entirely won over. At the conclusion of their long talk Pichon said: "Your brilliant exposition has aroused great interest in me. It will not be forgotten and will be put before my successor, no matter who he may be."

The outbreak of the war forced Nordau, a subject of belligerent Austria, to leave France for Spain. Nevertheless, Pichon, again foreign Minister of France, remembered their talks, and at a grave moment for the Allies a dispatch was sent from the Quai d'Orsay to the French Commissioner in Egypt, Georges Picot, to consult with British officials there about the possibility of exploiting Zionism for the allied cause. Picot consulted Sykes, and so the matter was delivered to the British Government in London, which, in turn, started negotiations first with Leopold Greenberg, then with Gaster, and lastly with Weizmann, who represented the Zionist organization in England during the Balfour Declaration.

Nordau, who declined to accept the official leadership of Zionism, although that was Herzl's last emphatic wish, was always considered the unofficial head of the movement. In 1919, when the war was over, he was asked to come from Madrid to London, to discuss Zionist plans. He knew what had to be done: Zionism had to prepare itself for decisive action. Six hundred thousand Jews should be promptly taken out of the Ukraine, Poland and Rumania, not only to save them from murderous persecutions, but also to secure, through their immigration to Palestine, a Jewish hold on the country. He knew that once Jews became a majority there, the country would be theirs, and so they would save millions of their brethren by enabling them to enter Palestine. He also knew that Arab opposition, which he never doubted, would necessarily abate in the presence of the *fait accompli* of a Jewish majority. But Zionist leadership did not accept his plan. Nordau shouted with despair: "You delay our redemption for a hundred years, if not forever!"

This declaration of Nordau indicated the deep rift, which developed between the official Zionist leadership and Nordau. The worsening relationship still enabled Nordau to visit the Jewish communities of Scotland with a brilliant "call to arms," but the larger plan for his campaign in America was ultimately abandoned by hardships placed on its way by both the Zionist leadership and Nordau himself, who was finally impeded by his deteriorating health. Nordau was forced to retire to his home in Paris where he concentrated on his last work,

The Essence of Civilization, which he brought to the point of the last chapter.

I do not think I could give this article a more fitting ending than the one I gave my earlier study of Nordau. I shall present it here again, therefore, in its original form, without subjecting it to the slightest alteration:

> On his death-bed he said: "This is the end, the definite end, for I do not believe in the immorality of the soul." He did not believe in it, but he was destined for it. His soul became immortal, *his* name everlasting. In the history of most ancient, most tragic and most remarkable people he has a place of honor beside Herzl, his friend, and beside their great ancestors—the ancient prophets of Israel.

Israel Zangwill
Chapter 4

Born in London in 1864, Zangwill was a renown writer. His play, The Melting Pot, coined that phrase. Zangwill later became an advocate for Zionism. He died in 1926.

(the following was originally published in *Road to Freedom*, "Introduction" [Hebrew], Hoza'a Medinit, Tel Aviv, 1938)

I

Max Nordau, Herzl's first famous convert to Zionism, was also the first who offered Herzl incomparably useful council in the service of their cause. It was he who advised Herzl to go to England, and by giving him a letter of introduction to Zangwill, he provided him with both a foothold and a key to future political activity. There was, seemingly, a wondrous chain of coincidence here. For in 1895, the year Herzl drafted Nordau to his cause, a new edition of Nordau's book, *Degeneration*, appeared in English translation and Zangwill wrote a highly favorable article on it. In that same year, Nordau visited London and had the pleasure of meeting his new supportive critic; and a few months, perhaps only a few weeks later, he was already making use of their friendship to further the cause of Zionism. But set against the overwhelmingly incidental nature of history, this string of events hardly seems the product of happenstance. It was the shared beliefs of Herzl and Nordau that brought them together, and it was the spiritual tie between Nordau and Zangwill that brought the latter to speak highly of *Degeneration* and to seek the company of its author. Nordau once remarked that his bond with Herzl was a "friendship born of spirit and blood;" and the same can be said of the amity between Nordau and Zangwill, as well as subsequently between Zangwill and Herzl. And it is certainly not coincidence that these three individuals, who admired each other to their dying day, were the world's first Political Zionists.

Louis Zangwill, the brother of Israel Zangwill, drew a finely composed sketch of his brother's initial meeting with Herzl. It occurred on a cold November day, as violent storms were followed by a heavy fog that covered the streets of London. The two Zangwill brothers sat by a blazing fireplace in their house, in one of the most distant quarters of the city, as Herzl—later described by Zangwill as someone who had "saved and led thousands of men and women, lost in the fog of modern life"— wound his way to their home, through the damp, murky weather. His only encouragement lay in the letter in his pocket, which was written by the renowned author, known for his astuteness, who had recently renounced half of Europe's writers as a bunch of semi-lunatics, and, by endorsing Herzl, attested, at bare minimum, to his sanity. Indeed, had Zangwill rejected Herzl's idea, or refused to offer him any assistance whatsoever, it is likely that the foreign guest, who knew nobody in London and nobody in that city knew him, would have soon retraced his steps home.

But, it seems as if the inherent laws of chance demanded a different outcome: the first man with whom Herzl discussed Zionism on English soil was, by his nature and general outlook, a potential Zionist. Like Nordau, he was captivated by Herzl's idea. Moreover, the meeting of the two immediately became a galvanizing factor, and just as the first supporter—Nordau—brings Herzl to Zangwill, so Zangwill— the second supporter—carries the process further and brings Herzl into the heart of intellectual Anglo-Jewry. It is before them that Herzl reveals, in his first public speech, his rescue plan for the Jews, and it is in their newspaper—*The Jewish Chronicle*—that he first publishes his "Proposal to Solve the Jewish Question." Henceforth, this plan would not leave the pages of *The Jewish Chronicle*, which became a steadfast organ of expression for political Zionism.

At this stage Herzl wanted Zangwill only as a middleman, in order that he may afford him access to the top circles of Anglo-Jewry. It was in their hands—he thought, possibly correctly—that lay the key to a Jewish state. Although Herzl enlisted this group with only limited success, he did succeed in another matter of utmost importance: enlisting Zangwill himself. For Zangwill, until then unknown to Herzl and vice versa, had already reached a respected position in English literature. Although he had yet to reach the peak of his fame and influence, he was by then already well-known, and his books graced the bedside tables of Gladstone and Queen Victoria. Zangwill was a member of Jewry's intellectual elites, which Herzl wanted to recruit to his side no less than he wanted to bring on board Jewry's political and financial forces. His acquisition was a great success, especially since Nordau and Zangwill were the only reputed authors he managed to sway.

Just as he failed to enlist the Jewish barons (Hirsch and Rothschild) and the opinion shapers of Austria's Jewish press (Bacher and Benedikt), he similarly failed to convert the great authors who were of Jewish origin (Schnitzler and Brandes). Even the budding Jewish authors, who in time gained fame and influence, remained beyond his reach. Jacob Wasserman, whose works Herzl disliked because of what he considered their pathology, shunned Zionism; Stefan Zweig, whose talent Herzl was the first to recognize and publish, demurred as well. And the same reaction to Zionism applies to the writers of today like Franz Werfel, Ludwig, Maurois, or any of the oft-mentioned Jewish authors who have acquired international fame. It is clear that all of them (although Zweig gave a different reason) were touched with what Zangwill termed a "modern Jewish Marrano-ism"—inducing them, like the forced converts to Christianity of the past, to cloak their Jewish identity, or, to use Zangwill's phrase, "causing our famous members to see a profit to themselves in ignoring their origins." But we will not deal here with the phenomenon of the Jewish author who flees his Jewish identity, even though the Opera Platz bonfire in Berlin attests that he flees in vain. We must merely note the uniqueness of Nordau and Zangwill and take into account that while Nordau turned his back on Judaism before returning to it, Zangwill never left it.

We are touching upon a main trait of the man. Zangwill was the sole famous non Hebrew-writing Jewish author to place the Jewish Question and Jewish existence at the heart of his work. Browse through the volumes of his collected works and from each page of them blows a strong gust of Jewish idealism, arising from Judaism in all its splendor and disgrace, from its dreams of redemption which never realized, as from its tragedies which were all too real. In short, he unfurls before the Jewish and non-Jewish reader alike the great problems facing his people. But it seems that his Jewish preoccupation did not detract an iota from the standing which his literary talent brought him. For England took interest in his "Jewish" works and his "general" writings in equal measure. In America, where he was read in the original, he was regarded with profound respect. France and Germany followed suit, as did Japan, where they had a long run of his prototypically American, even prototypically Jewish, drama—*The Melting Pot*. Clearly, his talent, as noted, dictated this response. But it seems that even his talent was to a certain extent an expression of his Judaism, or to be precise: it adapted itself to the many needs—personal, national and universal—of his Jewish character.

Like Herzl and Nordau, he was multi-talented. He was a journalist and a publicist, author of novels and novellas, reviewer and essayist, poet and playwright. His pen, flashing with brilliance in each of the literary professions, turned like the edge of a sword, arousing the admiration of readers and reviewers. I will not speak here of the skill with which he described character, a sculptor's sure-handed art, melding his icy style with the inwardly burning "fire of sacred indignation." I will not speak here of the remarkable originality of his thought, his talent for analysis, his penetrating gaze, which, Nordau said, saw into the heart of things. Suffice it to say that he was a towering figure in both the fields of high literature and philosophy; that the most important societies and the most venerated literary and political clubs considered it a high honor to host him; and that he secured a top spot in the lofty world of English letters.

I should perhaps fortify this statement by mentioning that the great English writers of his time, from H.G Wells to Jerome K. Jerome, from Arthur Conan Doyle to George Bernard Shaw, regarded him with universal admiration, and to this I shall add that every English newspaper from the *Times* to the *Standard*, from the *Pall Mall Gazette* to the *Westminster Guardian* to the *Observer*, published unsparing praise for his works. When he wrote *Blind Children*, a volume of poetry, England's most important critics hailed him as "similar in many ways to the greatest modern poet of his race—Heine." When he wrote *The Melting Pot,* the papers proclaimed that "since the days of Walt Whitman no other man has given such an in-depth description of American life" and that "his humor is precious and unique, like that of Dickens." When he wrote *Plaster Saints,* a satire, it was acclaimed as "on a level with the best dramatic works of Brielle," the most caustic and famous French dramatist of his day. When he penned *Italian Fantasies,* a book of essays, he was equated to Montaigne; when he published *Without Prejudice,* a book of articles, the reviewers reached the conclusion that "he unites the expansive intelligence of George Meredith with the keen wit of Shaw." Indeed there were many who compared Zangwill to Shaw. Like Shaw, Zangwill was known throughout England as a man who could coin a brilliant phrase. But for all that Zangwill resembled Shaw, the two were rather different. For Shaw was an Irishman who assimilated among the English, while Zangwill was a Jewish nationalist who emphasized his affiliation to his people. His god was the one who had spoken to Moses at Mount Sinai, while Shaw worshipped Marx as a new materialist-idol. Therefore, if Shaw's aphorisms were paradoxes which seemed like facts, Zangwill's were facts that seemed like paradoxes. In that, too, he resembled Nordau.

II

If it's true that the first are not necessarily the best, then it's also true that in many instances, being the best does not guarantee being the first. It appears that in the case of Zionism, or to be precise, of political Zionism, its first proponents required not only extraordinary originality of thought and unlimited idealism, but also a new attitude toward all the phenomena of human society. Nordau, who judged all matters with strict rationality, rendering sacred ideas mere "conventional lies," somehow became an enthused admirer of an idea that contains a good measure of utopia. Of both he and Zangwill it must be asked: How did this come to be? For all plans or theories promising redemption to humanity were subjected to Zangwill's critical eye. Not one was exempted—save Zionism. Nordau's "conventional lies" were, to Zangwill, "organized hypocrisy," and Christianity, which influenced European culture as a whole and constitutes its basis, was to him a symbol of that hypocrisy. He was possessed of too keen a sense not to notice the many contradictions that exist between the ideas left over from the eighteenth century and, all the more so, from the ancient world, and the rapid development of societal, national and political structures of the modern period. It is no wonder that a man such as him wrote, as early as 1908, to Henrik Senkevich: "In place of the Germany of Goethe and Schiller, of Kant and Beethoven, there arises a Germany of blood and steel—militaristic and pagan."[1] It is also no wonder that a man like him examined the eternal laws of war and predicted, during the first World War the coming of a second. There is no other man who, duty-bound, fought as hard for peace, and, out of a recognition of reality, so strongly objected to pacifism.

I've noted elsewhere that Nordau turned his back on human society before calling on his people to follow suit. The same may be said of Zangwill. For one must note: He did not believe in European Humanism, which was at the root of European Jewry's Emancipation. He did not believe in Cosmopolitanism, the bedrock of Jewish assimilation. He did not believe in Socialism, the high hope of the Jews who doubted Emancipation under the rulers of the time. In short, he shared the same ideological framework as Nordau and Herzl, hence the unity of their approach to Zionism. For political Zionism is, first and foremost, a complete abandonment of all Diaspora-based delusions of utopia. It is a return to nature, but not in the sense of the well-known romantic ideal, but in the sense of serious regard for the laws of existence and wars of survival between peoples. And therefore, when Herzl came to

---

[1] Zangwill, *The War for the World*, 1916, pp.10-11

Zangwill, he found in him a believer not only in nationalism, but in ethnic origin—in that same idea which stirred the national recognition of the first modern Zionist: Hess.

"It was with considerable ease that I drew Nordau after me," Herzl noted after his first conversation with Nordau about Zionism. Zangwill followed similarly. And if they, responsible thinkers who examined every problem with more than ordinary thoroughness, so readily identified with a new idea, which was seen by almost everyone as merely a delusion, then it must have perfectly coincided with their already formulated worldview. It is clear they had toyed with the general idea of Zionism, but had failed to develop it to its conclusion. And if Herzl preceded them in formulating the idea consciously, they preceded Herzl in sensing the idea "unconsciously." In fact, before Herzl ever spoke to Nordau about Zionism, he once heard Nordau saying that if he only had Hirsch's millions, he would make himself king of the "Jewish state" in Argentina![2] Of course, we will never know how a great idea is born in a man's mind, because for the most part he himself does not know. How did Zionism take form in Herzl's mind? He pondered the matter again and again without ever arriving at a clear conclusion. Ostensibly, it was the Dreyfus trial, yet he also speculated whether a bottle of wine from the Jewish colonies in Palestine, which he once received from a relative, was its source. "It is possible that this bottle contains the Jewish state!" he remarked—a remark which is deep and wondrous indeed. And again let us remember the long introduction to this topic in his diaries and how he methodically traces his steps backwards.

Indeed, the greater the force of an idea that has conquered a man's mind, the deeper its roots linking it to his childhood. And if it is difficult to find in Herzl's Zionism the childhood influence of his parents, this influence is evident in each of the other founding fathers of Zionism. From his grandfather, who was a rabbi, Hess imbibed more than a fondness for the Bible and the Babylonian Talmud. Pinsker's father was a Hebrew scholar, with strong national feelings. Nordau's father was a Hebrew

---

2   Herzl, *Diaries* I, 1928, p.200

grammarian and poet and Nordau himself studied Hebrew until the fourteenth year of his life. Regarding Zangwill's father, it must be noted that before his son became a Zionist, he himself settled in Jerusalem.

At this point it is appropriate to consider another influential factor: dignity. The same sense of dignity that allowed Herzl to feel the degraded existence of the emancipated Jew and spurred Nordau to his side, also stirred Zangwill. Is it necessary to point out that dignity is nothing but the reflection of freedom? Like Herzl and Nordau, Zangwill, too, was a product of the Emancipation. If the primary effect of the Emancipation was, as Herzl said, to re-instill a political sense in the Jewish people, it was also assuredly a return to dignity. And if someone considered it fortuitous for Zionism that eastern European Jewry had not gained Emancipation, one should also remember that western Jewry, although it sank into assimilation, contributed to Zionism the political genius of the Jewish People. In any event, it was a total deviation from truth when Ahad Ha'am said that western Zionism was a result of antisemitic harassment, while the Zionism of *Hovevei Zion* stemmed from internal spiritual causes. The fact of the matter is that the movement of *Hovevei Zion* sprang from the pogroms of 1881. Pinsker, Lilienblum, and all the rest of its leaders came in its wake. On the other hand—those who formed political Zionism were not drawn to it by pogroms. They were drawn in mainly by spiritual causes, even if not the same ones that Ahad Ha'am talked about. Herzl, Nordau, and Zangwill were all emancipated Jews, and, as has been shown time and again, only someone who became free, only a Spartacus, could create a movement of emancipation in a people of slaves.

Zangwill, born in a London ghetto to a family of poor Jewish immigrants from Eastern Europe, could not avert his gaze from that ghetto. The exodus out of the ghetto, which also took Zangwill with it, failed to abolish its existence, due to a steady replenishing stream of poor Jewish immigrants from the East. But it was not the process of entry to the ghetto that worried Zangwill, but rather the process of leaving it. This happened, he astutely noted, not because the physical walls of the ghetto collapsed, but because the greater and more mighty wall which held it in place—the fiery wall of faith—had been razed. Was it possible to rebuild that wall of Jewish faith? This issue preoccupied Zangwill before he came to Zionism and would do so again towards the end of his days.

"The power of place is immense!" Zangwill writes in his essay on nationalism. The eighties and nineties of the 19th century represented the high tide of Anglo-Jewish patriotism, a tide strong enough to awaken Zangwill's deep anxieties about the future of Judaism. Herzl, based in Paris, where the Dreyfus trial raged, and in Vienna, where the Deckert[3] trial was held, knew that if the fiery wall of Jewish faith had fallen, it had been replaced by a wall of hate against the Jews. In the same year, 1893, that Zangwill wrote tragic tales about the old ghetto, Herzl writes the tragic drama about the Jews who are surrounded by a new ghetto wall, a social and spiritual wall worse than the old one. While Zangwill recognized that the departure from the old ghetto was necessary, Herzl already understood the same to be true of the new ghetto. But where to? Two more years had to pass before the lightning of the Dreyfus trial struck, and Herzl discovered the way out of both types of confinement.

III

Zangwill, like Herzl, was concerned with the Jewish ghetto before he became concerned with Zionism. In 1893, largely through Zangwill's influence, the Maccabi club, a circle of "artists and writers, poets and scholars" before whom Herzl gave his lecture on the Jewish Question, was founded. Zangwill sought to bring Judaism's leading lights together, those who were proud of the ancient ideals, to form a modern alternative to the old faith which had been destroyed. But the expansion of the club, which aspired to encompass the spiritual powers of Anglo-Jewry as a whole, came at the expense of some of the founders' original motives. The club members were not all birds of the same feather. Zangwill and

---
3   Dr. I.S. Block, *Memoirs*, II, 1930

Solomon stood in contrast to men like Lucien Wolf and Philip Magnus. Though they all aspired to advance the status of the Jew, this was to be within the framework of the British nation. Thus the Maccabi club members, who were meant to serve as symbols of Jewish patriotism, were for the most part devoted British patriots. It was typical that at roughly the same time that the club hosted Herzl, it also hosted Sir Saul Samuel, a Jew who already held several ministerial portfolios in Australia. Not one word concerning Jewish matters was mentioned at the Samuel party, and there was tremendous enthusiasm at Sir Saul's announcement: "I can promise you that the Australian colonies will be loyal to England to the last man, to the last shilling!"

It's important to recall that their chief argument against Zionism, which Herzl needed to counter, pertained to the relationship between English patriotism and Zionism. Undoubtedly, their English patriotism outweighed their Zionism. In view of this, it becomes clear why these "Maccabis" could not serve Zangwill as a model for Jewish revival. One need not stress that he, focused on the "ghetto", could not comprehend their excessive English patriotism and saw them leading a dual existence while imbued with a Marrano-like mentality. For before he had participated in the formation of the Maccabi club, he was among the founders of another association, "The Wandering Jew". Whoever saw the Jew as a wanderer could not see him as an English patriot, since someone who sees the Jew's tragedy in his endless wanderings could only aspire to the renewal of his deep link to the homeland—that which the historic Maccabis symbolized. If Zangwill did not attain that goal in the small English association, then he found it finally in the larger Zionist movement. Zionism was for him, as he said, "the end of the Marrano-like period and the revival of the Maccabi period."

It is impossible, to my mind, to comprehend Zangwill and his Zionist activity without paying attention to these matters. Zionism attracted Zangwill not because of its promise as an immigration center for certain Jews or its promise of cultural renaissance and economic prosperity. It seized him body and soul because the bright light of

Jewish independence beamed through the entire enterprise. "This independence, this liberty," he tells the opponents of Zionism, "which many nations have valued more than life itself, in whose name the Boers astonished humanity and our forefathers astonished the Romans—can it be nothing but an illusion? Can all of the human race be mistaken, and only you alone be sane?"[4] To him, freedom and liberty were the essence of Zionism, and their presence or absence were always the criteria by which he judged the goal and direction of any movement that sought redemption for the Jews. He was able to perceive the Jewish tragedy as a function, not of their enslavement, but as the absence of a thirst for freedom-above-all; not in their dire predicament, but in their inability to see a way out of it, even though it was as clear as daylight. "In our long period of wandering we have lost our political sense and love of independence; we have become blind as the fish that swim in the caves of Kentucky." And just as he saw the absence of those elements as the source of the Jewish catastrophe, so too, did he perceive their presence as the main condition for the success of Zionism. For Zionism's success or failure depended not on its ability to raise funds or such, but on whether love of independence, as well as political understanding, were present or absent. Here he saw the solution, and the problem.

He found these elements in Zionism, and therefore joined its ranks. But in all truth it should be noted that he was drawn in by the character of the movement's leadership, not its masses. "In Herzl," he said, "we've found our Disraeli!" Nonetheless, if his faith in the movement fell short of Herzl's during the early years, it stemmed from his dim view of the masses. "He did not know the Jews," he said of Herzl. But he, Zangwill, knew them well: He had delved too deeply into the messianic movement, particularly that of Shabtai Tzvi, to permit him not to fear that messianism and Zionism shared some of the same traits and that the two lacked maturity and political acuity. Certainly, those fears were not baseless. The masses were mostly former members of Hovevei Zion, a group he was well acquainted with and depicted in his *Children of the Ghetto* but refused to join. Hovevei Zion, which boasted

---

4   I. Zangwill, *The Road to Independence*, 1938, p.90

of its practicality and realism, was rife with the same kind of romantic delusion that defined the followers of Shabtai Tzvi. In fact, they showed even less logic than the dreamers of the 16th century. The latter had been sufficiently astute to recognize that redemption would not come under Turkish rule, and saw as a pre-condition the removal of the Sultan from his throne. They believed this will happen, because they believed in the divine power of the messiah. But this belief, in itself illogical, served, at the very least, as a logical basis for their plan of redemption. Hovevei Zion lacked even this basis. They even failed to notice that they had not pioneered their ideology of settlement: scarcely a century passed in which waves of Jewish immigration did not flow toward the gates of Palestine, only to be blocked and crushed time and again by the same elements that blocked the immigrations efforts of Hovevei Zion themselves.

Only his ever-growing respect and admiration for Herzl stirred in him the hope that the masses understood their leader's plan, even if he never rid himself of the feeling that their support was, as he wrote in *The Turkish Messiah,* a "plague of enthusiasm." Whereas Ahad Ha'am feared that the masses' enthusiasm would be disappointed and therefore cool, his fear was that their enthusiasm would cool and therefore disappoint. Ahad Ha'am believed that the movement's leader was unrealistic; Zangwill felt that to be true of the followers. Ahad Ha'am feared the masses would be disappointed by their leader; Zangwill feared the opposite. He saw the "terrible mud, which Herzl has to wade in up to his neck,"[5] and he wondered: "Can his soul endure all of this?" He knew Zionism's chief weak point, just as he knew its high point. For he was the one who, during Herzl's lifetime, uttered this very great remark: "It is not the mood of the Sultan which will decide the fate of Zionism, but the mood of Herzl!"[6] Indeed, his admiration for Herzl, his heartfelt concern for his well being and eager desire to ease his burden by creating a financial base for him that would free him from his work

---

5   Ibid, p.46
6   Ibid, p.66

in the *Neue Freie Presse,* were perhaps the deepest and most touching part of all of Zangwill's Zionist activity.

But his own actions were invaluable, and I cannot refrain from summarizing them now: no man, save Herzl, did as much to entrench Zionism in England and bind England to Zionism. I am passing over his Zionist public relations efforts within and without the Jewish people, I am passing over his great struggle with the Jewish Colonization Association to hand over "the millions without a plan to the plan that lacks millions"; I am passing over many other matters, in order to stress this one matter: Zangwill was the first to speak in a direct manner about Zionism to the upper circles of British politics. At the Article Club, where the rulers of Britain's financial and colonial affairs used to gather, and from which frequently sprang statements that served as the policy lines for the entire empire, Zangwill lectured in November 1901 on the future of Palestine from the perspective of Zionism and the Jewish Question. From then on, support for the idea spread, not only in the public but also in the government. The men attending those meetings— admirals and generals, ministers of the English colonies, Sirs, Lords and Viscounts, authors and men of renown (such as the African explorer Stanley)—were the spokes in the wheel of the English empire, and they were in regular contact with the leaders of the nation.

In fact, some of them were to hold important offices in the empire later on, during the time that the question of Palestine was being decided. It will suffice to say that among those present there was Hall Caine, a man who anointed Zangwill as "one of the brightest stars in the firmament of English letters," and repeatedly expressed—under the influence of Zangwill's speech—his great fondness for Zionism. He did so not only at the Article club meeting but also subsequently, at a meeting of the Maccabi club and on other occasions. This was the same Sir Thomas Hall Caine who played a major role in British public relations in the U.S. during the Great War [WWI]. Even the *Encyclopedia Britannica* notes that this campaign sought to rally America's Jews and, as such, was one of the reasons behind the issuance of the Balfour Declaration.

Sir Thomas's position on this pivotal matter is clear, as is Zangwill's role in shaping his stance.

For politics, like all other human matters, is but the fruit of ideas sown in that fertile field known as the soul of man. Policy borne of sudden invention is destined to a short life, as opposed to the approach that has taken deep root in human consciousness. It is clear therefore—and would be clear even without all the documents that provide proof—that it was during those years, and not a decade hence, that Herzl, Zangwill and Greenberg, in binding Zionism and Britain together, effectively produced the Balfour Declaration. Need I mention Lloyd George, a close acquaintance of Zangwill's from the start of his Zionist activity to the end of his days? Or Chamberlain, whose negotiations with Zangwill over a Jewish territory stirred such enthusiasm in him that he stood and said: "I will carry the thing out even if I have to break a wall down." Or for that matter Balfour, who himself admitted, in his introduction to Sokolov's book on Zionism, that he "became a Zionist while the government [he] led offered Uganda to the Zionists." Lord Robert Cecil was Zangwill's personal friend. Lord Landsdowne, who was Foreign Secretary at the time of the Uganda offer, held Zangwill in such high esteem that he voted in favor of the Balfour Declaration, even as Opposition leader. Churchill, one of the most influential men in the empire, wrote of Zangwill's letter to the *Times* in December 1905: "I concur with all my heart to the spirit of Mr. Zangwill's letter. I understand the noble aspiration of a scattered and beleaguered nation for a secure home of its own. Such a plan has spirit and it relies upon enthusiasm and forces, which no plan of individual settlement could put at its disposal. I do not suppose that it is possible to allow this noble vision which was unfurled before your eyes, to pass like a shade." Indeed, apart from the aforementioned there is a long list of names. For not merely in Herzl's day, but even, and especially after, his death, Zangwill steadfastly fixed the thoughts of British statesman to the need of solving the Jewish Question through the establishment of a Jewish state. Even in America, he was the first to obtain (in 1904) the formal consent of American policy makers to the Zionist solution: Theodore

Roosevelt, who attended the premiere of his play, *The Melting Pot,* and Hay, the US Secretary of State, gave him permission to publish a statement, in the name of the United States of America, in favor of Zionism.

"The center of gravity has shifted to England," Herzl wrote during his trip to England on that November day in 1895. The center of gravity remained there for the subsequent decades. And if it is not yet clear whether this was for the good or ill of Zionism, it is, at any rate, very much due to the man with whom Herzl first discussed his idea on English soil.

IV

"The last Zionist Congress," is what Zangwill termed the seventh congress; the one that forever pulled Uganda off the Zionist agenda. It may well not have been the final congress, even according to Zangwill's criteria, but it was the last one he attended. He created the territorialist movement—political Zionism's fiercest response to spiritual Zionism (of Ahad Ha-Am). Indeed, no man opposed spiritual Zionism as staunchly as Zangwill. He claimed, quite justifiably, that the Jewish people did not aspire to turn Jerusalem into a spiritual center, for Jerusalem had been a spiritual center for 1,800 years, and such it continued to be. If Judaism was not content just with that, it was because it had never aspired to spiritual centers like Mecca or Medina; rather, it longed to see Jerusalem as the capital of a great Jewish kingdom, because "Judaism requires a place of concentrated and concrete settlement and not a point hovering in mid-air." But, while Zangwill's opposition to spiritual Zionism is understandable, Ahad Ha'am's opposition to territorialism is not. For it is incomprehensible how this man—who was sure that the Land of Israel was incapable of solving the Jewish Question, who was sure that the majority of the Jewish people would remain in the Diaspora since to him, Palestine's absorption capacity was extremely limited[7]—could

---

7   See for instance his clear remarks on this point: *At the Crossroads*, II, p. 25-26

have allowed himself to interfere with a plan that strove to concentrate a fraction of the Jewish People in some place outside the Land of Israel, which was, to his mind, beyond reach at any rate.

But unlike Ahad Ha'am, who interpreted territorialism as a threat to the "spiritual Land of Israel", Zangwill felt the movement was of great aid to the *actual* Land of Israel. For Zangwill's territorialism was not borne of despair regarding the possibility of acquiring Palestine, nor was it a surrender of the notion of the Land of Israel, or a replacement for it. Anyone who believes that to be the case is either unfamiliar with Zangwill's writings or does not understand them. The Turkish government's refusal never led him to doubt the eventual acquisition of Palestine by the Jewish people. Just as the refusal failed to rattle his faith before the Uganda offer[8], thus it did not also in 1905, when he predicted a "council of the major powers, which will meet and decide to give us the Land of Israel." He saw the Uganda offer as more than an emergency shelter, a means of rescuing masses of Jews. To him, the offer held importance for the Land-of-Israel Zionism as well. He believed that "any Jewish territory, over which the Jewish flag will fly, shall serve as a lever, a school for experience in self government and a source of political influence for the future obtainment of Palestine."[9] Indeed today, as extreme antisemitism takes over one country after another, as the countries of refuge across the seas are closing themselves off to Jewish refugees or minimizing their influx to the most meager quantities, no man would hesitate to acknowledge the fact that the Jewish people in general, and Zionism in particular, would be immeasurably stronger had that plan, which was rejected by the Seventh Zionist Congress, been realized. And it is likewise certain that it would not have been to the detriment of Jewry if those masses of Jews, who today are tormented or threatened by the Nazis, were removed from the domain of German rule to become a politically independent force. In any event, Zangwill could not understand why Jews should remain in countries where they are subject to contempt and harassment, if they could find a land that would

---

8 Zangwill, *The Road to Independence*, p.53-54
9 Zangwill, Speeches, Articles and Letters, London, 1937, p.212

provide, at the very least, for a life with respect. Therefore, he said, "If a Jew tells you that he chooses to be born in Kishinev and not on Jewish soil and under a Jewish flag, he is nothing but a madman."

Those who railed against the Uganda offer claimed that Zangwill lacked vision, that he was too wrapped up in the narrow demands of the present and paid no mind to the eternal aspirations of the Jewish People and the existential conditions of the nation, while they, the true Zionists, acting out of the above, would wait patiently for the receipt of the Land of Israel in the future. In truth, as noted above, Zangwill's support for the Uganda plan took both the urgent needs of the Jewish People and the political aspirations to acquire the Land of Israel into account. But the "Comedy of Contradictions," which so often prevails in human affairs, showed itself in this matter too. If the majority of those who fought the Uganda offer were later prepared—whether in theory or in practice—to forfeit the greater part of the Land of Israel in the name of "urgent needs," why then was Zangwill forbidden to demand the receipt of a certain territory, which did not require any forfeiture of the Land of Israel, in the name of those very same needs—or, more accurately, in the name of far greater and more urgent needs? Today, they are willing to forfeit most of the Land of Israel in the hope of immigration for, at best, a million Jews, while the supporters of the Uganda offer were aiming at saving several millions. The offer, after all, came in response to the hardship of six million Jews who needed immediate rescue, and in whose name Herzl spoke before the royal commission in 1902 and, afterward, before Chamberlain and Lansdowne. Indeed, if they were to offer the Jews a plot of territory for autonomous settlement today, they would readily accept. But today the Jews are no longer offered a charter for Uganda, but rather private settlement without any rights in Kenya, or, worse and far more perilously, scattered settlement all over the world, which will bring about the spread of anti-Semitism to every corner of the earth.

Zangwill did not pay heed to the general opposition stirred up by the opponents of the Uganda offer. Even Nordau's stand, opposing the offer, did not budge him. He was certain that the Jews needed a safe haven immediately and that they would move there en masse at the first antisemitic attack. Today, no one could doubt that if conditions for Jewish immigration to that country had been established during the thirty years that passed between the Uganda offer (1903) and the rise of Hitler (1933), Jews would have moved to eastern Africa, just as they do now to South Africa. Certain that a free Jewish state would enhance the standing of Jews in the world, he also believed that it would buoy the spirits of Jewry as a whole. Did not even the Kuzari state raise the spirits of Hisdai Ibn Shaprut? And when did that occur? At the height of Spanish Jewry's Golden Age! Additionally, he was sure that anywhere Jews could live in political liberty, they would reveal their inherent talents. In any place where a great Jewish center would be founded, a beacon for all humanity would be established.

Even if the Jewish state were founded in the heart of Africa, the Jews, with their immense drive and thirst for action, would utilize the land's natural resources, develop the culture and upgrade transportation, and, from the heart of Africa, electric cables of Jewish genius would run to all the continents of the world. He was of the opinion that any place the Jews enjoyed political self-rule was liable to become a global focal point. And, therefore, he did not attribute great importance to the location of the land of refuge. He sent missions to Angola and Cyrenica and conducted negotiations over settlement in Australia and Canada. Moreover, he aspired to a land empty of white populations, because he was well acquainted with the central problem of settlement. And if such a country was not found for him, it was because other nations, not lacking a homeland, preceded the Jews in acquiring all available territories. Indeed, he was of the opinion that if the nations were fighting each other to realize their colonial ambitions, the Jews were also entitled to fight over their own unique colonial aims. If other people were willing to sacrifice considerable blood and treasure to gain territory, why should the Jews not accept territory, which was offered to them "for free" without a similar investment? He never doubted that the Jews would know how to keep such a territory should it fall into their hands.

He thought that just as the English defended Singapore with the same drive as they defended England, the Jews would defend that land, upon which they would revive themselves as a nation, even if it was not the Land of Israel.

The territorialist worldview was, as a matter of fact, a political view of Jewish immigration. Though the Jews were no different from other people in leaving for the Diaspora, they differed from them in the manner of their going. All nations migrate, but they aspire to lend their migration political form, an aspiration Jews never embraced. The Greeks migrated from ancient Hellas, but they founded independent Greek colonies ("New Greece"). The Phoenicians migrated from Tyre, but they founded the "New City" of Carthage. Behind all the migration of nations in the Middle Ages was a desire to seize control over the territories they settled in. That very purpose defined the modern migration of the English, French, Spaniards, Portuguese, Dutch, and Germans. The dissemination via settlements of all the nations was accompanied by the aspiration to power. Only the Jews migrated like a herd, never attempting to concentrate their efforts in a way that would lead to the acquisition of their own territory. Was Mordecai Emanuel Noah not a lone voice in the wilderness? For Zangwill, the concept was but a reversal of the usual process: other peoples, living in their homelands, immigrated to settlements; the Jews, who were not in their land, would proceed from a settlement to their homeland.

But would not the success of the Jews in some other territory lead to estrangement from the Land of Israel? Zangwill, who expressed his deep regard for the Land of Israel in inimitable lyrical poetry, would reply in the negative. All nations have their colonies and that does not stop them from loving their homelands. Moreover, when the Jews no linger live by the figurative rivers of Babylon, he said, they will recall Jerusalem more than ever, "because they will not need to hang up their harps again."[10] But what I want to stress particularly in his attitude to Uganda is: He never thought that a territory of 5,000 square miles,

---

10   Ibid, p.102

which was offered by the British government, would solve the question of Jewish immigration, or to put it another way, the question of the territorial-political concentration of the great Jewish nation. In his eyes Uganda was nothing but a first territorial foothold for a people, which required considerable territorial expansion. And therefore: just as he speaks in 1905 of the greater Land of Israel, which spreads from the Euphrates to the Nile,[11] so he stresses again, in 1919, that only a Land of Israel "on a broad scale, with room to expand, would be capable of solving these problems." In short: Zangwill's territorialism demanded a certain imperial inclination, or at the very least, a national-political-colonial inclination, which the Jewish People, then as now, lacked.

The English government backed away from the Uganda offer not only in light of the opposition of the local white population, but primarily because of the opposition of the Zionists. As late as 1906 the offer had not been completely taken off the table, and Balfour, a great British statesman who knew well that the annals of Europe, as it emerged from the Middle Ages, were nothing but a chronicle of colonial struggles, was perplexed at the refusal of a nation, which lacked "a single square acre of national land," to accept territory offered to it without a fight. But if rejection of the Uganda offer was, possibly, the result of a lack of political sense, it is likely that this lack of political sense did the Jews well. For to the great, frequently asked question about whether the Jews would have been successful in Uganda, there is no answer but this: they would have succeeded, had they been led by a strong political leadership; they would have failed, had they been led in the manner evident during the decades after the publication of the Balfour Declaration. Despite the fact that Herzl and Zangwill would not have started any settlement without firm political agreements, it is safe to assume that they would have faced obstacles. For the conquest of any land involves obstacles. And would the Jews of the Diaspora not have chosen leaders in their own image? And would they not then have been quick to forsake what they had been promised? If even in the Land of Israel, which the Jews transformed from a wilderness to a settled

---

11   Ibid, p.100-101

country, where they invested hundreds of millions of dollars, sacrificed fifty years of sweat and blood, they were ready to surrender most of the land after the first serious confrontation, it does not require a great deal of imagination to foretell how things would have turned out in Uganda!

It is possible that things would have turned out badly, indeed. But since national-political leadership was Zangwill's first condition for settlement of any kind, he could not take that reasoning into account. In any event, his great inner conviction told him that the path he had proposed was not only desirable, but also feasible. Since he truly believed this, he never changed his position. He was not a man of compromise. He never gave up on what he thought was true and never subordinated spiritual liberty to personal comfort. That explains why, as a boy, he rejected an offer from Lord Rothschild to study at his expense at Oxford, the same man who later did his bidding as president of the territorialist movement, to which he devoted ten grueling years. The fact that his movement encompassed only a tiny minority of Jewry did not weaken his resolve and did not deter him from forcefully fighting for his views. The words of Ibsen—"He is strongest who is most alone"—were often on his lips. Indeed he did not utter these words for naught. Years of utter isolation waited in the wings.

V

The outbreak of the World War led to a turning point in Zangwill's politics, focusing his attention on Palestine. But just as his territorialism was not a result of despair in implementing Zionism in the Land of Israel, his renewed Zionism was not borne of despair of territorialism. The ten years he devoted to territorialism did not serve as proof for him of its failure, just as the first twenty years of the Zionism, devoid of any real political gains until the publication of the Balfour Declaration, did not serve as proof of that mission's failure. True, he thought that the Jewish People should attempt to obtain another territory so long as Palestine remained under the Turkish government, since he was sure that the latter would persist in its refusal to hand that territory over to the Jews. But as soon as it seemed clear, based on objective conditions and his own political observations, that Turkish rule in Palestine might end, he redoubled his efforts to acquire Palestine. In his view, the right policy was, as Nordau defined it, the art of accommodation to circumstances coupled with complete faithfulness to the entirety of the mission.

If the reader bears in mind what was noted above regarding Zangwill's Zionist public relations activities in the wider circles of the British public, if he agrees also to what was stressed above, namely, that every methodical political approach emanates necessarily from spiritual wellsprings that preceded it in time, he will not be surprised to learn that the first man during the war to raise the idea of a rebirth of Palestine as a Jewish country was, in fact, an English author, and that he turned to the person the English tied most closely with Jewish nationalist aspirations. Several weeks after the outbreak of the World War (in November 1914), H.G. Wells addressed Zangwill with an open question, published in the *Daily Chronicle,* that contained but one short sentence: "Mr. Zangwill! Is it not the hour for the Jews to purchase and establish the real Judea?" Indeed, Zangwill sensed that the time had come. H.G Wells, the quintessential Englishman, knew that only through such a bold approach would it be possible to motivate Zangwill, the quintessential Jew, into recruiting the Jewish People to the side of the Allies; Zangwill clearly grasped the underlying meaning of the message, emphasizing in his answer that the establishment of the Jewish homeland could be realized if Great Britain comprehended the future benefits of such a move for itself and pried Palestine from Turkish hands.

In July 1915, Zangwill called for concentrating all Jewish soldiers fighting on the allied side into their own separate Jewish brigades. Even while this offer was only aimed at strengthening the position of the Jewish people when the terms of the peace would be drafted, the statesman in him, who was accustomed to thinking only in the category of *do ut des*, stressed that the "brigade would draw volunteers both on ethnic and motivational grounds," something which, at the time, had special importance for England and later served as one of the main causes of the creation of the Jewish Legions. Later that year, when Patterson sent him notification of the founding of a "legion of mule drivers," he wrote, in a reply that for some reason did not find favor with the military censor, that this legion would assist the establishment of a British patronage over a free Land of Israel. In December 1915, he spoke before a group of British public leaders on the "Jewish element in war and settlement," and aggressively defended the *Manchester Guardian's* view that "Britain will not be able to ensure appropriate protection for the Suez Canal as long as Palestine remains in enemy hands." Indeed, just as he tried to stir British public opinion to move the war to Palestine's front in order to free the country from Turkey, he likewise strove to hammer home the point that, in the name of British interests, Palestine would be handed over to the Jews and that this would be in any case a rightful reward for Jewish services to the Allies: "If, through its alliance with Russia, England will advance toward victory with the lives of Jewish Russian soldiers, then handing over Palestine to their race shall be a salve to its conscience and a promise to the oppressed Jews of Russia, that they did not fight and spill their blood in vain."[12] He repeats the same view in 1916. In his book *The War for the World*, which was published that year, he stresses that the granting of Palestine to the Jews would not be charity, but a payment for services rendered. In May 1917 he published an invaluable article in which he discusses the future of Palestine and the connection of Zionism with England with a certitude jolting even to those who believe in human clairvoyance.[13] In July of that year he brought the Territorialist Federation into collaboration with the Zionists, aware that Palestine was within reach and that the time had come to combine their forces. Six months later, on December 2, 1917, he stood on stage during the "Meeting of Thanksgiving," which, under the presidency of Lord Rothschild, expressed gratitude for the publication of the Balfour Declaration.

---

12   *The War for the World*, p.342
13   Zangwill, *The Voice of Jerusalem*, New York, 1921, pp. 96-98

Thus, he stubbornly scaled that hill that from its top one can view "the cape of good hope," the hope of a new Cyrus Declaration, and he succeeded in standing on its peak during the great days of the Balfour Declaration. But perched on the peak, he did not devote himself, as others, to euphoric self-satisfaction; rather anxiously, he looked with the responsibility of a statesman to the depths and obstacles that lay on either side of the knife-edge ridge, cognizant of how one misplaced step would squander all the efforts of the past and the hopes for the future. Indeed, the first man to bind Zionism and Britain together was also the first to warn Jews of their mode of behavior toward Britain. For the behavior of the Zionist leadership stirred real fears in him already in December 1917, and at that very "Meeting of Thanksgiving," he saw the first deviation from the proper course. It was clear to Zangwill that it would be of no use to Zionism for Jews to show an outpouring of gratitude for the generosity of Britain; instead they should regard the promise contained in the Balfour Declaration as something naturally theirs, deserved by right and until then perverted by tyranny.

Thus in December 1917 he saw fit to stress—and clash with the prevailing expressions of gratitude being heard at the time—that he was not "coming to the government with a bow and a scrape" but that he has long contended that "after the war which is waged in the name of freedom and the rights of smaller nations, they would have to give this compensation to this miserable, scattered and ravaged people, which shed blood and suffered alongside the combatant states."[14] And just as he warned the Jews to take a dignified stance in their negotiations with Britain, so too, did he warn them to adhere to the full aim of Zionism. "I will not devote my powers to anything," he said that same December 2, "that will contain any mockery of Jewish aspirations." And on that very occasion he defined those aspirations as "an independent national Jewish home." The reader who takes note of what was said above about Zangwill's Zionist approach, will realize that he could not have defined them in any other way.

---

14   *Speeches, Articles and Letters*, p.331

For just as he perceived the greatness of the moment that history had presented to the Jewish People, so too, did he dread the possibility that they would miss it through "lack of nerve and will-power."[15] He knew that Jewish settlement in Palestine was a most difficult undertaking, which could be brought to fruition only by a daring and imaginative policy that weighed matters on a grand scale. In contrast to all those Zionists who boasted about their "practicality" and "realism", Zangwill saw clearly that the main difficulty of Palestine stemmed from the presence of a alien population within the land, whose attitude towards the Jewish endeavor he did not for a moment doubt. He stressed this difficulty in 1905,[16] and again five years later in 1910,[17] and, more aggressively, five years hence in 1915,[18] when he demanded that the British grant Palestine to the Jews. This obstacle, never out of his sight, kept him riveted on the only solution that would remove it for good. Indeed, in 1917, as Zangwill publicly presented his plan, the great catch phrases regarding the new and equitable distribution of the territories of the world sprang up. In that same year Zangwill announced with unparalleled certainty, that the only solution to the difficulty posed by the Arabs lay in that same radical method he proposed and insisted upon in 1905, 1910 and 1915. Thus he suggested transferring the Arabs, in whom he saw an element that would never meld with the national and cultural persona of the Jews, that would always serve as a source of racial tensions, would always offer an excuse for foreign intervention— he suggested transferring them to Saudi Arabia, Iraq, and Syria; in any case, to remove them from the Land of Israel. He noted that the Jews would pay their travel expenses, the price of their property—as valued by a neutral government—and compensate land holders of all kinds. In short, he was certain that no price would be too dear to put this plan into motion.

---

15 *The Road to Independence*, p.300
16 Ibid, p.99-100
17 In his article "Zionism and Territorialism" which appeared in Fortnightly Review; compare: *The Voice of Jerusalem*, p.93
18 In his lecture before the Fabian Society; compare: *The War for the World* pp.318-342

Moreover, he demanded that negotiations on the very same basis be conducted with the German settlers there, so that they would also vacate the Land of Israel. Why? Because he was of the opinion that even if the Jews overwhelmingly outnumbered the non-Jewish population in their midst, the ethnic minority, here as elsewhere, would see the majority as its enemy. Those who read his essay on the principles of nationalities will see how much attention he paid to the eternal law of racial tensions, which lie at the root of all conflicts in modern and ancient nation-states. Truthfully, he thought a thriving nation was what he termed a "simple nation"—concentrated in one country, populated by only one race, sharing a single religion and language. Indeed, even if he believed that strong nations may overcome the presence of minorities, he saw this task as immeasurably difficult for a state not yet born and in the process of settlement. He knew that even the smallest minority can serve as a pretext for foreign intervention. And he, who always regarded Germans with deep antipathy, seemingly saw ahead of time what might become of this nest of German settlement in the Near East. Thus, he did not want any minorities in the Land of Israel; he did not want, as he said, to introduce "a spoonful of oil into a barrel of wine." Even the matter of the holy sites did not dissuade him. "The Holy Sepulchre," he declared firmly, "will be guarded by Jews who were baptized, and Omar Mosque—by Jews who've embraced Islam!" It was for him a matter of course that, for Jewish settlement to reach its goals without dangerous disturbances, Palestine had to be completely clear of all foreign elements and decidedly available for Jewish settlement alone.

In *The Social Contract*, Book One, Chapter 9, Rousseau wrote that if one of the nations of the world owns a tract of land greater than its requirements, it is completely just that another nation, lacking sufficient land for its existence, should seize this excess. Indeed, the Zionism which was taught about "national morality" by Ahad Ha'am—a morality which was not, as a matter of fact, anything but the fruit of Diaspora servility and which made no real distinction between "private morality" and "national morality"—did not justify Rousseau, just as it did not justify Zangwill. But Zangwill, who was accused of immoral goals by the Zionists, did not learn morality from those who turned "Jewish morality" to "Christian morality", which he always defined as "organized hypocrisy" since its essence was opposed to the fundamental laws of existence. Zangwill saw grave immorality not in transferring the Arabs of Palestine to the vast territories standing at their disposal, but rather in leaving them in Palestine and letting them take up the place of the most harassed, despondent race, which had not a piece of land in any part of the world. Not to clear Palestine for Jewish settlement seemed to him a grave misdeed—"to use modern democratic ideas about a population which has done nothing in Palestine—except for causing it to be desolate—and allow it to overwhelm the Jewish minority" and the hope of redemption for the Jewish People. He knew that this plan required the use of force, but he understood that the fulfillment of the Zionist plan with an Arab presence in the land would require immeasurably greater force, or, as he said, "the force of the British Empire, which will eventually take the form of bombs and gas." He knew that "one enforced action is better than endless friction and conflict, just as pulling a sick tooth is better than a neverending ache."[19] He warned the Jews against rosy-eyed delusions of "settlement through good will and mutual agreement," since it was clear to him that if a political plan is not based on force it is neither political nor planned. And he instructed the apprentices of ghetto morality that history had swept them up in a torrent towards the realms of a kingdom, from which they had long been absent—"the kingdom of power, which is the essence of national politics."[20]

But those who saw themselves as the guardians of morality also viewed themselves even more as the keepers of practicality and realism. Zangwill's plan was greeted with cries of "absurd!" and "this has no historical precedent whatsoever!" History though, which has witnessed the wanderings of free and defeated people alike, did not pay much mind to the Zionists' ridicule: the "unprecedented" was repeated in 1923, when more than a million Greeks were transferred from Turkey to Greece.

---

19 Ibid, p.189
20 Ibid, p. 265 and p. 294

Today, the notion is no less new. It is considered the simplest way to settle an ethnic and nationalistic struggle. Indeed the most astonishing thing is that those very same Zionists, who scorned Zangwill's plan, took seriously the proposal of the British Peel Committee to transfer 250,000 thousand Arabs, residents of the area offered as a Jewish state, to the domain of an Arab state. But—if it is possible to transfer 250,000 human beings from one country to another according to a methodical plan, why is it not possible to transfer in that very same manner another 350,000? And if the Peel Commission proposal came in order to clear a space for Jewish settlement in the narrow area set aside for it, it must be remembered that Zangwill justly saw the entire land of Palestine a none-too-broad absorption point for the vast emigration of the Jews, and recommended his policy on the grounds that the 600,000 Arabs settled in the land would, by their natural rate of reproduction and by the lands which they would be forced to keep in their possession, take up space of 2,000,000 additional Jews. If the royal commission's proposal was to prevent ethnic friction in the Jewish area, why then Zangwill spoke in the name of the same cause.

Today, August 11th 1938, as I write these lines, I happened to glance at the daily newspapers where I read that the *Pornai Courier*, the semi-formal organ of the Polish government and one of Poland's most important newspapers, sees a possible solution to the Palestine question only if the 600,000 Arabs living there are transferred to Arab territories and if the 500,000 Jews living in Arab lands, where they suffer torment, are transferred to Palestine. But it appears that even the Polish statesman who wrote these words understands that this desirable policy is not possible now, while the Land of Israel is gripped in the flames of rebellion. Indeed, even in 1923 Zangwill said: "The policy of expired rights which was possible at the time of the vast tragedy of the war, cannot possibly be recommended today." He was not as naive as the Zionists to take that policy seriously today, were he alive, since it would have been clear to him that it would require the use of too much force and might involve untold difficulties. He made his proposal while Palestine was in ruin, ravaged by war, with many of its residents on the run, while the land lay untreated, unappealing to Arabs; while the Arab nationalist movement was still in the early stages of formation, if at all, and the Arab race was grateful for being released from the yoke of the Turks, enjoying their newly bestowed territories and the promise of self-rule; and while the immensely powerful allied forces had complete control over the area—it was at that moment that he envisioned such a policy and felt it feasible, and it would have been so had the Zionists desired and demanded it, and the major powers, charged with enacting it, acquiesced. Today those circumstances no longer exist. Instead, the world is in turmoil, further fueled by each new disagreement. Since there has been a change in the situation, there needs to be a change in the proposals. But alas—the trouble with small politicians is that they always remember the old proposals, when the circumstances upon which they had been founded have long since disappeared.

Zangwill and Nordau were troubled by the very same issue, at the very same time: the need for a Jewish majority in Palestine. Both stressed the need to address the issue a *priori,* so that Zionism would not be endangered from the start. While Zangwill proposed to transfer the 600,000 Arabs in Palestine, Nordau sought to draw 600,000 thousand Jews to the land in one mass wave of immigration. He would have been satisfied with a Jewish majority, but Zangwill did not want even an Arab minority. Others saw this as a maximal demand; in his view it was a minimal condition.

VI

Zangwill's proposal for population transfer was, to him, an important factor in the success of Zionism, but it was not a critical factor which might cause the movement to flounder and fail. Indeed, the condition which he saw as a binding necessity for the realization of Zionism was the same one laid down by Herzl in his negotiations regarding Palestine, Sinai and Uganda and on which Zangwill insisted during negotiations for Cyrenica and Angola: Jewish rule over the land of settlement.

Hence, from the very moment that the Zionist leaders returned from the Peace Conference and brought with them what they had demanded, nearly nothing, when it became clear to Zangwill that Zionism had not insisted on rule over Palestine, had not, in fact, even included it among its demands—from that moment forth Zangwill waged war with the Zionist leadership. They had "renounced Zionism," he said, and "sabotaged" it, because they failed in fact to grasp its essence. He had been certain that the one thing the Zionist leadership would demand, the one thing they would fight for and insist on, would be a Jewish state in the Land of Israel. He was certain that they would do this not only by relying on the promise of the Balfour Declaration, but also by seeking compensation due the Jewish people for the sacrifice of hundreds of thousands of Jewish soldiers, who fought on all major fronts with the allies and as reward for the military and espionage services provided by the Jews in Palestine, as well as payment for the considerable diplomatic and public relations rendered on Britain's behalf by American Jewry. But those who spoke in the name of the Jewish People did not demand a Jewish state; in fact, they took pride in not having demanded it, heralding their stance as political shrewdness. If the shrewdness of this behavior eludes the reader, he should refer to Dr. Weizmann's own remarks. He accounted for his conduct by saying that had the Jews demanded a Jewish state, they would have been denied. Apparently he would have us believe that he secured the Jewish state by *not* asking for it. If this argumentation may seem perplexing, Dr. Weizmann's second reason is even more confounding. According to him, the Jews were not entitled to demand rule, because they were not capable of it. Trotsky, who once said to Passfield: "Whoever doesn't feel it within his power to rule, should not take rule into his hands" would possibly have seen this step of Dr. Weizmann's as clever and praiseworthy.

But if Weizmann felt that he, or the Zionist management on whose behalf he spoke, were not capable of ruling, he was not entitled to attribute this weakness to the entire Jewish People. He should have resigned this decisive role to people like Nordau or Zangwill, who believed in the power of the Jewish People to rule and would have demanded for their people, all 16 million of them, the same political rights that the Powers had allotted to the Lithuanians who number one and a half million, to the Finns who number not much more, and the remainder of the small and enslaved nations whose contribution to humanity was as naught compared to the massive contribution of the Jews. "Why that very same claim," cried Zangwill, "that the Jews are incapable of rule, was always claimed by the anti-Zionists, yet the Zionists still carried on with their project!"[21] And they did so because they believed in the power of the Jewish race to manage a state of its own, and it was on the shoulders of this belief that their plan to solve the Jewish question rested.

This was in any event a belief shared by Herzl, Nordau and Zangwill, and Zangwill was forced to prove to the Zionists what he had previously stressed to the non-Zionists: that the Jews were a nation capable of ruling and were even particularly gifted in this regard. "The race which gave birth to people such as Beaconsfield, Reading, Montague, Klotz, Eisner, Trotsky and formed a Zionist Congress even in the Diaspora—is incapable of political rule?" No. It was impossible for him to agree with the supposition that "Jews are not capable of doing what even the Eskimo do and what the illiterate Arabs are now going to do." He pointed out that "Hijaz, whose residents lack even a sense of private property, has been accepted as a member of the League of Nations," and in contrast pointed out the great Jewish administrators of domestic affairs, which even the greatest of empires—Britain—uses for its purposes. He pointed out the Jewish multitudes longing for a homeland, those being wiped out in the Ukraine and other areas where war was being waged at the time, who were ready to immigrate at the first call. Foremost, he pointed to the military, to those same hundreds of thousands of Jewish soldiers who were not long ago demobilized from the different fronts and were ready to enlist for the defense of the their own land. He pointed out the "Jewish General of genius Sir John Monash" who played an important role in the World War and because of whom one need not look any further for a Jewish governor of the

---

21   Ibid, p. 176

land.[22] "People, governors, administration—nothing is missing."[23] What was lacking? Political leadership, imbued with the understanding that one had to demand the essential element and insist upon it with steely determination; a movement which appreciated the opportunities offered by the current state of affairs; and loyalty to the great principles in which—and in which alone—Herzl believed lay the essence of Zionism.

Indeed, there was not another man in the Zionist movement, save Nordau, who was so immersed in Herzl's teachings and who understood them as fully as Zangwill. For what did Herzl say? How did he formulate the meaning of Zionism? He did so with exceeding clarity: "If I were permitted to express myself in the form of a paradox," Herzl wrote, "I would say that the land, which according to public law belongs to the Jewish People, but may be in its entirety allotted privately to non-Jews—that is the land which is the ultimate and permanent solution to the Jewish Question."[24] Herzl sought, therefore, a land which would belong to the Jewish People according to public law—where it would rule its territory and residents, with its treasures and real estate, even if private assets remained in non-Jewish hands. He aspired to *political* rule over a certain territory; that was the crux of his aspirations. Herzl understood that the fate of immigration and settlement depended on it, and that property would in any case switch hands as the Jewish population would expand. He was certain, as I have shown elsewhere, that Jewish settlement alone would not lead to the creation of Jewish rule, since the settlement itself would not be possible unless it were preceded by Jewish rule supporting it. Zangwill had understood this and therefore argued and declared at every opportunity: "Immigration cannot bring about the creation of a Jewish state unless the Jews take the management of affairs into their own hands from the first moment."[25]

"A minority will rule the majority!"—was his great cry. For he knew that if the Jewish minority did not rule the Arab majority, the Arab

---
22 Ibid, p. 210
23 Ibid, p. 210-211
24 Theodore Herzl, *Zionist Writings*, Mizpeh edition, 1934, p. 166
25 *The Road to Independence*, p. 191

majority would rule the Jewish minority, or—a possibility which seemed not much better to him—the British would rule Jews and Arabs alike. The Zionists, who chose the latter course, objected to his plan in the name of democracy. "And exactly how many Englishman will rule Palestine?" Zangwill asked in bitter irony. "The English, you see, do not pay any attention to the principle of democracy." Indeed, if the policy that relinquished the demand of self-rule was in his view short-sighted, then the emotional causes at its root were Zionism's greatest flaw. For the unrelenting efforts of the Zionists to prove to him that Jewish rule was immoral and the Jews incapable of using it illustrated something else: that the element of fear borne of the long Jewish existence in the Diaspora had crept also into the Zionist movement and that "twenty years of Zionism have not managed to revive the crushed sense of national pride." For he, who saw all Zionism as nothing but expression of longing for liberty and independence, who stressed time after time that "the Jewish ideal is not only 'Next Year in Jerusalem', but also 'Next Year to be Free Men'," could not gaze with equanimity at the fact that "while the Indians, the Egyptians and the Irish are competing with each other in their aspiration to doff the English yoke, the Jews are struggling, out of crazed enthusiasm, to put that yoke upon their necks."[26] The bitterest of surprises for him was to see how that same movement, which came to put an end to slavery and stir the Jewish power to action, was turning into a movement of subjugation *of their own accord*, hanging their hopes on the power of their masters.

Emerson wrote somewhere: "Our heroism stems from our weakness." And indeed what is heroism, but the effort of weakness to renounce itself? The Zionist leaders lacked this understanding. They thought that the weakness of the Jews obliged them to continue in the same vein for all eternity.

---

26   Ibid, p. 219

VII

Those who attribute significant value to the ideas that Zangwill opposed should remember that those who doubted the importance of Jewish rule also doubted the premise that the essence of Zionism was a Jewish state. The essence, for which Zionism was created, was distorted by other goals which had infiltrated the movement and began to bear their fruit as early as 1919. The Zionist movement's formal organ, *The World*, published articles that strained to prove that the essence of Zionism was not a Jewish state, but, rather, the movement of Jews to the East and so forth. In contrast—Zangwill's insistence on a state and self-rule were dubbed by Sokolov, "theatrical demands". But—Zangwill roared in anger—"I do not know a claim, which was said with more brazenness than this, which describes the very aim for which Zionism was formed as a theatrical object!" The same people attempted to prove that a Jewish state was not even Herzl's objective—offering the Basel plan, which did not refer to a Jewish state, but to a "safe haven", as proof. Nordau, who formulated this offering, had to speak up and proclaim that what they "meant by the Basel plan was a Jewish state and nothing else." These are the depths to which Zionism has sunk! But this alone did not suffice.

The same people who took the trouble to demonstrate that the meaning of Zionism was not a Jewish state, went to great lengths to prove, as if their very lives depended on it, that the Jews had not been promised their own state in the Balfour Declaration, and that they were therefore barred from voicing this claim at all. Zangwill had to undo one by one these self-perpetuating anti-Zionist arguments, dreamt up by Zionists. Indeed, he proved that although Weizmann never demanded a Jewish state, the Balfour Declaration had intended nothing but that. For the Declaration had not been given to Weizmann, but to the Jewish People, whose assistance the powers sought during World War I, and who, the Powers understood, lent them their strength and assistance in the hope that their eighteen-hundred-year-old dream of freedom would become a reality. In fact, during that very same year, when Ahad Ha'am took the trouble to prove that the Jews had been promised a national home in Palestine and not Palestine as a national home, Zangwill proved that Palestine had been promised to the Jews particularly as a national home, and that a change of phrasing, which had been made by the subtle cunning of the clerks of the Colonial Office, could not change the fact that the intent of the Balfour Declaration was that which a whole world understood, and which Britain's statesmen reinforced at every opportunity.

No man, he said, would make himself "ridiculous by thinking that even when the Jews return to their land they will have less liberty than the Negroes in their republic of Liberia."[27] And indeed, no man did think so. Britain's own statesmen did not think so. And if the reader opens up the state documents on the matter and reviews them, he will find immediately that what Britain's statesmen thought and what they promised to the Jewish People, one after the other, was—Palestine as a national home. It is possible to bring proofs of this not merely from the period of the Balfour Declaration, when British statesmen spoke clearly of a Jewish state, but even from the year 1920, after Arab opposition reared its head in the form of Jerusalem's first pogrom.

On July 12, 1920, there was a mass meeting held in the Albert Hall in London in honor of the inclusion of the Balfour Declaration in the peace treaty with Turkey and the promise of a British mandate over Palestine. The most senior statesmen and leaders of Britain sent their congratulations and public statements to this meeting, which Balfour himself attended. And what do they write in those statements? The Marquis of Elsberry writes: "I sent my blessing to the day on which the Jewish People will find itself raised up again in accordance with its claims for full rights of self rule and an independent country." Sir Martin Conway, MP, writes the following: "I look forward to the day, when Palestine, which shall be in the main part Jewish, shall serve as an important cultural centre and focal point of the Jewish forces, which are capable of making a highly valuable contribution to human civilization." William Graham wrote simply: "My best wishes for the success of your campaign," which will ensure the renaissance of "Palestine as a Jewish

---

27   Ibid, p. 175

national home." Lord Kinnaird wrote clearly that "Palestine (not part of Palestine, but the whole country) which was liberated from Turkish rule, is destined to be once more a national home for the Jews"; in the same vein MP Lieutenant-Colonel White wrote: "I fully understand the joy of those who have raised their eyes for so long to the day on which Palestine would once again be the Jewish national home." Mr. Neville Chamberlain, the same Chamberlain who later served as Prime Minister, did not hesitate to add in 1920 his own promise to the Jews, a promise that the investigation committees sent by the government he led, were charged with verifying. "I would like to express to you my admiration for the purpose of your assembly, which celebrates the granting of a British mandate over Palestine as a Jewish national home. I am pleased at the thought that the aspirations of the Jewish people, which so appealed to the feelings of my late father, have been fulfilled at last."

If I cite those remarks here, it is because I want to stress that Zangwill attributed extraordinary importance to the Jews' regard for the promises they had received, and because he became certain that the hour had come for the great public political battle for the fulfillment of those vows. Realizing that Palestine was still populated by Arabs, who had rapidly become passionate enemies of the Zionist endeavor; realizing that the Jews lacked any rule over the land; that Zionism was becoming what Lord Curzon, head of the Colonial Office (1920) wanted it to be: a tool for the development of the land in order to serve the needs of the British empire;[28] in short, since he saw in advance the anti-Zionist policy that was to be pursued in Palestine, he showed his people the only way in which they could change this policy for the good of their own goals. Indeed, just as he accused the Zionist leaders of giving up on the Zionist goal in so far as foreign relations are concerned, and just as he accused them of distorting this goal internally, so he accused them of being unskilled and unable to wage the Jewish People's difficult campaign. For they were, "sons of the Pale of Settlement, who have not

---

28   Lord Curzon's speech in the debate on Zionism, which was held in the House of Lords, is in my view one of the most important documents, accounting for the present fate of the movement. The reader may find it in the Jewish Chronicle dated VII.2.1920

been accustomed to the atmosphere of freedom and stand in fear and trembling before a foreign civil servant."[29] He declared that "they are like go-betweens, the groveling representatives of Judaism in the ghetto period," and that in truth, "they have not, from beginning to end, filled any but the most passive and worthless role of British political agents."[30] He saw both the disgrace of Zionism and its end "if it becomes the blind and obsequious agent of the powers that be."[31]

What, then, was the right path for the Jewish nation to follow? Zangwill defined this way clearly: "*Obsta principiis!*" "Oppose plans at their onset!"—he cried to the Jewish American Congress—"For if you do not oppose things from their beginning they will go from bad to worse." [32] True enough: the Jews did not voice opposition from the start, and the situation indeed worsened. The leaders of Zionism found it necessary to constantly blame the Jewish People for the reduced power of Zionism, because, in their view, the people did not respond satisfactorily to their financial demands. "They thought that the cure for all evils was in that very thing that is often thought to lie at the root of all evils." They forgot that in politics, when laying claim to a land, money takes merely fourth place in importance. Did Baron Rothschild's millions assure the Jews' rights in Palestine? The political path, mobilization of the masses, and the formulation of public opinion decide the fate of nations, the Jewish people included.

Obsta principiis! Zangwill saw the policy of capitulation leading directly to the loss of Zionism, its certain ruin. He declared, "The path of least-resistance leads nowhere" and that "this path is neither the course of true statesmanship, nor the highway to national rescue." But he knew that a firm and opinionated path was worthless without a readiness for sacrifice and effort. He saw a possible end to Zionism, not in the expected attacks from without, but in its having "lost its initial readiness for sacrifice and candor," in that its leaders and masses were immersed in a mood of peace-time when "the level of requirements that need to be

---

29 *The Road to Independence*, p. 220
30 Ibid, p. 218
31 Ibid, p. 298
32 Ibid, p. 316

laid upon every Jew even in peace-time is the level of requirements of the time of war." He saw that the hour had come, that Zionism needed to learn the well-worn route to national liberation travelled by other nations. He found it necessary to remind the Zionists that "Garibaldi did not offer his followers comfort and wealth, but suffering and death, and that behind the free Irish state was hidden the death throes of tens of thousands in torment." Although he recognized the Jewish People's capacity for sacrifice—"the Jews do not recoil before suffering and death any more than Garibaldi's followers recoiled before them"—he also knew that the great tragedy of the Jews was that those capacities had "never been dispensed in an effort made for saving the Jews and under Jewish leadership."[33]

"Zionism needs to rise to the heroic heights of our times!"—this was his great cry to Zionism. This was also his cry to the Jewish People. Yet Zangwill felt his voice was alone in the wilderness. Dispirited to the very core by Zionism's meager accomplishments and by his life's work, he decreed that "political Zionism was dead."[34] But the great question remained unanswered: "Do the Jews have to continue for another two thousand years under the shadow of the sword, prey for every outbreak of racial hooliganism, and nowhere will be heard the sound of the trumpet, betiding the buds of a brighter future?"—And since he saw clearly that the leaders of Zionism were not providing an answer to this question, since he saw clearly the future to be shaped by them—"a few hundred thousand Hebrew speakers in Palestine—which will be, possibly, an interesting episode and spectacle, but will not cause any radical change in the condition of the Jewish people," since he saw clearly that this endeavor which they were making "shall not result in the quantity of mass rescue, nor in the quality of independent political status"[35]—he began thinking anew about the ancient means of existence, which preserved his people in the darkness of the Middle Ages. For like Herzl and Nordau, he, too, saw that the Middle Ages were being renewed against the Jews in their global scope and their cruelty. And even in

---
33 Ibid, p. 284
34 Ibid, p. 301
35 Ibid, p. 227-228

1920 he declared with certainty, that "in all the countries of the world there is due to be a mighty outburst of antisemitism," and therefore, he took care to ensure for his people a defensive weapon in the dynamic war before which it stood. Thus he began to brood again over the revival of the Jewish religion, of "that same faith, which buoyed the spirits of our mothers at the hour when they leaped with their children into the fire, just not to hand them over to apostasy." He began to think over that same alternative to the ancient walls, over which he had brooded before Herzl and Zionism were known to him. He concluded in despair what he had begun in hope. "The hunter is back from the woods." The Eagle returned to its nest.

*****

Jerome K. Jerome said in his eulogy, on the thirtieth day after Zangwill's death, that he admired Zangwill the author no less than Zangwill the dreamer. But he protested against what Zangwill had written of Jesus, that "he died for the sake of dreams without knowing that even dreams die in the end." "But he was mistaken," said Jerome K. Jerome, "or at any rate impatient. Dreams do not ever die. They are the wandering souls of their owners, frequently visiting our thoughts. The 'lost idea' will once more find a redeemer. Somebody else's feet will trip upon it in its hiding place—God's trumpet in the dust of the earth!" How accurate are these remarks. "Dreams do not ever die." Such was the case for political Zionism. Herzl's great dream, to which Zangwill devoted the better part of his life, did not die. In 1923 it seemed to Zangwill that his words had gone up in smoke. But they did not. "The lost idea once more found a redeemer." And "God's trumpet, which rolled in the dust of the earth" is today in the brave hands of a new and young Jewish generation and from those hands it will not fall until the day independence comes for Israel—the independence dreamed of and fought for by the greatest dreamer of the ghetto—Israel Zangwill.

Ze'ev Jabotinsky
Chapter 5

Born in the Ukraine in 1880, Jabotinsky was a famed writer and Zionist orator, who during World War I created the Jewish Legion of the British army. Later, he formed and led the main Zionist oppositionist party, advocating active resistance to the anti-Zionist policies of the British government. Jabotinsky died in 1940.

(the following was originally published in a Haifa University publication, 1981)

I. The Rise of Resistance (1918-1922)

Ze'ev Jabotinsky was the last of the founding fathers of Israel's renewed statehood. He shared with his forerunners an appreciation of the importance of diplomatic activity, utilizing this method time and again to achieve breakthroughs in the advancement of Zionism. Similarly, like his predecessors, he recognized that the Jewish people would approach its end if there were not a sharp turn in the course of its life and if it did not gather and focus the remainder of its divided forces on national resurgence.

Nevertheless, he differed from his predecessors in one important matter. His main political activity commenced at the period meant to implement the realization of their ideas. But this implementation set a problem before the Zionist Organization that its leaders did not succeed in solving, thus endangering the future of the Jewish people. This was the background to Jabotinsky's work in the last eighteen years of his life. It aroused in the Zionist movement differences of opinion and flare-ups, which cooled only for short periods. In those years, Jabotinsky was almost constantly in the eye of the storm.

1. The First Clash

The problem just mentioned had to do with Britain's policy towards the Zionist movement, and it involved neither all of Britain as a monolith nor any single or fixed position. It was a wondrous combination of circumstances that, in the decisive years of the First World War, the British government which had risen to power was headed by David Lloyd George and Arthur James Balfour, who were called by the British diplomat Mark Sykes "the Uganda Zionists". He called them and some of their supporters by this name because their sympathy for Zionism had been formed in the period when Herzl was discussing a charter for Jewish settlement in Uganda with the British officials. Zionists of this kind, or close to them in spirit, included the distinguished journalists Charles P. Scott, editor of the *Manchester Guardian*, Henry Wickham Steed, foreign editor of the *Times*, and Herbert Sidebotham, to whom those two newspapers served as platforms for furthering the cause of Zionism. In 1916, Jabotinsky wrote: "Since 1903, when Chamberlain offered the Zionist Congress the opportunity to settle in Uganda, the Jewish people has had solid faith in British sympathy towards the Zionist program." A year later (1917), this faith was confirmed, and even gained new strength, by the publication of the Balfour Declaration and the formation of the Jewish Legion. The British "Uganda Zionists", we may add, had complete faith in the Jewish people. They believed in the Jews' capacity to renew their national life and in the Jews' future support for Britain. And they kept faith with Zionism.

However, there was another Britain. Zionism knew this Britain in the form of the military administration set up in Palestine by the General Staff of the British army that occupied Palestine in 1917-1918. This administration took an anti-Zionist stance from its first day, and quickly turned out to be antisemitic as well. Several of its officials were in fact extreme antisemites. Their anti-Jewish stance was strengthened by the recent Communist revolution in Russia, which had Jews in its leadership. We may assume that their newly bolstered antisemitism spurred these officials to further their anti-Zionist activity. Jabotinsky was aware of this and was deeply troubled, so much so that occasionally he came to doubt the wisdom of the "English orientation" that was underlying Zionist policy and which was to a great extent due to his own influence.

Jabotinsky would not have gone so far if he had not feared that the conduct of the military administration in Palestine might be a reflection of the attitude of the General Staff headed by General Allenby, and that this position was likely to be supported by influential political entities in Britain. In any event, in a letter that he wrote to Weizmann on 12 November 1918, while still an army officer, he cautiously avoided drawing a final conclusion on the matter. He made do with describing the attitude of the administration officials toward the Zionist movement, and in indicating the changes needed, in his opinion, in the process of appointing such officials. What characterized their attitude toward Zionism, he stated, was total disregard of the Balfour Declaration and the National Home program and contempt for the rights of Jews in the country (including the Hebrew language). On the opposite side, they displayed sympathy for the Arabs which was expressed, first of all, by appointing Arabs to the overwhelming majority of local administrative positions, as well as by using the Arabic language whenever addressing Palestine's population. This clear preference for the Arabs over the Jews, Jabotinsky pointed out, caused "the Arabs to interpret the situation in the only way it could be interpreted." Consequently, the Arabs' position changed "from resignation when they accepted the 'Declaration', to insolence when they gradually began to think that it was nothing but a mere 'promise'." He saw correction of the situation mainly in placing a "pro-Zionist" (Jew or non-Jew) at the head of the Palestine administration, in appointing Jewish advisors for every district governor, and in publishing a manifesto in the country that would confirm the promise of the National Home.

In his next letter to Weizmann, written about two weeks later, he defined "the general feeling of the Jews in Palestine as similar to the feeling of being in exile. They were admonished not to move to and fro, not to sing loudly, not to pass through the Jaffa Gate (in Jerusalem) or similar central places in large groups, and even to avoid joining processions of joy to mark the entry of the British into Jerusalem." As for the political aspect of it, "The Balfour Declaration", he stated, "is treated as a document not to be mentioned." While assigning direct guilt to the administration, he added a warning of what would happen.

> "If the Arabs try to initiate a pogrom", he said, "I would not place the responsibility for it on them. The responsibility for it will fall on those whose policy entices or—more than that—compels those who have a primitive mentality to believe that such acts will be treated indulgently or even be received favorably."

He rejected Weizmann's proposal to set up "an advisory body for Jewish affairs" instead of demanding direct Zionist supervision over the appointments of all leading officials. Likewise, he repeatedly stressed that, "if in the future, too, British officials ruling Palestine would be appointed without any Jewish supervision, this administration would undermine our settlement, deprive us of our rights, and harm our honor as it is doing now."

In a letter to Weizmann, written a month later (in December 1918), he presented the demand of the Provisional Committee of the Jews of Palestine (which was about to send delegates to the Peace Conference). Their demand was that, *"The Zionist Congress must supervise, through an undersecretary in the British government, appointments of members of the administration in the country"*—a demand that has Jabotinsky's stamp on it. However, no signs of action were seen on Weizmann's part in the suggested direction. He continued to disregard Jabotinsky's demand. Instead, he sent a series of proposals to the delegation of Palestine's Jews, which was to leave for the Paris peace conference, where it intended to submit its proposals. The first items on the list were that, "The administration in Palestine will be organized so that the country will become a *Jewish community under the trusteeship of*

Britain," and that "the Jews will take part in the administration in a way that will ensure achievement of this goal." These were, of course, general proposals regarding the future, without containing any answer to the problems that had been created by the existing administration.

Meanwhile, the situation in the country was going from bad to worse. On January 22, 1919, Jabotinsky wrote to Weizmann again: "48 hours do not pass without fiery speeches calling on the Arabs to wield the sword. The authorities in the country, by their behavior, openly hint to the Arabs that the administration does not intend to implement the [Balfour] Declaration. Your proposals are unsatisfactory, because they lack the most important thing: *the appointment of the Palestine government must be made in coordination with us.* I do not believe that this would be difficult to achieve. But even if they don't accede to this demand of ours, I believe that we will not be forgiven if we don't demand it. You seem to be declaring that you rely on the English to choose people who are sympathetic to us. You have no right to grant them a certificate of honesty when you well know that we are surrounded here by enemies and that the Foreign Office does not lift a finger to improve the situation."

Throughout 1919, it was difficult to discern any sign that Weizmann was acting in accordance with Jabotinsky's demand. Time after time, he proposed a substitute that Jabotinsky did not see as a suitable solution. Most likely, Weizmann's mode of action was that, when he considered a demand to have only a small chance of being fulfilled, he avoided making it. After Balfour had dismissed the head of the administration General Money, who had demanded to get rid of the Balfour Declaration, two governors came in his place. The second of these, Bols, was the worst of all. The atmosphere in the country was suffocating. On 12 March 1920, Jabotinsky wrote to Weizmann: "I don't know whether Allenby himself or his people want to destroy Zionism, but all of their deeds since the day that they entered Jerusalem have been directed at this goal. It seems to me that this strategy was born here and not in London (although it has already caught on in

London, too). I believe that most of public opinion in England still supports us, but it is necessary to bring Allenby and his policy into confrontation with this public opinion. And this must be done before he succeeds in misleading the whole public, as if all of England's difficulties derived from Zionism. Because this is the objective of his tactics." Jabotinsky concluded the letter with the warning: "There is an immediate danger of pogroms. This correspondence may be taking place on the eve of a terrible disaster."

Indeed, several weeks later, on April 4, 1920, the pogroms that Jabotinsky had all along foreseen finally broke out. In the same way as in Czarist Russia, the role of the government in planning the pogroms became obvious in the ban on bearing arms that was imposed on the Jews, in removing military forces from the area of the riots, and in refusing to allow members of the Jewish self-defense group to come to the aid of those attacked. However, nothing revealed the character of the government, its attitude toward the Jews, and its political intentions, as did the jailing of Jabotinsky, leader of the Jewish defense, and as did the sentence issued against him by the government judges: fifteen years in prison with hard labor.

The government officials believed that this sentence would strike a crippling blow against a man who vigorously and ceaselessly fought them and demanded their expulsion from the land. In fact, they had made a grave mistake which harmed themselves. Their hatred for the Jews caused them to lose judgment and refrain from thinking through about the possible results of their extreme measures. As Englishmen, ignorant of the Zionist movement, those results would have been difficult for them to comprehend. Indeed, what occurred was unexpected even to the Zionists, because it belonged to the kind of events that very seldom happen—the kind that suddenly transforms a people's stance and, as a result, causes a chain of reaction that creates a new historic situation. Jabotinsky's arrest and sentence created such a situation, transforming the anger and bitterness of the Jewish people over the pogroms in Jerusalem into a vast protest against the unjust regime that abused the Jews of Palestine and into a thundering demand for the release of Jabotinsky and the members of the defense league who were arrested with him. The facts were publicized in newspapers in Europe and the United States, particularly in the British press, whilst their significance became clearer from day to day. Such newspapers as the *Manchester Guardian* and *The Times* sharply attacked the British administration in Israel, while showering praise on Jabotinsky. And what was most important: the Jewish protesters were quickly joined by Jabotinsky's British admirers who embarrassed the government with numerous parliamentary questions. The government, in turn, delivered to Allenby a sharp criticism of the strange sentence, and he immediately announced a reduction of Jabotinsky's punishment (to one year!). This only exposed the corruption of the administration and intensified the demands for the immediate release of Jabotinsky and his fellow prisoners.

Even a quick survey of these developments indicates that they came as a natural response to the grave wrong done to Jabotinsky. Indeed, if Jabotinsky had not been included amongst the twenty defense league members arrested and sentenced, the protests over the pogroms and the sentence would not have gathered such strength and accelerated so quickly, until they became a kind of a avalanche. No organization could have produced anything like this protest movement. The force that brought about the release of Jabotinsky was Jabotinsky himself.

The Secret of the Revolution

What was it about Jabotinsky that the attack on him changed the Jewish community overnight from one accustomed to restraint and a bowing of the head in the face of humiliations, while suffering the blows of the taskmaster into a people rising up, defending its honor and rights? Indeed, some of its sons, if required to do so, were ready for an extreme response. There is no doubt that what caused the change, was, to a considerable extent, the admiration they held for Jabotinsky.

In no small measure, this esteem derived from Jabotinsky's resistance to the British administration over the two years of its rule and from his position as leader of the defense league and a prisoner of Acre. But, it is clear that the reverence for him could not have spread over such broad expanses and risen up to such a high peak, had it not rested on the prevailing admiration for Jabotinsky as creator of the Jewish Legions in WWI.

Indeed, no phenomenon like the Legion creation had ever appeared during the long years of Jewish existence in Exile, and we would need to go back in history 1300 years to find it even in the Jews' own land. The Jewish Legion that fought as part of the British armies to liberate the Land of Israel from Turkey reminds us of the Jewish legions fighting in 614 on the side of the Parthian armies to free Palestine from Byzantium. However, in order to properly evaluate Jabotinsky's achievement, we need to pay attention to the differences between the conditions in which the aforesaid phenomena were created. The Jewish army that fought on the Parthian side was established by the leadership of the Jews in Palestine, whereas the legion that Jabotinsky set up was created by him *as a private person* without any support from the Jewish leadership—indeed, despite its opposition. Likewise, the soldiers of the Legion were not recruited from among a people living in its own country, that aspired to regain its freedom, but from amongst fragments of the Jewish Diaspora in Britain, whose members at first vigorously and angrily opposed their very participation in the war. Out of these fragments, Jabotinsky created a legion which was intended to fight on the front in Palestine in support of the Jewish people's claim for a senior status in its ancient homeland. Who could have imagined that such a project could be brought off, and who but Jabotinsky could have done it?

The masses of Jews never properly understood how unique Jabotinsky's feat was, although they had a clear feeling that something special and extraordinary had been achieved. This fact alone was enough to produce widespread admiration for Jabotinsky. Yet, in reality, the admiration was also fed by Jabotinsky's outstanding abilities as an orator, writer and thinker—abilities that helped him clarify his positions on issues of diplomacy and settlement, and on matters of language, literature and history. All these factors turned Jabotinsky—as was stated by one of the labor movement organs in Palestine—into "a symbol for our hopes, our aspirations, and our demands," into a manifestation of "the national genius that cannot bend or surrender," and into a faithful expression of "the determined desire for revival and resurgence."

Weizmann's Reaction

Among the many declarations of this kind, the absence of any public reaction from Weizmann stood out. Finally, when his reaction came, it noticeably differed from all the others in its evaluation of Jabotinsky's endeavors, on one hand, and in its evaluation of the actions of those responsible for the pogroms, on the other.

It was on April 25, 1920, after the Conference of the Powers at San Remo had decided to incorporate the Balfour Declaration as part of the peace treaty with Turkey, that Weizmann first reacted to Jabotinsky's sentence and to the pogroms in Jerusalem, in an interview with the reporter for the *Manchester Guardian*. Perhaps no words reveal his ways of political reasoning and his way of defending Zionism as do the remarks he uttered in this interview. "The leaders of the Arab pogroms," he said, "openly boasted that they were aided in their actions by the British." Weizmann then stated that he *"doubted the correctness of this claim."* Weizmann was in Palestine at that time, he was in contact with the local Zionists' Delegates Committee and was aware of the facts that clearly attested to the assistance offered by the British to the pogromists. Nevertheless, he did not refrain from objecting to the claim of cooperation between the British and the Arabs. While "such an impression has been created," he added— merely an "impression"—he, Weizmann, could only "regret" the fact.

Speaking about Jabotinsky's trial, he described his actions as organizing "defense against *acts of repression that the authorities could not prevent.*" But had the defense league been created for the purpose of preventing "acts of repression" (subject to various interpretations), rather than for the purpose of preventing phenomena that from the outset were clearly *acts of murder, robbery, rape and looting*, acts that can be summed up in one word: *pogrom*? Here, too, he attempted to whitewash the administration of guilt for cooperating in the pogrom. But he not only expressed doubt about British guilt, but he also claimed that the Jewish defense had taken into account the possibility that the authorities *could not prevent the pogroms.* Did Weizmann really not know that the Jews had never doubted *the ability* of the authorities to prevent the pogroms, only their *willingness* to do so—although only a few must have actually imagined that the British would actually *assist* the pogromists to perpetrate their activities in the ways outlined above.

No less perplexing was Weizmann's reaction to the sentence pronounced on Jabotinsky—a reaction that was clearly in line with his statements about the pogroms. Although he criticized the sentence very harshly (defining it as "judicial murder"), he explained it as a product of a "weakness of vengeance seekers"—that is, as the reaction of people of weak character who couldn't tolerate the criticism which Jabotinsky hurled at them personally. Every Jewish leader in Palestine, however, clearly realized that British cooperation with the Arabs sprang not from Jabotinsky's criticism of the British officials, but the other way round—that his criticism stemmed from the behavior of those officials, which was demonstrably anti-Jewish. To justify, however, his strange explanation, Weizmann added a peculiar reason.

"There is no doubt," he said, "that Jabotinsky was *technically guilty.*" But this addition, with its admission of guilt, further mystified his argument. Consequently, Weizmann found it necessary to clarify the meaning of his claim, saying that "*if Jabotinsky was guilty of something*, his guilt was that of *political transgression* by organizing a means of defense." It is hard to believe that a leader of Zionism saw organizing defense against murderers and rapists not as a natural right but as a *political transgression*, and what is even more astounding: Weizmann—who was in Palestine during the pogrom, as mentioned above—knew that Jabotinsky had organized and led the defense not as a private individual, but at the request of the Zionist Delegates Committee. Therefore, if his action involved any guilt, it was shared by the Delegates Committee—a body which constituted the Zionist leadership in Palestine and whose members had been appointed by Weizmann himself. Indeed, if someone were to assume that the role played by the Delegates Committee's in Jabotinsky's actions were not known to Weizmann when he gave the interview, then he could no longer assume so after Jabotinsky had presented to the Military Council in London a demand for abolition of the sentences pronounced on himself and his comrades. In that demand, Jabotinsky indicated that he had not acted as a private person, but at the request of the Delegates Committee, and on these grounds, he viewed it as appropriate to request the Zionist Organization that it reimburse him of the expenses involved in presenting his case to the Military Council. But Weizmann did not allow the Zionist Organization to pay these expenses. Could this merely be a result of personal attitude of Weizmann, or was it another manifestation of his policy? No one can say for sure. Perhaps Weizmann was not certain that the sentence would be cancelled, and he did not want the Zionist Organization, of which he was the leader, to assist a person whom a high British judicial body might find guilty of improper conduct towards Great Britain.

We don't know how Jabotinsky reacted to the refusal of his request. But there is no doubt that he understood the degree of unfairness that Weizmann demonstrated towards him in that refusal. Nevertheless, we do not have any sign that this influenced his attitude toward Weizmann. It is nearly certain that he behaved in this case according to the rule of *pulchrum ignoscere* (it is more fitting to ignore). This is because Weizmann's diplomatic talents and his capability for benefiting Zionism were immeasurably more important to Jabotinsky than the flaws he found in Weizmann's conduct—*if only Weizmann would agree to use his strength in other ways than those in which he was using them.*

2. The Trial that Failed

Apparently, Jabotinsky secretly hoped that such a change would take place—and it seems that at the same time, Weizmann was also ready for close cooperation with Jabotinsky. At any rate, it is clear that he needed his help. He believed that Jabotinsky, with his talent for agitation and the widespread admiration for him amongst the people, could help considerably in raising the huge funds that would be needed for sustaining the institutions of the Jewish community in Palestine, and for laying the foundations for a program of settlement by Jews, which Weizmann sought to begin. However, Jabotinsky agreed to this proposal only on condition that Weizmann would be obligated actively to work towards achieving the following two goals: the appointment of district governors for Palestine in agreement with a Zionist body, and setting up a Jewish military presence throughout the country. Without the government's assent to these demands, it was clear to him, peace and security would not be obtained, and waves of Jewish settlers would repeatedly be smashed, time after time, on the rocks placed by the opponents of Zionism. Weizmann agreed to Jabotinsky's demands and promised to act with all his might to implement them. He even set up an inner commission which would deal with all high-level political matters (it would include Weizmann himself, Sokolov, and Jabotinsky), and as a member of this triumvirate, Jabotinsky helped Weizmann a great deal in all areas of diplomatic activity, as well as with the public campaign for raising the required funds. It seemed to him that Weizmann was starting on a new road. Weizmann was rather firm in everything relating to obtaining a suitable wording of the Mandate, as well as in the negotiations he conducted with the British over the northern border of Palestine. These were the major matters that his diplomatic activity revolved around at the time. Yet, he acted forcefully on these matters only as long as it seemed to him that he had the support of Lloyd George. As to the issues that formed the basis of his accord with Jabotinsky, Weizmann treated them from the beginning in an offhanded manner and eventually cast them altogether aside.

Weizmann did not do so because he differed with Jabotinsky over the importance of these issues. There is no doubt that he believed in the two goals that he had undertaken to achieve. But he must have retreated from his commitment because he believed that working for them in those times might severely weaken his political work. His method of activity was based on four principles from which he was not ready to deviate.

Weizmann's Policy

These principles guided him throughout from the beginning of his diplomatic activity to the end of his life, and they can be briefly summed up as follows: 1) abstention from demands to the government of Britain which had, in his opinion, a minimal chance of being accepted; 2) abstention from public criticism of the actions of ministers or high officials, even when these actions seem to him clearly harmful or destructive to Zionist goals; 3) the negotiations with government representatives must be conducted by way of personal persuasion alone, and therefore, it is necessary to avoid presenting demands that have no chance of acceptance in this manner; and lastly, 4) in any situation in which he might find himself during his talks—whether in agreement or in a difference of opinion—he must appear as a loyal friend of Britain, who understands its problems and is considerate of its interests. Weizmann was opposed to Jabotinsky's opinion that it was necessary not to accept a refusal by the British government as final, that it was indeed necessary to insist forcefully on vital Zionist demands, and if need be, even to fight for them openly.

Weizmann's method became doubtlessly set in his mind under the influence of his first experiences. He knew that this method that he advocated carried him this far, i.e., to a status of esteem amongst the British statesmen to which Weizmann ascribed the greatest importance. It probably never crossed his mind that the results that could be had through negotiations with personalities like Balfour and Lloyd George could not be had with some of their successors—and under conditions different from those that were in place during the World War. As a result, he remained bound to his four principles which very much weakened his political strength, his maneuvering ability, and the influence of his arguments—all despite his sharp mind and the astute points incorporated in his arguments.

Jabotinsky, of course, discerned the lines of Weizmann's policy and thought that it was leading to only one result: *retreat*. Distraught, he decided to resign. But Weizmann did not accept his resignation. He appealed to him in an emotional letter, in which he asked him to continue carrying the burden with him. Jabotinsky, a generous man, assented, perhaps also because he may have viewed the appeal as a sign of a remote possibility that Weizmann might finally change his ways. In these circumstances, he had to face the problem of the civilian administration which kept worsening the Zionist situation.

The Illusion Called Samuel

No problem connected with British rule in the period before the signing of the Mandate caused the Zionist movement so many surprises, so much worry and so much disappointment, as those evoked by the conduct of Herbert Samuel. He was supposed to establish—according to Balfour and Lloyd George's plan—an administration in Palestine that would be sympathetic to Zionism, and ensure establishment of the Jewish National Home.

In his memoirs, published twenty years later, Samuel revealed how he had first reacted to the question posed to him by Lloyd George. Could he, in his opinion, serve as head of the civilian administration that would be established in Palestine? Samuel responded that he would be ready to take on any role assigned to him in the country only if he could help in fulfilling it. He explained this attitude, with which he was supposed to have been imbued, by *"the deep interest that I had in the Zionist idea* and by my readiness to make *any sacrifice necessary* in order to increase the chances of realizing this idea." In a subsequent conversation about this matter with Lord Curzon, Samuel recalls, Curzon mentioned Allenby's warning that, "appointing a Jew as High Commissioner in Palestine might cause an outbreak of rioting which might include attacks on Jewish settlements and perhaps even invasions from across the border." Samuel responded that he was "ready to take on any personal risk" that might be involved with the office; but since Allenby's warning was not aimed at him alone, he added, but at the Jews of Palestine as well, he believed that he would do the right thing if he consulted on this matter with a delegation of Jews from Palestine who were then in London. Their response put his mind at rest, he indicated. As a result, he thought that he could answer Lloyd George positively and without reservation. On this occasion, he again promised the Prime Minister that he would act for the sake of the goals that he had been appointed to attain, and only expressed the hope that the Zionists would understand, out of consideration for the circumstances, that fulfilling the Zionist program would be "gradual," and that they would display "patience" in this regard, out of their clear understanding that the "pace" of progress would be determined by a man who had "full sympathy for the final goal" of Zionism and the Balfour Declaration.

We may already discern in this last comment by Samuel the main aspects of the problem that he faced. On one hand, he was eager to obtain the office that to a large degree satisfied his aspiration for honor, which at that time he had not found any other way of fulfilling. On the other, he wanted to alleviate as much as possible the worry that gripped him, the fear for his life—which he was supposedly ready to "risk," as he said, for the sake of the Zionist goal. In truth, his readiness, which he had quietly proclaimed, was nothing but a pretense that covered his cowardice. This was one of his basic character traits, which Weizmann had had an opportunity to sense even before Samuel was appointed high commissioner, and that Lloyd George discerned only afterwards. In our opinion, this trait was the chief factor inclining Samuel towards the program which he tried to implement as High Commissioner.

He displayed his cowardice in his first steps as head of the civilian administration. Instead of dismissing the administration officials known to be enemies of Zionism, he treated them as friends, and even appointed some of them as advisors. Likewise, he appointed the leader of the Arab pogromists, whom he, Samuel, had pardoned, to the chief religious office amongst the Arabs in the country, overriding the choice of the Arabs themselves. In this way, he believed, he had won the hearts of those who were likely to dominate most of his opponents. Thus, he calmed his fears considerably. However, riots broke out in May 1921 and his request to Congreve, the British military commander in Egypt, to suppress the riots by force, was rejected with the explanation that, if harsh measures were used, an Arab "revolt" would break out. Samuel's cowardice then turned into panic. He immediately proclaimed a cessation of Jewish immigration and shortly thereafter decided on a policy that may already have been in his mind before his appointment, after hearing Curzon's warning, as to what he would do if he were in danger. The main points of this policy were: demonstrating sympathy towards Arab aspirations whilst systematically reducing the progress of Zionism.

He knew very well what the Balfour Declaration had intended when he proclaimed his desire to strive for its fulfillment. In a speech that he gave in December 1919, he himself had defined its principal purpose as creating "a solid majority" of Jews in Palestine. Yet in his speech of June 3, 1921, he declared that the Balfour Declaration merely intended to establish in Palestine a Jewish "Spiritual Center" into which "some

Jews" would enter "with limits to their numbers, to be determined by the size and the interests of the present population." Likewise, he had completely understood the reason the Balfour Declaration had limited the rights of the existing Arab population of the country only to "religious" and "civil." Yet he now shamelessly claimed that the Declaration promised the Arabs national-political rights too, while the "Spiritual Center," as implied by his remarks, did not grant such rights to the Jews. In his memoirs he indeed admitted that he had been appointed to the office "by His Majesty's Government *principally thanks to his support for the Zionist ideas.*" But despite this, he claimed that he was in Palestine in order to care for all its inhabitants, not only a portion of them, and that he had been "appointed to this office not by the Zionists, but by the King." By this reasoning, it was as if he had been appointed twice by the government, to fulfill two functions contradicting one another. In order to emphasize this contradiction, he pointed to remarks that Weizmann had uttered—at an "unfortunate moment," according to Samuel. Weizmann had expressed the hope that "Palestine will be as Jewish as England is English." These remarks, Samuel explained, naturally aroused the concern of the Arabs. "They saw that thousands of Jews were coming from Europe to Palestine, buying land, building villages, founding industry. How long would this process continue? Wouldn't this bring about the removal of the Arabs from the country, so that in the end there wouldn't be any room in it for them when they grew old or for their children after them?" Samuel failed to mention, of course, that no such danger existed from Jewish immigration, and that Jewish settlement was actually attracting masses of Arabs to Palestine, in fact increasing their numbers. He presented himself as an "objective" high commissioner concerned to prevent the phenomenon referred to in Weizmann's quoted remarks. He went on to say that any change that he might want to introduce into the country's administration, and the latter's laws and authorities, would be meant only to strengthen the Arabs' status. In this vein, he proposed setting up a legislative council in which the Arabs would have elected representatives who would be likely to ensure anti-Jewish legislation. Likewise, he wanted to set up an Arab Agency as a counterpart to the

Jewish Agency. We have not yet mentioned that he brought down a heavy blow on Zionism in the first months of his reign, by limiting Jewish immigration to "the country's absorptive capacity." This was meant to prevent formation of a Jewish majority. If none of the other proposals, but only the last-mentioned limitation, was actually put into practice, that was because the Arabs were not satisfied with them or because the Colonial Office, headed by Churchill, saw them as a violation of the Mandate. Thus, Zionism was saved from the extinction that Samuel had designated for it, no doubt intentionally.

We said above that Samuel's plan was induced in principle by the panic which took hold of him after the pogroms of May 1921. But there is no doubt that some of its parts were influenced by the advice of the anti-Zionist officials under him. He formulated explanations for his policy that were supposedly based on his "liberalism," but in fact also flowed from his desire to appear as a "British" high commissioner in all respects, who was concerned first of all for Britain's interests, rather than as a Jew who favored his own people. In this way, the man, who Lloyd George and Balfour trusted for his Zionism and moral honesty, became the inventor of rights supposedly promised to the Arabs and the denier of rights promised in fact to the Jews. Needless to say, all his "interpretations" of the Balfour Declaration were a result of his readiness to betray his earlier commitments. Therefore, Weizmann viewed his actions as no less than "a terrible disappointment," while Jabotinsky judged him as dangerously harmful, someone to be rid of as soon as possible.

The Last Efforts

Several times Jabotinsky implored Weizmann to influence the English government to remove Samuel and to cancel the limitations he had imposed on Zionism. This was Weizmann's wish, too. For this purpose, he enlisted Balfour and Lloyd George. They both supported Weizmann's position and at the same time they also totally negated

Samuel's interpretation of the Balfour Declaration, stating clearly that by "National Home" they had always meant a "Jewish state." However, since at the same time they were compelled to deal with other political matters, Weizmann too, stopped his efforts against Samuel, which had been in any case restricted, in his usual way, to back rooms, never emerging to see the light of day. In public, he avoided making any criticism of Samuel, even going so far as to defend his administration. Jabotinsky, who had been surprised by Weizmann's conduct in this regard, held his disappointment in check and awaited the signing of the Mandate, which he hoped would display a forthright position validating the Zionist claims. This hope was indeed fulfilled, but publication of the Mandate did not bring any change in the administration's conduct toward the Jews. The principal local officials, who were enemies of Zionism, remained in their posts, acting as usual. Jewish immigration remained restricted as it had been, and no easing was granted to the Jews in purchasing real estate or in settling. None of these facts brought about any Zionist reaction, which might have, in Jabotinsky's opinion, held back a process which had one goal: the destruction of Zionism.

Jabotinsky was now a member of the Zionist Executive and urged it to demand from the British government a basic change in the administration of the country and to allow Zionism to advance in accord with the rights explicit in the Mandate. These demands, he argued, must finally be expressed in a political struggle which would continue until it had yielded the desired results. But Weizmann reacted with vigorous opposition. He knew from experience how difficult it had been for him to effect any change in favor of Zionism since Balfour's departure from the Foreign Office, whereas now, after the fall of the Lloyd George government, he stood defenseless. The government was now headed by Bonar Law who was openly hostile toward Zionism, while Shuckborough, director of the Colonial Office, consistently acted as an anti-Zionist, though under disguise. Weizmann feared that if he changed his approach, which had always been marked by restraining his criticism, he might only intensify their opposition to Zionism and broaden the limitations that they might impose on it. He believed that Zionism could achieve something worthwhile only through concessions and compromises, and could not advance except within the limits set for it by the government. We must always bear in mind, he used to stress, that we do not have any power to force our will on Britain.

This was the point around which most differences of opinion between him and Jabotinsky revolved, and these differences became more pronounced day by day. Jabotinsky argued that Zionism had effective means of fighting for its rights, with the Mandate being the most important of them. It included clear obligations toward Zionism that could not be blurred in any way. It would be enough for the Jews to remind Britain and the United States of what Britain had promised to them and of what it was actually doing, for various friends of Zionism to come to their aid. These friends had given fair and enthusiastic consent to the alliance that Britain had made with the Jewish people. Jabotinsky thought at the time that it would not even be necessary to bring the case before the League of Nations which gave Britain the Mandate over Palestine. He was certain that British statesmen would consent to have their nation's reputation for reliability and its political prestige damaged so, by openly betraying an international obligation.

Jabotinsky now no longer believed that he would succeed in changing Weizmann's methods. But he did believe that he would succeed in obtaining the support of most members of the Zionist leadership. The time had come, he thought, for them to understand that diplomacy does not only need to take the form of conversations with statesmen and heads of governmental departments, but that in certain situations, the Zionists had to enter the arena of public struggle. It seems, though, that the members of the Zionist leadership did not understand this. Likewise, they were apparently not influenced by the letter directed to them by the National Council (the Jewish leadership in Palestine), in which the open, bitter truth was stated as follows: "Since the approval of the Mandate till now, there has been no change for the better in the attitude of the government towards us, rather there is a definite slant against us in all matters." Even the grave conclusion that the National Council had arrived at—that "This method contains a concealed aspiration to thwart all the promises and declarations given to the Jewish people"—did not make an impression on them. Members of the Actions Committee who convened on January 2, 1923 unanimously supported Weizmann, and Jabotinsky saw the need to resign from the leadership and even to resign from his membership in the Zionist Organization.

3. The Turn towards Independence

Jabotinsky knew that this crisis in the relations between him and Weizmann was not temporary, but constituted a rift that would never heal. He understood that he had been mistaken when he focussed his efforts on attempting to influence his fellow members of the leadership, almost all of whom had been Weizmann's partners for a long time. Finally, he clearly perceived a fact that ought to have been known to him long before. With all their honest concern for Zionism, these leaders in the main were not capable of freeing themselves from the mode of thought acquired by Jews in their centuries-long exilic existence. This mode of thought dictated their reaction to every difficult situation, and it was based on three principles: caution, moderation, and self-restraint. This was a behavior that Jabotinsky no doubt would have considered fitting and advisable in normal times, but not for all circumstances, and certainly not during emergencies which may sometimes require quick and daring actions. What separated him from them, he now understood, was not only a difference in opinions and outlooks, but also in behavior-affecting character—such as the ability to withstand dangers, to look at them without flinching and draw the necessary conclusions without faintness of heart, and to act accordingly without hesitation.

It seemed to Jabotinsky that he had exhausted all possibilities in his efforts to fortify the Zionist movement, but he found it difficult to come to terms with this conclusion. His friends' arguments intensified his predicament, as they did not share his opinion about the limits of his abilities. They belonged to the Zionist Organization and they all pleaded with him to come back to the organization and set up a party that would fight for his ideas and try to take over the Zionist Organization. For a man who had "wearied of keeping" his prolonged silence, their pleading held a certain temptation: He would *appeal to the masses of the Jewish People*. He thought that such an appeal had a chance of success. There are always healthy elements in the people, with common sense and natural patriotism. But the shortcomings of exilic existence, he knew, are found among them too. Moreover, he was aware that every leader in the Zionist movement had already enlisted a group of supporters, and these leaders would surely recruit additional supporters if they understood that their status was in danger. The chance of arriving at a majority under these conditions appeared to Jabotinsky remote. Although he agreed to act in this direction, he did not see it as a solution to the problem. So what was the answer, and where should he seek it?

He recalled Trumpeldor's plan to set up a large body of Jewish youth who would dedicate their lives to serving the people. When Trumpeldor had expounded this plan to him, Jabotinsky had called it unrealistic. But now, considering the matter again, his attitude changed considerably. He had no doubts any longer: here was the solution to the problem! It was necessary to educate a new generation of Jews imbued with faith in the principles of Zionism and free from the complexes of Exile, a generation strong in mind, powerful in character, that would also be ready to brave war in defense of its people and future.[1] He knew that fulfilling this task would require immense time and mighty

---

1   We may clearly see the image of the generation that appeared in Jabotinsky's imagination, as well as Trumpeldor's decisive influence in this regard, in Jabotinsky's poem "HaNeder" (The Vow) (*Shirim*, tashaz [=1946-47], p 260, in the paragraph "Enlistment") and from an account of Trumpeldor's program in Jabotinsky's "Megilat haGdud" (= Scroll of the Legion) in his *Ktavim Nivharim* (Selected Writings), II, 1943, p 183 (Heb.).

efforts, but he reached the conclusion that there was no other way, and decided to go in that direction.

In order to arrive at such a far-reaching decision, one requires unique qualities: a huge desire to save the people, readiness to take on a burden almost too heavy to bear, and in addition, a sense of obligation to a duty which cannot be avoided. After ten years of systematic preaching in this direction, years of teaching certain values and expounding truths, which won over many thousands of young minds— the hoped for generation had been established. This was a generation that had only one single goal—liberation of the Land and redemption of the people. To achieve this aim it was ready to make any sacrifice and fight any enemy, whoever he might be. We have mentioned above the singular accomplishment represented by the establishment of the Jewish Legion. But perhaps even more wondrous was the creation of that generation which filled the ranks of the liberation fighters of the underground resistance and which forced the British to leave Palestine. When Weizmann informed General Smuts that the UN had decided to establish a Jewish state, the great commander and statesman commented that Weizmann had indeed received the state, but *it had been Jabotinsky's fighters who brought it into the world.*[2]

II. From Resistance to Rebellion (1923-1940)

The history of a real liberation movement is not expressed merely by a survey of events, but also by examining the beliefs which guided its actions and constituted its strength. This strength is what is responsible, in the long run, for the developments that determine the course of history. In our following comments, we shall try to clarify several elements of Jabotinsky's political thought which he meant to instill in the Jewish people. It was both realistic and idealistic, and comprised a set of values and principles which on one hand, were

---

2   See Richard Meinertzhagen, *Middle East Diary* (New York: Thomas Yoseloff, 1960),1973—p 154.

rooted in a glorious past, and, on the other, could serve as sound basis for solutions of many unsettled problems. This kind of thinking captured the minds of many, especially among the youth thirsty for knowledge. It is the kind of thinking which doesn't lose its value over time, because truths that have been clarified, proven, and confirmed in the course of several generations, are considered certainties and not fleeting conjectures.

1. Submission and Resistance in Jewish History

When we examine Jabotinsky's writings and scrutinize the ideas that he expounded, we see clearly that one great principle guided his thought and public activities. This was the principle of *resistance to subjugation*, which was accompanied by his stress of the need to create a multifaceted force, including military force, as an instrument of resistance. Perhaps few today are aware that at the time this principle was an innovation in Jewish thinking. This only attests to the great change that Jabotinsky brought about in Jewish outlook in this regard. In order to properly evaluate this change, we need to cast an eye on Jewish history and observe the general trend of the Jewish people as it relates to resistance to submission.

There is no need to stress that in ancient times the Jewish people were distinguished by the power of resistance. We did not allow anyone to humiliate us without being hurt by our reaction. Even less did we allow others to endanger our existence, to annul our freedom, or to attack our rights without reacting strongly. I need only mention our vigorous responses to attempts at subjugation by the ancient empires, and afterwards by the Hellenistic (Seleucid) and Roman empires. These latter responses took shape in repeated, bold uprisings over a period of eight hundred years, from the Hasmonean revolt (against the Seleucids) to the war against Emperor Heraclius in 614 A.D., which ended in the expulsion of the Byzantines from the Land of Israel. Our capability to resist did not vanish during the first few hundred years of Exile, but it dwindled, and eventually it eroded to almost nothing. Some historians view the laws that denied the Jews in Germany the right to bear arms—laws that may have been put into place as early as the twelfth century—as the beginning of the humiliation of European Jewry. There is much truth in this view. Indeed, after that we became "Protected Jews"—considered powerless and incapable of self-defense. Albeit, in the other center of Jewish life in Europe—that of Christian Spain—we still find in the twelfth century fortresses whose defense was entrusted to Jews alone. We also find Jewish battalions taking part in the Christian wars against the Moslems, and we find Jews bearing weapons in the cities even at the end of the fourteenth century. However, these instances continually diminished. By the time the great pogroms broke out in Spain in 1391, there are no clear indications of Jewish attempts to resist the pogromists by force. In the middle of the fifteenth century, the bishop of Jewish extraction, Alfonso de Cartagena, who was the son of the convert Pablo de Burgos, described the Jews as a people known for their cowardice and inability to partake in military action. The Jew had lost, he said, the bravery in battle that his forefathers had excelled at, and considering the context in which these remarks were made, they appear to have been true. This quality, pointed out by Alfonso de Cartagena, became a known trait of the Jews in Exile, especially in Eastern Europe where the Jews lived for eight hundred years. What was even worse: the lack of capacity to resist by force, which was originally considered one of the humiliating and detrimental effects of the Exile, became over time a praiseworthy trait. An ideology emerged which justified and praised it. This ideology even penetrated the ranks of the national movement which had arisen at the beginning of the 1880s. In 1894, Bialik wrote in his poem *On the Threshold of the Synagogue*: "From being a lion among lions, I prefer to perish among the sheep."

This was not Jabotinsky's position nor the position of Political Zionism, which arose a few years after Bialik wrote his poem. Jabotinsky's stand, as reflected in his writings, may be summarized as follows: You can cultivate a dream of perpetual peace and even work to advance and attain it. But if you want to reach the day when this dream is realized, you must in the meanwhile wage a war with predators. Therefore, you must use your teeth and nails; and if you do not have these, you must grow them. When Jabotinsky wrote his article, "Man Is Wolf Unto Man" (*homo homini lupus*), he was referring more to relations between nations than between individuals. In other words, he understood that the domain of politics is a zone of tests of strength and that the main forces at work in this domain are embodied in aspirations of expansion and domination. Either you recognize the existence of these aspirations, and find a way to use them in the struggle for your goals, or you ignore them and will be defeated. Whoever enters into the arena of this struggle must learn its rules.

We can see then how great was the revolution that Jabotinsky introduced in our thinking, in our values of morality and our view of our problems as a nation among nations. *He taught the doctrine of resistance to a people who had not known what resistance meant for hundreds of years.*

"Resistance" and Independence

In order to fully comprehend the meaning of this doctrine, we ought to recall that according to Jabotinsky's understanding, the principle of resistance he espoused was merely a manifestation of the principle of independence. We may state his equation as follows: If you resist those who undermine your rights, you resist those who strike at your independence. This equation would not be vitiated—from his standpoint—even if the value of independence were replaced by such values as freedom, self-respect, and the like. Each one made up a cornerstone in his world-outlook, or more precisely, in the structure of his thinking about human society, both the actual and the ideal. We shall not analyze Jabotinsky's general outlook here concerning these principles, but only what they meant for his political position. And what it meant was clear: *Vigorous resistance to any concession of any right whatsoever*, or any position that the Jews were entitled to as individuals or as a people. He saw such concessions as harming the independence that in his view was the paramount principle. Consequently, such a concession was to him not a generous or tolerant or moral act; rather it was immoral—and to the highest degree. After all, if you have a right and you concede that right, whether voluntarily or involuntarily, even if out of supposedly "pragmatic calculations," then what is taken away from you is, simply, theft. Hence, you have fundamentally surrendered to robbery, even if you pretend to having been magnanimous. Likewise, he did not see any practical sense in surrender. On the contrary—because the nature of violent extortion is that it grows when fed. When the tiniest crack opens up, the extortionist makes an effort to enlarge and deepen it. This is how we should understand Jabotinsky's stormy opposition to the Zionist leadership's "patient" and acquiescence to the British administration's actions in Palestine, at the beginning of its rule and many times after.

Those who are not conversant with the stages of development of Zionist thought's might be surprised by it, but whoever is acquainted with its history will agree that Jabotinsky's position at that time resembled that of Nordau and Zangwill. These two great Political Zionists also severely and bitterly criticized the policies of the Zionist leadership. We recall especially Zangwill's slogan: *Obsta principiis*—that is, resist bad things at their beginnings, in order to prevent their development into mighty forces. Jabotinsky advocated the very same approach. In his letter to Weizmann of 1919, he spoke about the conduct of the British authorities in Palestine, which was hostile to Jews and to the Balfour Declaration. He became more and more critical of Weizmann for not having fiercely resisted the "beginnings"—namely, the political and administrative foundations which the British were laying in the country. "The fact," he said, "that the Foreign Office is getting accustomed to the thought that the Zionists will swallow and digest anything and everything, lowers the value of our diplomatic moves. I am amazed that you don't understand this yourself."

And from these two principles that he advocated, resistance to tyranny and insistence on independence, flowed the activist-maximalist conception that formed the main part of his doctrine and from which flowed his principal contributions to Zionism. I find these in three areas: fostering a military capacity among the Jews, education for political struggle, and his position in respect of the Arab Question.

Military Capacity As A Condition For Political Independence

We begin with the topic of an army. Here we ought to mention, of course, that the idea itself was already present in Herzl's writings. He had affirmed the vital necessity of a Jewish military force to defend the state that would arise. In *The Jewish State*, he wrote: "We will have to maintain a professional army armed with the best modern equipment, for the defense of the state internally and externally." In his speech to Hovevei Zion in London in July 1896, he stated: "*I want only such settlement that we can defend with our Jewish army.*" This requirement appeared in all the proposed charters that Herzl drew up. Moreover, he viewed military service as not only a duty performed for the sake of honor, a civil and human duty, but even a sublime value that the state is based upon. Therefore, he agreed to introduce into the Jewish state even hardened criminals who had served out their sentences, while refusing to let in army deserters from any country. However, this stand and similar ones did not deeply penetrate the minds of the Zionists, or more correctly, the Zionist camp as a whole. Only some apprehended their full meaning, while only a very few connected the notion of military service with the general world outlook of modern Zionism.

Jabotinsky was among those few. His approach to the issue of the military and the whole notion of the use of force was pursued by him in practice. First of all, he founded Jewish self-defense in Russia, later founded the Legion, afterwards the self-defense force in Jerusalem, and subsequently advocated reinstatement of the Legion. He then fought against the non-retaliation policy of the Jewish Agency toward

Arab terrorism in Palestine, afterwards headed the Irgun Zva'i Le'umi (National Military Organization), and lastly, he supported an armed uprising in Palestine against the British government. We see that in his military activism, Jabotinsky went far beyond Herzl, although his outlook on this matter rested on fully Herzlian foundations. He also went far beyond Herzl on another matter of very great importance. He perceived that Herzl's remarks in this area had not been absorbed into Jewish thinking, and he understood that the time had come to *bring into* Zionism not only awareness of the need to form an army, but also awareness of the value of *military capability* as a positive factor in the life of the nation. Therefore, he spoke not only of a professional army that would serve the needs of internal and external defense (as Herzl had done in *The Jewish State*), but of educating the youth as a whole as soldiers so that the people could withstand the harsh struggle for national revival. Likewise, he viewed it necessary—for the very same reason— to explain that there is good and bad militarism, just as there is good and bad nationalism, and that military education also contains certain exalted values, which only it can impart.

Jabotinsky's approach was not accepted by most Zionists, who continued to deride him for his opinions. In this struggle over a new education for the youth, the wide gap between Jabotinsky and his generation came to light. Today it is difficult to understand the intensity of the resistance which Jabotinsky encountered in this matter, because his demands seem to us today elementary and obvious. But at the time, these things did not seem elementary, but superfluous and damaging, and at any rate—revolutionary. Here I will merely quote briefly from Mr. Medzini, a well-known journalist in his time, who criticized Jabotinsky. "Let us state the truth," this journalist wrote. "A large part—perhaps a majority—of the Jewish population in Palestine, did not display, for various reasons, excessive enthusiasm for the very idea of the Legion. *The military world-outlook*, which for Jabotinsky and his disciples is an inseparable part of their 'imperial' world-outlook, is *remote and alien to many of us.*" Of course, we do not find any "imperial"—today they would surely say "imperialistic" world-outlook—in Jabotinsky's writings. At any rate, what was called in his time a *military world-outlook* refers to everything that Jabotinsky wrote in praise of "militarism" without his ignoring the negative traits that it might take on under certain conditions. He wrote in praise of the qualities that military capability develops—discipline, the capacity to act as a group, mutual assistance, the spirit of self-sacrifice, daring and the aptitude for heroic deeds. All these traits which he advocated and which his opponents called "Jabotinsky's militarism" became those of the youth movement that he created, and in time became those qualities which the Israeli army today instills into its troops—virtues which the citizens of Israel are proud of.

2. The Doctrine of The Political Offensive

I now move on to Jabotinsky's special contribution in the area of political struggle. This contribution was embodied in his emphasis that the most important means of political struggle is *public pressure*. We must know what he meant by public pressure in order to properly understand the nature of his viewpoint. In the first stage, the pressure is primarily presenting claims, argumentation, and vigorously insisting on one's demands. Essentially, the claim or argument must rest on the support of public opinion. This pressure is one of the instruments of power which show up in struggles within peoples and between peoples. "There is no friendship in matters of state," Jabotinsky said. "There is only pressure. What is decisive is not the positive or negative qualities of a particular ruler. It is the quantity of pressure which comes forth from the subjects themselves." Therefore, "If the pressure comes only from our opponents, while on our side there is no counter-pressure sufficient to cancel out and overcome it, then everything that will be done in this country will be *against us*, even if the man who heads the government is called Balfour, even if he is called Wedgwood, even if he is called Theodore Herzl." This is because, "The slightest change in matters of state is not obtained except by pressure and struggle. And whoever has no energy or daring, or no talent, or has no eagerness to fight, will not obtain even the slightest change in our favor, even from a government made up entirely of our most loyal friends. This is because the machinery of government is primarily a machine which is subject to the laws of public pressure, just as a machine made of iron is subject to the laws of physical pressure."

Many Zionist leaders argued against the doctrine of pressure, stating that it was irrelevant in the case of the Jewish people, which could not rest its claims on real sources of power. Jabotinsky did not agree with this argument, rejecting what he called "the well known refrain since ancient times," that is, the refrain which claimed that "we are weak and small, helpless and powerless. We can be crushed with a finger. No one is afraid of us and so on." Not so, he said. "Our side is closer to the truth than the composers of the hymns about our weakness and nothingness. For if we are nothing, let us not interfere in politics at all. Let's not go off on flights of fancy about our rights, about territory; let us not struggle—let's simply close the store and go home. But, in reality, we are struggling, we are making a breakthrough and moving forward, step after step, simply because we are a world power. It is difficult to mobilize a force like outs, it is difficult to concentrate it, but it exists, and our enemies believe it to be so."

Jabotinsky wrote these words in 1915, at the beginning of the First World War. He repeated these words ever more intensely after the war. The doctrine of public pressure was the very first chapter in his entire political doctrine. It contained the bulk of the criticism that he directed toward the Zionist leadership's policy. He did not place much hope on the so-called diplomatic method or in negotiations between Jewish representatives and British governmental leaders as a means to remove the stumbling-blocks that had been placed in the way of Zionism *as long as these negotiations did not simultaneously rest on the promotion of public pressure*. "The diplomatic method," he said, "may have been good some time before, during the days of the *shtadlanim* [Jewish emissaries who petitioned the ruler], when a conversation between a court Jew and the Austrian chancellor was sufficient to save a Jewish community from a decree of expulsion. Then, the whole government was embodied in the chancellor, maybe even the state. He did not need to consider the press or parliament or public opinion. But now there are no chancellors like that...A political action of broad scope must nowadays appeal to the public...Look at England and you'll learn that every such action begins with a series of group demonstrations. The groups of citizens that are interested there act on their own, and the ministers listen not to delegations but to the voice of the masses."

At the Sixth Congress, Max Nordau said: "From the day the world was created till today, only two ways have been found to achieve something. These two ways are taking [by force] and demanding. We cannot take and we do not want to take. Thus, only the second way remains: to demand." "It's amazing," Nordau added, "but it is absolutely correct: before Zionism came, we had in fact made no demands. The change that we introduced into the situation was to all appearances a trifle, but in fact it was very big. We demanded." Political Zionism indeed made a demand, and it directed its demand both toward the governments and toward world public opinion. From this vantage point too, we may say that Jabotinsky followed in the footsteps of Herzl and Nordau.

From Public Relations to Confrontation

Nevertheless, we ought to indicate the distinction between actions of the above two in this field and Jabotinsky's proposals. He not only called for presenting the Zionist demands and creating public opinion by stating arguments that would win friends for Zionism and defend it from false accusations. Political Zionism had already conducted propaganda of this kind, and such propaganda was conducted by Jabotinsky too, during and before the First World War. What he now demanded was somewhat different, what he called "a political offensive," a sharply critical attack on British policy, meant not only for the British public, but for world public opinion. What this implied, of course, was *confrontation* with the British government along the whole international front. Here was the principal difference between Jabotinsky's position and that of the Zionist leadership which had made every effort to remain within the confines of public relations and within the boundaries of a loyal opposition. Their activities mainly meant defending positions within the bounds of consensus.

In April 1925, Jabotinsky said: "Zionism is not separate from political offensive. We must prepare *world* public opinion and the governments, even hostile governments." And in August 1925, at the Fourteenth Zionist Congress: "It has been asked here, and outside the hall too it has been asked: From where will you get the power to compel the British government? But they used to ask Herzl too: Where is your strength? You want to transform Palestine into the Jewish State. But where is your authority? What will So-and-So tell you, and what will Such-and-Such say? And this was Herzl's position: I cannot tell you how I will convince So-and-So and Such-and-Such. Maybe [political] parties can not be convinced. But the world is not a party, and the world *can* be convinced if we demand logical things from it. If that is so, then we need demonstrations, we need what we call a political offensive in order to instill our demands, until they are accepted. However, either one or the other is true: Either it is possible to convince the world to accept the truth, or it is not. If not, then we are finished, because we want something impossible. But if it is possible, then let's make the effort to convince it."

Weizmann responded. The confrontation that Jabotinsky was demanding, between the Zionist movement and the British government, the greatest power in the world at that time, seemed incomprehensible to him. In a statement made in the eve of the 1927 Zionist Congress, he wrote: "The starting point of our diplomatic work in the future must be—as it was in the past—maintaining our friendly relations with the Mandatory authority and with its emissaries in Palestine. *This is a truth that should not be refuted.*" Further, "We must not allow any part of the [Zionist] Organization, or any individual Zionist, to place obstacles in our way by means of irresponsible demonstrations in Jerusalem, in

London, or anywhere else." His readers knew of course which method and which "individual Zionist" he was referring to. Nevertheless, not all Zionists agreed completely with his opinion. Even Mr. Medzini, Weizmann's sworn defender, was compelled to confess that on this issue Jabotinsky was right "to a certain extent" in criticizing the prevailing method. "There is no doubt," Medzini said, "that the leaders of the Organization made a *big* mistake in that they did not find it necessary to conduct broad political propaganda in England and that thanks to our silence, the impression was created there that the Jews were completely satisfied with everything done in Palestine by the British authorities, that it's only the Arabs who protest against and oppose the authorities." It goes without saying that Mr. Medzini did not thoroughly comprehend Jabotinsky's thinking, or merely limited the extent of his agreement with Jabotinsky by speaking about appealing to Britain alone. We have already stressed that Jabotinsky meant both a struggle within Britain and on the international front. Here I want to touch on another matter. Jabotinsky wrote: "We want to convince public opinion in England and in all other countries and prove to it the *justice* of our demands. We believe that a truth, which is uttered in the ears of the civilized world and defended with respect for one's stand, will always win in the end."

Today, when the political world has changed so much from what it was before the war, there are many, of course, who doubt the validity of this belief, at least for our times. Nowadays, when we see how justice is trampled upon and hypocrisy parades about openly, even in places where we used to believe that the principles of decency were treated with respect, it is extremely difficult to rely on the faith that "the truth will always win out in the end." Nevertheless, even today, we cannot doubt one fact. All those who appeal to public opinion, no matter how vile their demands, appeal to it in the name of justice. This is because it would be *totally impossible* to appeal to public opinion in any other way. But Jabotinsky believed honestly in the justice of our demands, *completely and in full*. Moreover, without this absolute faith, he saw no basis or hope for our struggle. It should be borne in mind that even from this viewpoint, the moral one, he demanded not only a defense of our positions, but also—and mainly—a political offensive, a frontal attack on enemy positions which would leave no room for compromise or concessions. Without such an attack that would provide a renewed foundation for the standing of our full, valid, and clear right in Palestine, we would not win this battle, he argued; and it was important—so he believed—not only for winning over public opinion; it was necessary not only for our friends throughout the world; it was necessary for ourselves and our children too, because we are Jews, because without our being totally convinced that we are struggling for a just cause, we cannot fight with the same devotion and resolution that we need in order to be able to win the struggle.

3. The Arab Problem

I have arrived at a third point where I see Jabotinsky's contribution to Zionist political thought—his position regarding the Arab Question. The opinion is widespread that this problem was first discerned by those called Practical Zionists, or by those who spoke of Jewish-Arab rapprochement from the beginning of the British mandatory period. Herzl and his associates, we are told, did not take into account the Arab Question at all. Yet nothing is further from the truth than this conventional notion. Whoever is familiar with Herzl's writings knows that he opposed the Hovevei Zion program precisely because he was *certain* that opposition on the part of the existing population would precipitate under conditions of Jewish settlement that lacked support by governmental authority. For that reason, he demanded a treaty with international guarantees that would ensure the necessary defense of the settlers and the undisturbed progress of their activities by hostile acts. And as far as Nordau and Zangwill are concerned, it is sufficient to read their articles and speeches from 1919 on in order to understand that they viewed the danger of Arab opposition with concern and gravity. Their political proposals at that time mainly derived from this concern, as did their criticism of British and Zionist policy.

Regarding Jabotinsky, no one saw as early or as profoundly the full meaning of the Arab problem in the period after the British conquest. He saw the birth of Arab opposition, fostered and supported by British policy, and realized the possibility that this opposition might quickly develop into an independent force and consolidate in a manner that would be difficult to restrain. This was because he discerned the natural basis of this opposition, as did Herzl and Nordau—and in this he saw the source of the problem. True, he believed that if this growth had been nipped in the bud, it could have been uprooted and removed from the world. But it was not nipped in the bud. To the contrary, it was cultivated. And he realized the danger of this cultivation, and as early as 1918 saw an urgent need to fight against British policy, which was inciting the Arabs to hostile acts against the Jews. From here also flowed his severe criticism of the Zionist leadership, which did not realize the full gravity of the British activity and did not oppose it with sufficient vigor. In June 1920, in his letter to the Jewish population of Palestine from the Acre fortress prison where he was held, he wrote: "Weizmann is a brilliant diplomat. But he has never understood the political situation in Palestine. He never saw the decisive value of everything happening here as a *precedent* for the future. He choked off—over the course of all these years of continuing pogrom— the protest that was gathering, until the insolence of our enemies increased, became established, and struck deep roots. We've become an easy target for them. During the last Passover [the 1920 Passover pogrom in Jerusalem], he saw with his own eyes the results of this strategy. But, even after the destruction, he learned nothing and forgot nothing, and now he continues the policy of blindness and leads us to a greater destruction."

After Arab opposition had consolidated and developed with British support, it became an established fact that required special treatment. Here, we ought to bear in mind that Jabotinsky felt neither ill will nor contempt towards the Arabs. What he wrote in his poem—"There the son of Arabia, the son of Nazareth, and my own son will happily live together in abundance" was without question his genuine aspiration.

Nevertheless, he did not believe that the abundance and happiness that the Zionist enterprise could offer the Arabs would serve to sufficiently compensate them for giving up their aspiration to drive us out of the country. Therefore, he defined the hope, that the Arabs would agree to the realization of Zionism in exchange for the advantages (cultural and economic) that we could bestow on them, as "a childish fancy." In contrast to all the peace plans and peace preaching that then flooded the press and the Jewish public, he wrote: "The source of this daydream, of those among us who are fond of the Arabs, lies in fact in a feeling of contempt towards the Arab people. It seems, in the opinion of those fond of Arabs, that the Arab people is nothing but a rabble chasing after money, which is ready to sell its patriotism in exchange for a well developed railroad network. Such a conception is groundless. Of course, individual Arabs can be bribed, but that does not mean that the totality of Palestine's Arabs are ready to do what even the Papuans are not. Every native people fights settlers as long as there is a spark of hope of getting rid of the danger of foreign encroachment. The Arabs of Palestine, too, are acting this way now and will so act in the future as long as a spark of hope nests in their hearts that they will be able to prevent the transformation of Palestine into the Land of Israel." On another occasion, he wrote with greater emphasis: "As long as even a spark of hope nests in the Arabs' hearts that they may succeed in getting rid of us, there are no pleasant words and no attractive promises in the world for which the Arabs will be ready to give up this hope of theirs—and this is precisely because the Arabs are not a rabble, but a living nation. And a living nation is ready for concessions on fateful issues such as these only when no hope is left for it to change the situation and when every breach in the iron wall has been sealed."

Thus, what is the answer to the Arab Question? The answer is the Iron Wall. That is, a strong military and political force that in the last analysis will convince the Arabs that they will not succeed in driving us out of here. The Iron Wall does not mean that there will not be attacks on it and attempts to breach it. In 1885, Nordau explained as a general principle, without connection to the situation in Palestine, that, "Where two peoples are fighting over one country, the problem can only be resolved by force of arms." And in 1926, in a period when things in the country were quiet and peaceful, Jabotinsky wrote: "I admit that there are moments when I dream about a Jewish-Arab agreement over Palestine. This happens in moments of weariness, when a man is too tired to bear up." In fact, he did not believe that there was a chance for this dream to depart from the sphere of illusions. And he summed up: "I fear that we will obtain the Land of Israel only through war."

The question is whether Jabotinsky's outlook has been confirmed by the political reality of our times. The Arabs received all the states that they had dreamed of. They also received most of historic Palestine and they already have a Palestinian state that takes up 75% of the Mandatory territory (i.e., Jordan). Yet, they want all of Palestine "from top to bottom." Insofar as we have obtained the Land of Israel, we have obtained it through war, exactly as Jabotinsky had foreseen. But Arab opposition still continues. It not only has not diminished, but has increased. It has taken on a world-wide scope in accord with the magnitude of the territory under their control. The Arabs also enjoy the support of great powers and the great majority of states in the world. According to Jabotinsky's theory, their opposition will not cease as long as they have even a spark of hope of erasing our political presence in Palestine. And who will deny that they have such a spark today, in fact much more than a spark? Hence, according to Jabotinsky's theory, there is no room to hope for peace with the Arabs—real peace—at this time. After all, they still have not been convinced that they cannot destroy us or to push us into the sea.

4. The Test of Time

Now to sum up. I think that in these three ways, fostering military capability, emphasizing the value of a public struggle, and presenting his novel approach to the Arab Question—Jabotinsky made his greatest contributions to the political thinking of Zionism. I have shown that when outlining the main directions in these three matters, Jabotinsky started from the basic positions of Political Zionism. However, he went far beyond these positions and conceived methods of action that, whether they were accepted then or not, are understood in our time much better than they were at the time that he expounded them during a bitter struggle. The idea of having military capability, that many condemned in his time, has become a dominant idea in our time, not only in Israel but throughout the world. When Jabotinsky began his fight over this idea, many believed that the days of the messiah were approaching, that the world was advancing toward general disarmament, toward peace and friendship among peoples. Nevertheless, today we know that this is not to be, or that the chances for it happening are extremely scant. Indeed, added to the usual dangers of conventional war, the danger of atomic war has become ever more real. Who would disagree nowadays that military capability is a value of the highest order for our lives in Israel?

The same is true regarding political struggle. Public pressure—a means of political struggle that Jabotinsky advocated—had already been in use, of course. Its importance greatly increased after the First World War, when democratic principles spread throughout Europe, all the way to the border of Soviet Russia. Jabotinsky believed that under the new circumstances, public opinion was capable of influencing nations and governments more than it had in earlier periods. And on this point he was right without a doubt. But what happened afterwards—from the time America entered the Second World War and became fully involved in the international political arena, and especially what happened after the war—raised the factor of public opinion to an importance unprecedented in human history. This is because public opinion in America, more than any other force, can determine policy and change it, raise governments to power and topple them. All nations and states today compete to influence this force and use it. Hence, Jabotinsky's affirmations and opinions seem correct, valid and realistic on the matter of military capability, in regard to public opinion, and about what he called a political offensive, even more than in the past.

The same goes without saying concerning the Arab Question. Clearly, he saw the Arabs' position as much more stubborn, less amenable to compromise or to coming to terms, than many others saw it in his generation. It is also clear that the force that today prevents Israel's destruction is the Iron Wall alone, which we erected with our own strength. Who would dare to give up this Iron Wall? Who would dare recommend weakening it? Indeed, it is not the exact wall that Jabotinsky had in mind, because he was thinking of a political wall no less than a military wall, and of a spiritual wall no less than a political wall. Because the greatest *preventative* against an attack on a people that has enemies who want to destroy it, is contained not only in its system of defense or in the instruments of war at its disposal, but also, and principally, in its *inner strength* which is stamped in its character, in its beliefs and behavior—the strength that will enable it to make a counter-attack that will rout the enemy that wants to wipe it out, and punish him in a way befitting the gravity of his extermination schemes.

In all these matters, Jabotinsky demonstrated political realism and a sense of reality—with an understanding of world-wide historical processes—more than we can discern in any other Jewish leader in his time. We may say that through his teachings and activities he uprooted us from the idyllic, naive and provincial world of a Zionism, which during a large part of the Mandatory period immersed itself in wishful thinking. He brought us into the harsh world of our age and taught us to look at it with open eyes. From this standpoint, Jabotinsky, who essentially belonged to the nineteenth century, judging by his outlooks and ideals, was the man who *took us out* of that century and placed us in the midst of the twentieth—a century of hellish events and catastrophes. And he was the man who gave us direction, a compass, and rules of navigation for steering our ship in an age of storms.

*****

These were Jabotinsky's principal contributions to our national-political thought, and I could conclude my remarks here, did I not feel a need to comment on another important matter relevant to the subject. This matter does not touch on his basic positions, but has to do with his method of determining these positions. That is, with his method of drawing conclusions from which Jewish national positions logically follow. I refer to Jabotinsky's prognosticating of political developments which he brought to a very high level.

From this standpoint too, we may comprehend his outstanding ability only when we compare his actions and achievements in this realm with the achievements of the Jewish people through their entire history. A dividing line stands out in this history—a kind of cross-section between two great periods. The Jews, which in the distant past produced many personalities who excelled in prognosticating the future, became during the Exile a people that seemed to have become virtually blind in this faculty. It is a cause for wonder that in no period of our life in Exile, up to the beginning of the struggle for Emancipation, do we find insight into events taking shape, or a prognosis of developments in the near future. We did not discern the greatest disasters (such as the expulsion from Spain) even a short while before they occurred. For that reason, they always seemed to us like thunder on a clear day. This was a period of which one may say, in the words of the sages: Vision disappeared from the people of Israel.

During the Jewish struggle for Emancipation, we may find the beginnings of an effort to set a comprehensive national policy by making prognoses of political or social developments. In fact, those were not prognoses, but one prognosis: The world is "progressing" towards equality of rights, and in the framework of this process the Jewish people will find its healing. This determination guided the actions of personalities like Riesser and others. In contrast, as we know, the national movement asserted, from the time of Hess on, an opposite prognosis: Mankind was progressing toward equality (of one kind or another), but the plague of antisemitism would not vanish from the world through progress alone. This determination too led to far-reaching conclusions, as had the previous one. Yet, once again there was only *one single* prognosis, which of course, did not satisfy the multi-faceted needs of a developing national policy. We may say that *systematic* prognostication, capable of aiding the Jewish people in setting its course, began only with Political Zionism. Making prognoses stands out especially in Herzl's activity, as Herzl viewed it as a need of the first order; because more than others, Herzl understood that no policy is possible without prognosticating, and no *correct* policy is possible without correctly foreseeing the future.

This ability to predict the future that we speak of is not something mysterious; it is not the fruit of some connection with the supernatural. Rather, it is a faculty within man's capacity. It is one of the abilities that man is endowed with. In fact, foreseeing the future is nothing more than perceiving the meaning of current, ongoing processes, understanding their direction, their weight and their influence, and evaluating the outcomes of the clashes between these very processes among themselves. By properly understanding these matters, one has already touched the edges of future developments. Of course, this is not an easy thing to do. Not in vain does the Hebrew proverb say: Who is truly wise? He who foresees the future.

Jabotinsky, too, considered predicting future developments as an ability that is within one's capacity. Indeed, he viewed it as the principal part of statesmanship and of being a publicist, and as such writing on public affairs (indeed, he defined the Prophets of Israel as resembling publicists). His own writings are full of historical observations, which formed the basis of his forecasts, the great majority of which have been confirmed in their entirety. The chief method that he employed for this purpose comprised the cautious analysis of data, and the logical, meticulous weighing of the reasonable, the possible and the impossible. But it was not only these talents of judgment and analysis that enabled his accurate prognostication. As in every field of human investigation, we sometimes obtain through special illumination a clear perception of the phenomenon under study, a kind of intuitive penetration which clarifies the problem and its solution for us in a single moment. Without flashes of inspiration of this kind, one does not achieve great things in any field. Jabotinsky was obviously gifted with inspirations of that kind, as we may note in his writings.

I have already indicated above two of Jabotinsky's prognoses. One concerned the inevitably negative development of the Mandatory government's anti-Zionist policy (unless this policy encountered energetic Jewish resistance in time). The other had to do with chances for peace with the Arabs, which he viewed as not having any substance at all (unless the Arabs were confronted with the Iron Wall for a prolonged period). Now, I shall speak about a third prognosis that he made. This one had to do with the development of antisemitism or, more precisely, with the coming of the Holocaust. In this prognosis too, like those preceding it, his ability to forecast the future was in glaring contrast to the limited understanding of his opponents. And here too, as on other matters I have mentioned, a deep link can be seen between his conception and Herzl's.

The Zionism of Lilienblum and Ahad ha`Am believed that antisemitism would not disappear, might not even be reduced by the influence of Progress and Emancipation. But neither did it see that antisemitism would reach unprecedented heights. Pinsker, on the other hand, did perceive it. So did Herzl—and with greater clarity. By examining the processes of modern antisemitism and its special ideological elements, Herzl determined that antisemitism would continue to grow until it had the power to accomplish its goal, which was—the destruction of European Jewry. He described this destruction in clear terms that left no room for doubt. And he saw the solution in a quick departure, like the "exodus from Egypt,"[3] similar to what Jabotinsky saw and demanded several decades later.

It seems that Herzl's insights on antisemitism and some of his remarks on its final goal had become embedded in Jabotinsky's mind and guided his thinking. In any event, only a short time had passed after Hitler's rise to power and Jabotinsky had no doubt that the time of a

---

3   See my article on Herzl in the *Hebrew Encyclopedia* (*Encyclopedia Hebraica*), vol. 15, pp 373-381 (in Hebrew).

holocaust was coming closer. He arrived at this conclusion—just as Herzl had reached his conclusions on the matter—not out of a sudden nightmare, or a panic attack, or an eschatological vision, but out of a logical analysis of the facts as he saw them and perceived their meaning. "I warn you, dear readers," he wrote in May 1939, "against the natural inclination to take consolation in the notion that not all expected results will be realized; that maybe none of them will be realized; that my conclusions are based merely on theoretical logic and that life is not always logical. I warn you that at least where our Jewish troubles are the issue, life is always logical, and every stone will break glass and every spark will become a conflagration."

Out of this clear vision of the Jewish future in the context of general European reality, he had written as early as 1935: "A people of many millions...in its full strengths and talents... is rolling down to the final abyss of oblivion, and some whisper in its ear that it rightly should console itself with the assigned quotas of Jewish immigration to Palestine instead of *an Exodus from Egypt*..." (the same term which Herzl had used). And after repeated warnings of the *extermination* expected for the Jews of Europe, he wrote in January 1939: "To be frank, I sometimes fear that the time has already passed eleven o'clock; perhaps twelve o'clock has already rung. That means midnight. That means the end. However, it is best that we shake off this fear. Let it be only eleven o'clock. This is, therefore, the last hour. There is still the possibility of looking around us; it is still possible to make a quick accounting. Perhaps it is still possible to find some place on the enflamed horizon, where the flames have not yet reached. And perhaps we will still try to be saved."

In June 1939, Jabotinsky felt the closeness of zero hour, the time of great destruction or *hurban*, total ruin, according to the Hebrew term he used ("h-u-r-b-a-n, learn this word by heart," he wrote then). Thus, we have before us a series of prognoses repeated with increasing frequency, which had one content and one meaning: "oblivion," "the end," "*hurban*." It was clear to him that the time had come for performing a grand, daring, unexpected action, in order to make it possible to breach the blockade that the British imposed on Jewish immigration to Palestine, thereby shutting off rescue. Indeed, only by understanding *the full gravity of his prognoses* at that time, can we understand the plan that he proposed in August 1939, a month before the outbreak of WWII—to organize an uprising against the British in Palestine with his own personal participation, for the purpose of taking over the country, even for just a short time. This revolt was scheduled to commence in October 1939.

As strange as it may seem, in light of everything said above, there are still researchers and writers today who vehemently utter the old claim that no one foresaw the Holocaust. Of course, no one foresaw precisely the time, the place, and the special circumstances in which the Holocaust was to burst forth. But someone did see that the social, political, and moral conditions had been prepared for its coming. And someone did repeatedly warn and sound the alarm that it was coming in the near future. That "someone" was Jabotinsky, whose voice then was "a voice crying in the wilderness." I will not elaborate on this, nor is there need to. However, it is difficult for me to conclude my remarks on this subject without quoting at this point the following passage from Jabotinsky's speech in Warsaw on the Ninth of Ab (the day of the destruction of the Temple) in 1938. It can help us realize Jabotinsky's uniqueness as a historical prognosticator:

"It is for three years that I have been calling on you, Jews of Poland, the glory of world Jewry, with an appeal. I have been ceaselessly warning you that the catastrophe is coming closer. My hair has turned white and I have aged in these years, because my heart is bleeding, for you, dear brothers and sisters, do not see the volcano that will soon begin to spurt out the fire of destruction. I see a terrifying sight. The time is short in which one can still be saved. I know: You do not see, because you are bothered and rushing about with everyday worries... Listen to my remarks at the twelfth hour. For God's sake: May each one save his life while there is still time. And the time is short.

"And I want to say one more thing to you on this day of the Ninth of Ab: Those who will succeed to escape from the catastrophe will merit a moment of great Jewish joy: the rebirth and rise of a Jewish state. I do not know whether I'll earn that. My son, yes! I believe in this just as I am sure that tomorrow morning the sun will shine once again. I believe in this with total faith."